THE ALEXIS DE TOCQUEVILLE
LECTURES ON AMERICAN POLITICS

Christianity and American Democracy

Hugh Heclo

WITH RESPONSES BY
Mary Jo Bane
Michael Kazin
Alan Wolfe

HARVARD UNIVERSITY PRESS
Cambridge, Massachusetts
London, England
2007

ISBN-13: 978-0-674-02514-1
ISBN-10: 0-674-02514-8

Cataloging-in-Publication Data is
available from the Library of Congress.

CONTENTS

FOREWORD

IN EARLY MARCH OF 2006, AN INTERDISCIPLINARY group of students and faculty—political scientists, historians, sociologists, and others—assembled at Harvard University to discuss the mutual interplay of Christianity and democracy in American history. The focus was as much on the content of Christian beliefs as on the organization of religious institutions, and the principal lecturer, Hugh Heclo of George Mason University, analyzed not just how Christians and their beliefs and practices have contributed to society and politics in America, but also the ways in which American democracy has changed and challenged Christianity. Ranging over many decades of the American past, Heclo portrayed an unprecedented rupture starting in the 1960s, when, he argued a "secular awakening" emerged, fueled by movements and actors who have worked to displace Christianity from the hegemonic cultural authority it previously enjoyed.

Heclo's lecture—witty, learned, and provocative—was delivered in a semicircular conference room in the new Center for Government and International Affairs at Harvard, and afterwards the floor was opened for questions and debate from the surrounding audience. The next morning everyone reassembled, and three distinguished commentators explored new dimensions of the question and challenged Heclo's thesis, before he rejoined the discussion and the audience jumped in once again. Deliberately drawn from different disciplines and points of view, the commentators were sociologist Mary Jo Bane of the Kennedy School of Government at Harvard; historian Michael Kazin of Georgetown University; and sociologist Alan Wolfe of the Boisi Center for Religion and American Public Life at Boston College.

These presentations and discussions constituted the second Alexis de Tocqueville Lecture on American Politics. Made possible by a generous gift from alumnus Terry Considine, the Tocqueville series is an occasional set of debates sponsored roughly every year and a half by the Center for American Political Studies at Harvard. Following from the March 2006 occasion, this book makes Heclo's lecture, the three commentaries, and Heclo's rejoinder available to a broader audience. It appears at a resonant juncture, for we live in a time when religiously motivated Christian activists are playing major, highly visible, and contentious roles in shaping U.S. public debates, tipping electoral outcomes, and demanding shifts in public policy. Of course, as we are reminded by Heclo's lecture and by the rich commentaries of Bane, Kazin, and Wolfe, Christian religion and believers have *always* been in the thick of cultural and political developments in America. From the first and second Great Awakenings, through the crusades against slavery, to the clashes of Protestants versus Catholics, down to the civil rights movement of the 1950s and early 1960s, Christians have asserted themselves and remade our democracy. In turn, the dynamism of markets and the cacophony of civic participation in America have challenged and changed Christian practices and beliefs.

Heclo offers a fresh perspective on the past—and breaks new ground by arguing that this long-term, complex symbiosis may be coming apart in our time, leading to deepening estrangements between believing Christians and other Americans who are determined to promote fervently secular conceptions of public values. Heclo explores the possible consequences for government, politics, and society—and for different groups of citizens. The commentators, in turn, take issue with important aspects of Heclo's portrayal of American political and cultural development. Mary Jo Bane draws our attention to the distinct experiences and beliefs of Catholics in a Protestant-dominated nation, while Michael

Kazin further deepens our sense of conflict and diversity. And Alan Wolfe offers an alternative reading of American political culture, especially in our own time, suggesting that Heclo's prophecy of a "coming rupture" may be too dark. Heclo acknowledges the validity of much of what his critics have to say, yet reasserts and reinforces his own main theses.

Readers of these remarkable exchanges will decide for themselves, bringing new insights to the dialogue. That is as it should be, and the broadened engagement will further realize the purpose of Harvard's Alexis de Tocqueville lectures and books—to carry forward in our own time and through our own explorations the questioning about America that the namesake of the series so splendidly practiced when he visited these shores some eighteen decades ago.

THEDA R. SKOCPOL
Director (through June 2006), Center for American Political Studies, Harvard University

CHRISTIANITY AND
AMERICAN DEMOCRACY

1

CHRISTIANITY AND DEMOCRACY IN AMERICA

Hugh Heclo

I N THE FIRST TOCQUEVILLE LECTURE IN THIS SERIES, published in 2006, James Ceaser invited attention to what he called "foundational concepts" in American political development. Ceaser defined these concepts as high-level abstractions that serve to ground the explanations and justifications for a polity's other political ideas or general courses of action. The two foundational concepts he invoked were "history" and "nature." The three commentators on the lecture then inquired if "religion" might not also be a foundational concept deserving at least equal time in the discussion.[1] This is the direction in which I intend to turn.

We should begin with an obvious fact: Religion as such has had little significance for American political development. Religion in general can mean anything—from love your enemy's heart to eat your enemy's liver. Asserting the importance of generic "religion" in America is like saying that "economics" was important for Americans while ignoring the fact that the substance of the economic idea was private property; or saying that "geography" was important for American political development but glossing over a physical landscape of frontiers protected by oceans. In America—

and in every other place and time—religion affects political development as this or that *particular* religion, with a substantive content that includes its own distinctive features and variations.

Few people engaged in the myriad of actions that we, in retrospect, call American political development thought of themselves as engaged with some mere analytic category called "religion." If they had done so, they would have been mere social scientists. Rather, Americans filled in the academics' "religion" category with the substance of a richly variegated thing called Christianity. They did so as establishment clerics and radical dissenters, New Light and Old Light Calvinists, fundamentalist Bible thumpers and Unitarian Bible knockers, and on and on. The list of religionists is huge, but it is almost entirely a list, even if nominally, of alleged Christians. Similarly, in the case of those Americans who have not cared much about religion—and throughout our almost 400-year history, many have not—it has been Christianity they have not cared about. And the historically tiny, but increasingly vocal, minority of devout atheists in America has generally consisted of persons turning their backs on Christianity, not rejecters of Muslim, Hindu, or Zoroastrian faiths.

To focus on mere religion in American political development, rather than on Christianity, is to eviscerate any historical understanding. Hence my subject is not religion and American democracy, but Christianity and American democracy. Likewise, the historical presence we need to acknowledge in American political development is Christianity in general as well as Protestant Christianity in particular.[2] Thus the site of our inquiry is America and its political development as an ostensibly democratic, Christian, and predominately Protestant nation. That said, we must not lose sight of the central issue. For the last 500 years, Protestantism has typically defined itself against Roman Catholicism, and that oppositional self-identification is inherently too narrow for our purposes. It is Christianity as such that is the crucial specification of "religion" in all that follows. As we will see, in recent years both Protestant and Catholic versions of traditional Christianity have been coming to define themselves, not against each other, but against another Other, which is in some sense American democracy itself.

In the story line that follows I begin with an essential ambiguity and its historical resolution and go on to discuss a mutual and tensioned embrace between the democratic and Christian faiths. I then identify a growing estrangement and eventual turning point in the 1960s, raising the real possibility of a coming rupture between Christianity and American democracy in the years ahead. This story line is, of course, much too simple to capture everything relevant on this subject. However, I do think it is sufficient to headline the central tendencies of what has happened and is happening, as well as—in the spirit of Tocqueville—to offer a plausible warning about what lies ahead.

For a very long time, the scholarly community has neglected Christianity's role in American political development. I think it is not some accidental oversight that has led academics to resort to the abstract term "religion" rather than the substantive socio-political-doctrinal formation that is Christianity. It is instead a terminological dodge, which serves at least two main purposes. First, social scientists have been comfortable disregarding substantive differences in the content of different religions (and the political implications of any such differences) because to do otherwise risks having to examine their usually unspoken premise that all religions are essentially the same (wish-fulfillments, oppressors' tools, barbaric superstitions, archetypal myths, psychological projections, or just a touching human desire for the approval of supernatural beings). Second, modern social science arose with a determinedly secular outlook which privileged some voices and not others in accounting for the progressive march of democracy. Only the approved secular routes to democracy were highlighted. Those who counted in the pro-democracy movement were the champions of Reason rather than Faith, religious skeptics but not clerics. They were classical humanists inspired by the glories of pagan Greece and Rome rather than Christian humanists inspired by the Bible.[3]

The democracy-as-secularism blinders began to slip when scholars were surprised by the rise of conservative Christian activists in the 1970s. This eruption fit neither the secularization theory of modernity nor the "paranoid" thesis applied to culturally backward fundamentalists. And the scholars of secular academia have been playing catch-up ever since.

Recent events have made it still more academically acceptable to look at religious content. It is now common for western scholars to ponder whether Islam is compatible with democracy. A little reflection should show that to a devout Muslim this is an insulting way of putting the question; the more apt rendition would be to ask if democracy is compatible with Islam. Which way the question is put depends upon whether pre-suppositional faith is put in democracy or the Koran as the legitimate point of departure. Of course, being Americans, we know that the former and not the latter is the right way of putting the question.

But before that typically unthinking thought goes down too smoothly, let us replace the word "Islam" with the word "Christianity." We then would ask, is Christianity compatible with democracy? Or, to reverse the pre-suppositional faith, is democracy compatible with Christianity?

No doubt most Americans today would consider these to be silly questions. In what follows, I hope to show that to dismiss the issue is to take a myopic view of the past, present, and future of American political development. After all, in the larger historical scheme of things, it was not so long ago that Tocqueville identified "the organization and establishment of democracy in Christian lands" as the "great problem of our times."[4] Discerning a solution to that problem was a major reason Tocqueville commended the American experience to his fellow Europeans' attention. We would do well to begin with his insight.

Tocqueville's Insight

Modern readers have difficulty in appreciating how extraordinary the American scene must have appeared to a well-educated young French aristocrat like Tocqueville. Here was a society of vibrant democratic equality and liberty. But it was also a society of no less vibrant Christian institutions and fervor. To sense the surprise and admiration that Tocqueville felt, one needs to understand that at this time any sophisticated European intellectual would know that these two characteristics—democratic liberty and religious authority—did not go together. To think otherwise was to be intellectually naïve and historically ignorant.

The movement known as the Enlightenment, especially in French intellectual circles, had evolved from a complacent deism in the early eighteenth century to a militant, largely atheistic humanism of the *philosophes* by the end of the century.[5] Since "enlightenment" meant liberation of man's reason from tutelage under the guardianship of others, all religious authority could easily be construed as an unenlightened, superstitious fetter on free thinking and free men. Likewise, the religious-political structure known as Christendom, especially in French Catholic circles, had ample historical reason to see claimants for democratic liberty and free thinking as enemies of the one true religion. Thus Tocqueville came from a world of wretched consensus: the contending champions of faith and reason were in ruthless agreement that these were mutually exclusive commitments.

For a time, almost forty-one weeks, Tocqueville had expelled himself from this hothouse atmosphere of French intellectuals, churchmen, and politicians who were forever replaying arguments from the Enlightenment and the French Revolution. He injected himself into a new society, a wholly fresh atmosphere at the margins of an allegedly more "advanced" European civilization. The result for the young man in his late twenties was revelatory.

Tocqueville's observations in the raw new nation convinced

him that it was in Europe, and particularly his own country, where something unnatural had happened. In a "strange confusion" (10), the spirit of freedom and the spirit of religion had been sent spiraling in opposite directions. But in supposedly backward America, where one could observe the "natural quiet growth of society" (26), Tocqueville saw that the forces of religious faith and democratic liberty could exist in harmony and mutual support. Indeed, he saw that the partnership between the two must grow if something more than mere democratic equality was to survive. That "something" worth preserving at all cost was the God-given dignity and grandeur of human beings.

Thanks to the quick and dirty extracts from *Democracy in America* that are commercially produced for classroom use, Tocqueville is frequently misinterpreted as viewing religion mainly as a device for maintaining democracy. This view makes no sense, since Tocqueville clearly considered democracy as an irresistible historical development and inevitable wave of the future. The future of democracy-as-equality is not in doubt for Tocqueville. What is in doubt is democracy as a domain of liberty for preserving man's true dignity. Tocqueville considered the first thing that struck him about America—the religious aspect of the place—as key to preventing the only other more important factor he saw in America—the juggernaut drive of democratic equality—from running amok and degrading humanity.

Here, then, is a very brief sketch of some of the most important things Tocqueville observed about Christianity and American democracy.[6]

Tocqueville saw democratic equality as the God-inspired thrust of all history. This thought was in his first pages of Volume I, published in 1835, and in the concluding pages of Volume II, published five years later (pages 6 and 678–680). Such providential design expressed itself in direct historical movement as well as in the unintended consequences produced by those hostile to this purpose. This overall, apparently irresistible advance of democratic equality suggested to Tocqueville an intention coming from beyond history, and once this pattern is discerned, "effort to halt democracy appears as a fight against God Himself" (6). In the background of such a providential account is the recognition that "Christianity, which has declared all men equal in the sight of God, cannot hesitate to acknowledge all citizens equal before the law" (10). Much later, almost as something too obvious to discuss, Tocqueville describes the contrast with the most profound minds of Greek and Roman culture: "Their minds roamed free in many directions but were blinkered there. Jesus Christ had to come down to earth to make all members of the human race understand that they were naturally similar and equal" (404).

According to one of his biographers, Tocqueville himself was hardly a devout Christian believer.[7] This fact does not diminish the central importance of religion or Christianity in his analytic system. Tocqueville writes as a political sociologist, not a Christian, and generally argues that anything of political and social importance has multiple causes. But for all the importance he assigns to voluntary associations, decentralized administration, *mores* and the laws they produce, religion has the prior importance; it shapes the kind of people who will act in all these venues. "There is hardly any human action, however private it may be, which does not result from some very general conception men have of God, of His relations with the human race, of the nature of their soul, and of their duties to their fellows. Nothing can prevent such ideas from being the common spring from which all else originates" (408). In his last great work, Tocqueville views the inhuman outrages of the French Revolution as stemming from the preceding Enlightenment assault on religion.[8]

Tocqueville believes that for Americans or any other people, the circumstances of their origin are crucial to explaining all subsequent development. Fortunately for this strong claim about path dependency, America offers a unique case in that it allows one to see clearly—that is, undistorted by the travails of Europe's long history—the point of departure of a major nation.

Tocqueville cites several features shared by many early European immigrants coming to America: a common English language and notions of political rights, liberty, and local government; experience with the religious quarrels and intellectual battles shaking Christendom; the middling social status held by most immigrants; the frontier encounter with seemingly limitless supplies of land that undercut any pretensions of a landed aristocracy; and so on. And yet, given the scope and detail of what follows, these are only preliminary observations. Tocqueville clearly lays the main emphasis regarding America's point of departure on the New England colonists. And here is where Tocqueville's insight into our subject begins to emerge most clearly. In his view, it was in the English Puritan colonies of New England "that the two or three main principles now forming the basic social theory of the United States were combined." The New Englanders were distinguished from all other colonists by "the very aim of their enterprise . . . they hoped for the triumph of *an idea*." Tocqueville proceeds to describe their fervently sought combination of Christian piety, democratic self-government, and republican freedom. This foundation of Puritan principles, he says, spread its influence to enlighten "the whole American world" (29, 30).

Modern readers have little trouble grasping Tocqueville's point that Puritans scored well on the principle of democratic self-government. Neither rich nor poor, the Puritans at America's point of departure were a well-educated, middle-class, homogeneous people who knew how to form themselves into voluntary congregations and into a "civil body politic" of equals (32). Only in Puritan New England had the British Crown supported such organic communities of immigrant families—as opposed to individual adventurers farther south—to form self-governing colonies (33). Well over a hundred years before the Revolution of 1776 or the Constitution of 1787, New England's Puritans had become the founding fathers of American democratic self-government. "Puritanism was not just a religious doctrine; in many respects it shared the most absolute democratic and republican theories" (30). Unlike Europe, America came into political existence from the bottom up, democratic at its historically unencumbered roots.[9]

But these Puritans were also what today we would call religious extremists, and Tocqueville pulls no punches on that score. To the modern mind, he seems determined to undercut his own case by citing in detail the repressive penal codes that resulted from Puritans using the Bible to script their laws. He takes pains to quote laws punishing blasphemy, adultery, and disrespect of parents with death. Sins of idleness, drunkenness, intercourse among the unmarried, tobacco use, and long hair got off only a little more lightly with the Puritan lawmakers. And yet Tocqueville holds up such Puritan legislation as "the key to the social enigma presented to the world by the United States now" (34). How can he claim that these American Puritans set in motion America's "marvelous combination . . . the spirit of religion and the spirit of freedom"? (40)

In fact Tocqueville considered such penal codes shameful invasions of conscience and violations of human spirit. The key point, however, is that "these ridiculous and tyrannical laws were not imposed from outside—they were voted by the free agreement of all the interested parties themselves" (36). Alongside the penal codes was the great host of political laws embodying the republican spirit of freedom. Local independence, broad citizen suffrage with elected officials, free voting of taxes, trial by jury, government responsiveness to social needs—this broad sphere of political freedom was undergirded rather than contradicted by the Puritans' religious convictions. Clearest of all the examples were laws for compulsory public schooling. In good Protestant fashion, enforced taxpayer support for literacy was justified as promoting a knowledge of the Bible in its true sense and original meaning, unclouded by the commentaries and "false glosses of saint-seeming deceivers." Tocqueville answers the anti-religious sneers of France's Enlightenment *philosophes* with American facts: "In America it is religion which leads to enlightenment and the observance of divine laws which leads men to liberty."[10]

Here then was New England's gift of a national template—America's meta-constitution, so to speak—for harmonizing religious ardor and democratic freedom, doing so amid the irresistible historical trend toward democratic equality.

> Religion regards civil liberty as a noble exercise of men's faculties, the world of politics being a sphere intended by the Creator for the free play of intelligence. Religion, being free and powerful within its own sphere and content with the position reserved for it, realizes that its sway is all the better established because it relies only on its own powers and rules men's hearts without external support.
>
> Freedom sees religion as the companion of its struggles and triumphs, the cradle of its infancy, and the divine source of its rights. Religion is considered as the guardian of mores, and mores are regarded as the guarantee of the laws and pledge for the maintenance of freedom itself. (40)

Thus Tocqueville's insight into Christian New England saw that faith and reason, religion and politics, were distinct but, far from being separated in opposition, they could provide each other mutual support. One did not need to decide which blade in a pair of scissors does the cutting or which wing does the lifting.

In three large analytic blocs, Tocqueville subsequently expands his views on this cooperative relationship. The first of these discussions emphasizes Christianity as a main factor in maintaining a democratic republic in America (265–277). The direct influence is one of favoring self-government. This time without mentioning the Puritans, Tocqueville points out that England bequeathed to America a Christian immigrant population that was both democratic and republican: "From the start politics and religion agreed, and they have not since ceased to do so" (265). In the American context, Protestantism gave relatively greater emphasis to republican independence and liberty and Catholicism to democratic equality, but a single democratic and republican worldview prevailed.

Even more important to Tocqueville is the indirect support that Christianity gives to American democracy. Here he spells out the meaning of his earlier generalization that in America, religion takes freedom "by the hand" so as to "sanctify its striving" (10). The problem is that, left undisciplined, liberty loses its value as the means for human flourishing. Especially in a democratic republic, freedom without religious "oughts" and "ought nots" must become disorderly and self-destructive at both the individual and societal levels. "How could society escape destruction if, when political ties are relaxed, moral ties are not tightened? And what can be done with a people master of itself if it is not subject to God?" (271). The two questions are not quite the same.

As for the first question, Tocqueville finds that the needed tightening of moral ties occurs through a single Christian morality which unites the myriad of sectarian differences in America. To be sure, this morality may have trouble in restraining men seized by the many opportunities to enrich themselves in such an open society. But, he says, the balance is righted in domestic life, where marriage ties are strong and women take the moral lead. It is there that Christian morality is translated into the *moeurs* (moral attachments of the heart as well as ideas that shape mental habits) that do so much to maintain America's democratic republic. Men carry over the habits of moral order and restraint learned at home into the public affairs of state (268).

Tocqueville's answer to the second question has been generally underappreciated. The influence of American Christianity covers not only mores but also "reason" (268). With this term Tocqueville harkens back to his idea of politics as a sphere devoted to the free play of intelligence. Here everything is "in turmoil, contested, and uncertain" (40). The scope for political experiment and innovation seems limitless. But then the contempt for old ways and spirit of experiment "reaches the limits of the world of politics . . . in trepidation it renounces the use of its most formidable faculties; it forswears doubt and renounces innovation . . . it bows respectfully before truths which it accepts without discussion" (40). It is the reigning Christianity that checks, retards, and sets the primary assumptions and insurmountable barriers around the otherwise limitless world of politics. Later, in speaking of the American philosophical approach, Tocqueville puts it this way:

> In the United States there are an infinite variety of ceaselessly changing Christian sects. But Christianity itself is an established and irresistible fact which no one seeks to attack or to defend.
>
> Since the Americans have accepted the main dogmas of the Christian religion without examination, they are bound to receive in like manner a great number of moral truths derived therefrom and attached thereto. This puts strict limits on the field of action left open to individual analysis and keeps out of this field many of the most important subjects about which men can have opinions. (396)

No doubt thinking of the contrast with their French counterparts, Tocqueville points out that even American revolutionaries have their dreams circumscribed by the widespread respect for Christian morality and equity. He makes no judgment about Americans' religious sincerity; some profess Christian doctrines because they believe them, and others for fear of looking as though they do not believe them. In either case it is Christianity and respect for its morality that reign over both personal mores and public reason in politics (268–269). Liberty in America is ordered liberty because a people seeing itself as its own political master also sees itself as subject to God. Thus without speaking directly about freedom, religion teaches Americans "the art of being free" and so can be rightly considered the "first" of America's political institutions (267, 269).

What accounts for this powerful hold of Christianity on the American people? Tocqueville asks the question not as a believer, skeptic, or unbeliever, but as a political sociologist. His answer is the separation of church from state, of religion from politics. Again, however, we need to listen carefully to hear what Tocqueville is saying rather than what contemporary slogans in our modern minds are repeating. Tocqueville acknowledges and considers it irrelevant that most of education in America is entrusted to Christian clergy. The separated "politics" which he commends consists in the absence of clergymen from elective or appointive public office, their non-affiliation with particular parties, their disengagement in regard to particular policy opinions (even as they condemn bad faith and selfish ambition on any side of an issue) (272, 517). In other words, "the structure of religious life has remained entirely distinct from the political organization" (396). Eschewing this kind of "political" involvement with the apparatus of government and party competition, religion diminishes what Europeans would regard as its power. But that view, according to Tocqueville, simply reveals the distorted understanding produced by Europe's sad history of religious entanglements with worldly instruments of power. Avoiding those entanglements in America has increased Christianity's enduring strength and public influence, rather than its illusory temporal power.

At this point Tocqueville expands on the nature of religion in general. Religion's sphere comprises the universal and permanent longings embedded in every human heart as it faces the ultimate questions of its own existence (273). Alliance with the fleeting powers-that-be in the world can only diminish this natural claim that religion has on human beings, turning it into something as fragile and changeable as those earthly powers. And in a democratic republic, those political powers are very changeable indeed. Religion with political power is not merely prone to be intolerant, indolent, and unstable; it is prone not really to be religion. In America, organized Christianity assured its enduring influence by disassociating itself from the vicissitudes of political authority and power. The "political" separation of church and state does not safeguard liberty by protecting secular people; rather, it safeguards liberty by protecting religion from being corrupted into something less than itself. Thus religion is necessary to sustain the ordered liberty of democracy, but it must also be separated from the apparatus of political power to offer this necessary assistance (273–274, 410, 517).

Religion provides answers to the primordial questions by which men order their actions in the world. The more that claims of authority are weakened in the political sphere, the more important for human functioning is an authoritative foundation in religion's spiritual sphere. If both religion and politics become a free-form exercise in do-it-yourself living, the strain of this limitless independence will leave men disoriented and willing to seek order even at the price of their liberty.

Thus in looking at the subject in terms of "the interests of this world" (408) and "a purely human point of view" (410), Tocqueville describes the kind of religion that will be needed to sustain the ordered liberty of democracy in the centuries to come. To anchor the thinking of people afloat in a world of equality and freedom, religion must be clear, authoritative, and unchanging in its core doctrines and articles of faith. These doctrines must relate solely to spiritual matters, not human laws, science, or political maxims. In contrast to Islam, here the great merit of the Christian Gospels is that they "deal only with the general relations between man and God, and between man and man" (410). The beliefs that religion professes must accord with the democratic idea of a universal equality of men before the laws of a single God. To retain power in democratic ages, religion must also dispense with external ceremonies that are not essential to its core dogmas. Finally, religion must accept rather than attack the democratic passion for material well-being in this world, even while insisting that the admittedly good things of this life remain secondary to the spiritual kingdom of God (409–414).

Tocqueville clearly believes that Christianity in its natural American condition (that is, unencumbered by European history) does well on all these counts. But he also understands that the spirit of independent opinion pervading democratic populations will be an enduring challenge to any such religious authority. Some people will try picking and choosing among the various doctrines of their religion. But Tocqueville realizes that such efforts to finesse obedience and freedom are unlikely to be sustainable. In the future, the lines of division within democracy will be sharper. Those who take Christian doctrine seriously will move toward the single uniformity of orthodox authority (as he sees it, Catholicism). Others will completely abandon Christianity. Seeking unity in all things, these democratic unbelievers will be drawn to some version of pantheism and will reject Christianity's sharp division between the Creator God and His creation (415–418). As we will see, Tocqueville was not far off the mark.

Tocqueville usually frames his observations about religion and Christianity under the general rubric of their "usefulness." But it is a serious mistake to reduce his view to a narrow, utilitarian conception of religion as simply a means to political ends. The value of religion is not just that it is useful to democracy; it is useful to democratic man because it teaches truths about the human condition. Thus Tocqueville emphasizes that in America the doctrine of "self-interest properly understood" is crucial for countering democracy's tendency toward self-absorbed, short-sighted individualism. This doctrine, however, is ultimately religious rather than political. It appeals to man's reason by challenging him to look beyond his immediate desires and see that his behavior in this world is weighted with ultimate significance for the fate of his immortal soul in the next world.[11] And even with this utilitarian-style argument about Christianity's promise of heavenly rewards for good behavior, Tocqueville immediately goes on to insist that there is something grander than calculations of reward and punishment happening in the Christian mind (500). Faith brings man into thinking God's thoughts about well-ordered living, about doing good to others, and above all, about giving priority to spiritual realities.

Tocqueville has no doubt that the tendency of democracy to unleash passions for physical pleasure, to push individuals toward a short-sighted, brutish materialism, is fully on display in America. His claim is that it is therefore all the more important that religious beliefs counter these democratic tendencies by drawing attention to man's immortal soul and elevating his affections and mere natural reason toward what is majestic, pure, and eternal. Without the active presence of spiritual conceptions in society—the recognition that an integral part of each person is implicated in realities beyond this material world—human beings in the democratic age are in great danger of becoming degraded into something less than fully human (514–517). Becoming self-absorbed in mundane things, they will then be abandoning their true selves.

What can those who govern democratic peoples do to make spiritual conceptions prevail? For reasons already discussed, Tocqueville is firmly opposed to state-established religion or religious leaders officially taking on roles in public affairs. The only answer Tocqueville can see is for politicians to lead by example: "I think that the only effective means which governments can use to make the doctrine of the immortality of the soul respected is daily to act as if they believed it themselves. I think that it is only by conforming scrupulously to religious morality in great affairs that they can flatter themselves that they are teaching the citizens to understand it and to love and respect it in little matters" (517). On that hopeful and somewhat problematic note of incorporating a religious perspective into the high levels of governance, Tocqueville ends this analysis.

The Great Denouement

Spend enough time with Alexis de Tocqueville, and you are likely to come away feeling that anything you have to say is simply a gloss on some chapter, paragraph, or sentence of *Democracy in America*. However, with sufficient diligence, such humility can be overcome. At this point it is helpful to step back from Tocqueville and try to see the larger picture of which he—even with his brilliantly enlarged view—was only a part.

It is telling that when Tocqueville thought about how to make spiritual conceptions endure in society, he could come up only with the suggestion of politicians leading by example. And yet for well over a thousand years Christian church authorities had countenanced the use of any number of other means, fair and foul, to enforce conformity with various spiritual conceptions. They persecuted opponents, and used political power to do so, because they believed it was their sanctified duty to uphold the truth.

Strangely enough, after his discussion of the Puritans, Tocqueville says little about religious liberty in America and even less about the religious freedom clauses in the Constitution's Bill of Rights. He simply notes the common "republican" theme in Americans freely voting their temporal interests in politics and freely pursuing their heavenly interests in religion.[12] Even more striking is that Tocqueville seems oblivious to the vehement political debates swirling around the country as a result of evangelical Christian crusades concerning Cherokee removal, Sunday mail delivery, anti-lottery and temperance legislation, prison and orphanage reform, and a host of other Christian-led, "benevolent society" causes. While opponents of these crusades were complaining about the "Christian party in politics," Tocqueville was blithely assuring readers that Americans had found the key to keeping religion out of politics. Soon the young abolition movement would explode his notion that the underlying Christian consensus had set strict boundaries around political "innovation" and disruptions to society. In short, Tocqueville was touring America amid the political fallout of the Second Great Awakening and hardly seemed to take notice.[13]

My point is not to criticize Tocqueville but to suggest that by the time he visited America in the 1830s, something so important had happened, at such a deep political-cultural level, that it could hardly be noticed.

Coming from post-Enlightenment France, Tocqueville thought the problem was that the friends of democracy were anti-Christian and the Christian authorities were anti-democratic. But that was only one manifestation of the longer-term master problem: How can Christianity and civil government be reconciled with each other? In a thousand ways on a hundred fronts, Christians after the Protestant Reformation muddled their way toward an answer, one that pivoted on the idea of individual liberty of religious conscience. This profound historical achievement, centuries in the making, blended commitments to religious liberty and popular self-government. It produced the "twin tolerations" that we can now see are essential for modern democracy anywhere in the world—the political freedom of elected governments from control by religious authorities, and the religious freedom of individuals and groups from control by the government.[14] The term I have devised to describe this hard-won achievement is the Great Denouement, and it was first won in America.

The history of almost anything is not a pretty picture. (Instances where that is untrue could probably be assembled, but they would make a very small book.) Until we understand why governments could find it quite reasonable to couple religious heresy and political treason, we can never appreciate the monumental historical achievement that had occurred in America by Tocqueville's time. In fact if one simply considers the similarities between religion and government, it can seem quite odd that anyone would imagine the authority of the two should be anything but united. Religious and political regimes are both about governing people. Both lay down rules for doing so. Both regard these rules as expressing moral values, the way things ought and ought not to be. Both insist that these normative rules are authoritatively binding on people. Moreover, any religion is a comprehensive worldview which necessarily includes the political, social, and all the other dimensions of human life. From all this the conclusion would seem to necessarily follow: since God is Lord of all creation and since His truth is one, religious and political authority must be one. If they are not, social peace and godly order are impossible. Looked at strictly in these terms, the Taliban has a point.

But this tidy logic is speaking only of generic "religion." The substance of Christian belief introduces a vast disruption into the whole picture, for two interrelated reasons. First, Christianity from its outset has been a potential threat to any established civil order, whatever the form of government. This is because a Christian life is expected to extend its fundamental allegiance upward to God (loyalty to any worldly kingdom, nation, tribe, or family is always secondary to the Christian's current citizenship in a spiritual kingdom), and to extend its fellowship outward to a universal humanity (where there is "neither Jew nor Greek . . . neither slave nor free . . . neither male nor female"; Galations 3:26). These vertical and horizontal attachments threaten to break the normal boundaries of any political society.

This would be less of a problem but for a second feature: Christianity is committed to the opposite of a spiritual withdrawal from or indifference toward earthly human affairs. Following the model of God's incarnation, believers are taught that the world is to be penetrated, lighted, and salted by their Christian lives. Since their God is so deeply concerned with the affairs of the world, "The notion that we can be related to God and not to the world—that we can practice a spirituality that is not political—is in conflict with the Christian understanding of God." This "prophetic stance" toward government and society can be quite ambiguous, but the call is always to be engaged and critical.[15] Even the ascetic holy men and women of the "desert" in Late Antiquity were not in remote wilds but visible at the edges of towns and villages, where they counseled and bore witness to God's unsettling demands on settled society.[16]

In short, Christianity has some chutzpah: it makes profound moral claims on the powers-that-be while refusing any ultimate allegiance to, or even personal kinship or special friendliness toward, those powers.

After its first 300 years, the outsider Christian religion was brought inside civil power to become the state religion of the Roman Empire (the only way Imperial Rome knew how to think of legitimate religion). However, rather than eliminating the essential problem of Christianity and civil government, this move ultimately intensified it. This is because an "official" Christianity is even more dangerous than an outsider Christianity: it turns out to be dangerous both to itself and to any peaceful political order.

The danger to Christianity from entanglement with official state power is obvious. Worldly power, being worldly, is always ready and willing to use religion to win fights with political opponents. This innate inclination is something wholly inconsistent with the substance of a religion that disavows any dependence on or truck with worldly powers. Following their God's example, Christians are called to the unworldly ideas of loving their enemies and of defending the truth of their religion by suffering and dying, not by ruling and killing.

The second danger—an official Christianity's propensity to upset any peaceful political order—is less obvious to us today but is worth serious attention. For it is from here that we are set more directly on the path toward the Great Denouement.

This danger has its roots in the fact that of all religions, Christianity is inherently and fervently doctrinal in nature. It has been so almost from the beginning (that is, from the days of Paul, Peter, and disputes in the apostles' council at Jerusalem). This enormous doctrinal emphasis is not because Christianity's central core is a checklist of doctrines, but because its centerpiece is a very odd person. In a sense, this person *is* the religion. The essence of the good news, or gospel, is that this man died for believers' sins as foretold by the Jewish scriptures, was buried, rose again, and was seen alive by his disciples.[17] Doctrines have served to translate into human intellectual terms the fact that this person was born, died, and rose again. The fantastic claims and actions surrounding this peculiar person could not help but give rise to fundamental questions demanding answers. The answers were not being sought, in the first instance, by unbelievers but by believers, and not by believers who touched and knew the man Jesus but by the following generations of Christians, who were only going on reports. How are we to understand this person we are believing in? More specifically, how can God have a son? In what sense(s) was

Jesus both God and human? How can it be just for God to kill God to pay for humans' sinfulness? What logic allows God to be one and three? Officially endorsed Church councils tried, but even within the post-Constantine centuries of one empire/one religion, doctrinal divisions among Christians could never be settled. And given that enduring fact over the centuries, the temptation to use political power to settle doctrinal differences was even greater than that of using civil authority to squash mere political opponents.

This recurring temptation reached a climax in the sixteenth-century Reformation. Today we can read about the theological debates, social upheavals, political intrigues, and religious wars but still not fully grasp the shattering quality of what happened. It may help to imagine dropping all the labels that intellectuals later invented and pretend to be just an ordinary person who does not know you are living at the end of the "Medieval Synthesis," amid a "Protestant Reformation" and Catholic "Counter-Reformation," leading up to an "Age of Reason" and "Enlightenment." What you do know in a very general way is that people smarter than you have always said that philosophy (with knowledge from human reason) and theology (with knowledge from biblical revelation) both agree in giving a unified meaning to things, including your life and everything around you. Now into this scene comes crashing one monstrous, incontrovertible fact that people later will call the Protestant Reformation—namely, that all the best thinkers are violently disagreeing. Everything that might be considered traditional authority is at war with itself. How can there be multiple truths in contradiction? Where is there any authority for certifying what is true? The shattering effect of such questions on a once coherent worldview was felt across all aspects of European life.

Various approaches were tried to repair this shattering. The first was obvious: religious-political fights within Europe started, stopped, and restarted in vain efforts to impose the one right Christian and political regime. From this turmoil came legal initiatives for "toleration" (the 1598 Edict of Nantes in France, England's Toleration Act in 1689, and the 1781 Patent of Toleration in the Hapsburg lands). In effect, this second approach gave permission for religious minorities to exist in a nation without persecution or legal oppression.

A third approach sought a return to classic pre-Christian sources. Much of what we now call civic republicanism developed in direct opposition to the ideal of a Christian polity. Following in the footsteps of Machiavelli, who considered Christians too soft and passive for good republican citizenship, Rousseau argued that the two concepts of "Christian" and "republic" were mutually exclusive, particularly because of the former's intolerance.[18] For European thinkers like Rousseau, the problem was not what Christianity had become; the problem was what Christianity is when it is being its most true Gospel self. It unbinds the heart of a believer from the state and society and ties its allegiance to an otherworldly country. By definition, good Christians could not be good citizens.

Washing up from Europe along the Atlantic coastline, all of these approaches were tried in the scattered American colonies during the seventeenth and eighteenth centuries. There was energetic persecution of Baptists and Quakers in Puritan New England, toleration in Catholic Maryland, greater freedom for all sects in Pennsylvania and Rhode Island, mild Church of England establishment in Virginia, and flirtations with Enlightenment deism in various intellectual circles. From this confusing hodgepodge eventually emerged an answer to the conundrum of Christianity and civil authority.

The "doctrine" making for this Great Denouement was produced not by events nor by ideas, but by ideas about events. In the Americans' case, it is important to note that ideas about events were being forged during the late phases of Protestant Reformation and in an isolated setting. Lateness meant that any lessons of experience could be clearer, and that enough time had passed for a certain exhaustion to set in among all the combatants. Isolation meant that the colonists were relatively free to figure things out for themselves, with less interference from "old world" thinking and powerbrokers. The Protestant Reformation did not give the answer to the master problem of Christianity and civil authority; but it did precipitate the answer's emergence, and it did so in America.[19]

For one thing, the Reformation's proliferation of Protestant sects created more Christian heretics than it was generally practical to persecute. Well versed in the European tradition of using state power to settle and enforce doctrinal disputes, the New England Puritans tried persecution but eventually could not keep up. As many observers noted, this religious pluralism was especially prominent in the American colonies as a whole. The result was that Americans tended to be driven toward religious tolerance because there were too many sects to allow them to get away with the intolerance they might have preferred. Moreover, the colonial frontier exhibited a quite fluid sort of pluralism; refusing special privileges for any sect could be the safest course if the benefits for your group might tomorrow be grasped by others. In Massachusetts, for example, the Congregationalists (the original beneficiaries of state support) eventually came to favor disestablishment of religion when Unitarians began sharing the state funds in more localities. Thus James Madison would eventually be led to argue that a bill of rights was unnecessary in America's new Constitution because the true security for religious freedom lay in the religious diversity of the population.[20]

In the second place, the same proliferation created minority religious groups with a self-interest in advocating religious tolerance. Thus even Catholic communities, in contexts where they could not be the dominant church, found good grounds for advocating liberty of religious conscience. Through Catholics the colonists acquired the language of "free exercise" that would 150 years later work its way into the first line of the Constitution's Bill of Rights.[21]

Third, the upheavals of the Reformation spurred Christian

thinkers who witnessed the persecutions and turmoil—thinkers both inside and outside the minority sects—to reconsider the meaning of the Christian gospel in light of these events. The spiritual definition of the Christian church, rather than the worldly identities and props of a visible Church, came into sharper focus.

Finally, as time went on from the seventeenth into the eighteenth century, ordinary Americans in their colonial outposts could continually hear about, without themselves suffering from, the struggles going on in their British homeland—the Puritan revolution against Charles I, the Restoration of Charles II, Monmouth's Rebellion, the Revolution against James II, the Test Act, and so on. One did not need to be a philosopher or even particularly well-educated to learn about the futilities involved in the quest for an official Christianity. In all of this, we see that vital political phenomenon which scholars so often overlook: how thinking generated out of political uncertainties and controversies produced transformations in the meaning of old ideas and the emergence of new ideas.[22]

Since it has been done so well by others, there is no need here to recount the varied steps by which a consensus grew in America on the doctrine of religious liberty.[23] It is enough to highlight the central line of reasoning. The grounding of the argument was theological; that is to say, belief in the doctrine of individual religious liberty came from belief in the content of a particular religious faith called Christianity. The thinking developed mainly through debates in Protestant Christian circles, not between believers and secularists. Like their predecessor John Locke in England, American Christians like Roger Williams, William Penn, Isaac Backus, and many more individuals forgotten to history confronted other Christians. The latter thought that because they were right in their doctrine, they were right in persecuting error. No, came the response from the other believers. A Christian cannot be right in his doctrine if he thinks religious persecution is right.[24] Mostly without realizing it, American Protestants were reviving arguments used by a once-persecuted Christian as he tutored the Emperor Constantine's son. Religion cannot be coerced, but must be voluntary and promoted only by words. "Nothing," Lactantius wrote, "requires freedom of the will as religion."[25]

As the debate went on (and here I will confine myself to Madison's language because it so clearly expresses the emerging consensus on the subject), it became clear that the issue was not simply persecution. At bottom, government involvement with religion was not a political or philosophical mistake. It was a religious error. Authentic Christianity was the response of one's whole being to God's inner call; and that required that man's mind be left free from coercion. To say that government coercion is allowed in matters of a religion is *"a departure from the plan of the holy author of our religion, who being lord both of body and mind, yet chose not to propagate it by coercions on either."*[26] To say that religion should be encouraged by government support is another religious error. True religion could make it on its own, without government's financial support or legal weaponry. This abstention was the Christian thing to do, *"for every page of it [Christianity] disavows a dependence on the powers of the world."*

At this point the argument got to the heart of things. It is each person's duty to God that produces the right to religious liberty. Religion is an obligation produced by the fact of God's creative work *("the duty which we owe to our Creator")*. The right of religious liberty follows from this duty. *("The Religion then of every man must be left to the conviction and conscience of every man; and it is the right of every man to exercise it as these may dictate.")* Thus the right of religious liberty is an individual right, not a group entitlement *("the homage each person determines in conscience to be acceptable to the Creator")*. Authentic Christianity is not a problem of collective allegiances. It is a matter of God speaking to one person at a time, of people responding to God's call one person at a time. Far from logically leading to coercion, belief in the absolute truth of Christianity means understanding that faith is a gift from God and that neither the gift nor its acceptance is a work of man. Logically, the absolute truth of this religion absolutely commands individual religious liberty. From this sort of religious analysis, the political conclusions cascaded:

- The only legitimate authority and support for religion is *"the Governour of the Universe,"* to whose government each person is subject. Religion is *"wholly exempt"* from the *"cognizance"* of civil society or government.
- Any true church is a purely voluntary, spiritual association of individuals following the call of God in their innermost consciences. It can never be rightfully regarded as a creation or instrument of government.
- The right of religious liberty is something more than the obligation of a person to follow his own conscience. That leaves room for human authorities to question whether or not a conscience has been correctly formed in light of religious doctrine. The obligations of conscience are between each person and God, his or her Creator.
- Religious liberty extends beyond mere toleration. Toleration is nothing more than a government permission slip for some groups to practice their religion without official obstruction.[27] However, it is beyond any government's rightful power to permit or not permit religion. The doctrine of religious liberty requires that every government acknowledge its limits in the face of its *"Universal Sovereign."* No one using such words doubted that they were referring to the God of the Bible.
- Protection of religious liberty in society is not an affirmation of man's natural goodness. A free society is God's testing place for separating the wheat from the tares in a world that is corrupted but still in His sovereign control. Man's fallen nature fully and permanently justifies distrust of human power, whether in civil or ecclesiastic robes. Thus religious and political freedoms require the mutual support of each other.[28]

The preceding quotations use Madison's words from a Virginia petition opposing the proposal of popular Governor Patrick

Henry to give public support to teachers of the Christian religion.[29] Scheduled for adoption on Christmas Eve, the plan would
have allowed each taxpayer to designate the church of his choice
to receive his tax. A second petition, receiving well more than
double the number of signatures on Madison's petition, may have
been more important in eventually defeating the plan. This petition declared the proposed state support for teaching the Gospels
to be against "the Spirit of the Gospels."

Americans in these years were not inventing something new.
They were rediscovering something old, in fact something intrin-
sic to Christianity. But because they were rediscovering this in a
context of new historical circumstances, they were also innovat-
ing, and they were especially innovative compared to the theological and political dead ends prevailing in Europe. Americans creating the Great Denouement were doing something new because
they were believing something old. For centuries—and still today—would-be theocrats said, "Because our religion is true, it
must unite with the power of the state." In the Great Denouement, the American Christian impulse in effect said, "Because our
religion is true, it must do no such thing." This was more than
Protestantism speaking. As the Catholic Church acknowledged
two hundred years later, it is the Christian gospel itself that "recognizes and gives support to the principle of religious freedom as
befitting the dignity of man and as being in accord with divine
revelation."[30]

The cumulative result for Americans was something like an *entente cordiale* between the forces of Christian faith and Enlightenment reason. It was the doctrine of religious liberty that provided
the sturdy ship-lap joint in this alliance. To announce that "Al-
mighty God hath created the mind free" could be the preamble to
either a Christian tract or an Enlightenment essay.[31] Concepts revealed by the light of reason—inalienable rights of the individual,
limited government, social compact theory—were no less evident
to the Christian political theology developing out of the Puritan
heritage.[32] With two sentences, both making the same essential

point, Madison was able to encapsulate the entente between Enlightenment reason and Christian faith: the right to religious liberty is unalienable, first, "because the opinions of men depending only on the evidence contemplated by their own minds cannot follow the dictates of other men: It is unalienable also, because what is here a right towards men, is a duty toward the Creator."[33]

To be sure, such brilliant language could conceal important potential fissures between autonomous reason and divine revelation. To the former, separation of church and state could mean the state's indifference to religion as merely a matter of subjective private opinion and superstition; to the latter, it could mean that man's relation to God is something too important to be contaminated by all-to-human political institutions. For advocates of unimpeded Reason, the inherent rights of natural man could justify every democratic challenge to the divine rights of kings and churches. For believers in biblical revelation, human rights and democratic challenges to the divine rights of kings and churches could only be justified by man's duty to what is absolute and divine rather than finite and human. To champions of human reason, man could be seen as having an inherent right to rule himself; to champions of Christian faith, the divine right of the people could be seen as just another blasphemy. Americans' emerging commitment to religious liberty did not eliminate such tensions between faith and reason, but it did greatly help to diminish them.

The *entente cordiale* between faith and reason was vastly facilitated by the fact that virtually all of the individuals regarded as opinion leaders in America were much more influenced by Scottish common-sense philosophy than by the extreme rationalist claims of the continental Enlightenment. The former was at least loosely Christian, while the latter was aggressively hostile to anything resembling traditional Christianity. Precisely on that account Thomas Paine, despite all of his patriotic good work during the American Revolution, went on to become a *persona non grata* to Americans.[34] As Tocqueville emphasized, it mattered greatly that Americans-in-the-making were not a representative sample of semi-Christianized Europeans ranging from unlettered peasants to insouciant aristocrats. Instead the colonial core in America was a disproportionate sub-sample of Europeans, a marginal rump of common, semi-middle-class people who took their Protestant Christianity quite seriously. With the Great Denouement, such people were also gaining the capacity to mount a new kind of political revolution. The first great Protestant political uprising had been the Peasants' War in Europe (1524–1525), crushed by Protestant leaders using the biblical justification that earthly powers are ordained by God and must be obeyed. A second pulse-beat of Protestant political revolution, far more familiar to the American colonists, was the English Civil War (1625–1649) and the failed Puritan Commonwealth (1649–1660). Here, again invoking biblical justifications, Protestants had attempted to unite executive and legislative power to create an English "Christian nation." Having lived through this, people like John Milton and John Locke helped teach the colonists why this was a religious and political mistake. By 1776, again using biblical justifications, Americans had the capacity not only to fight a perceived oppressor (nothing new in history) but to understand their political revolution in a Christian context of individuals constituting a government to protect their God-given rights, grounded in their duty to God, without preference or penalty of state power in matters of religion. If *that* was what a revolution was about, it had meaning for every human being who would ever live.

In forging an alliance between faith and reason, American leaders demonstrated a hearty disregard for doctrinal differences among Christian sects. One reason was a prudent desire to avoid stirring up trouble while trying to persuade Americans to unite around common political endeavors (fight a revolution, create articles of confederation, empower a truly national government under a new constitution). The evidence is persuasive that the drafters of the 1787 Constitution produced a "godless" document not because of some secular agenda, but mainly because they wanted to avoid inviting sectarian disputes and diversions that might interfere with the ratification business at hand.[35] Gradually, alongside Christianity, Americans were constructing a "public religion," speaking of God in a way that unified rather than divided.[36] It was/is a God that created men in his image, endowed them with rights, took a "providential" interest in human affairs, judged individuals and peoples according to his righteousness and, not least, took a special interest in the American nation.

However, there was a deeper reason for the muting of doctrinal disputes. Alongside religious issues, a parallel debate was going on about the possibilities of republican self-government. The problems here had little to do with church/state tensions and much more to do with doubts about popular sovereignty. Whether a free people could successfully govern themselves for any sustained period of time was a question posed not only by the Founders' knowledge of classical antiquity but by the daily events in the former colonies. If freedom meant the absence of any controls, then the mob rule predicted by classical philosophy and history seemed inevitable. The proper design of republican institutions could help, but even an institutional engineer like Madison had to conclude that the ultimate answer lay in the virtue of the people.[37] A people lacking virtue would not be capable holding on to freedom.

Some were too politic to say it, but if the experiment in self-government was to survive, the nation had to deal not simply with the philosophical problem of virtue, but with a looming virtue deficit in the American people. There were intellectual resources that could be brought to bear from many sides—the intuitions of natural law in Scottish moral philosophy, deistic views of moral reason divorced from spirituality, the civic *virtu* endorsed by classical humanists, and the moral affections inspired by pietism. However, it is fair to say that the main body of American opinion addressed the issue of republican virtue by affirming the central role of religion in moral education. What has been called the "moral calculus" became commonplace in the new nation: republican government requires virtuous citizens, virtue requires morality, and morality requires religion.[38] Freedom, which posed such a problem for democratic government when defined as a lack of controls, was in effect reconceptualized into the idea of autonomy. Autonomy was not a lack of controls but rather self-control, a combination of personal independence and moral responsibility.[39] What was Christian and what was republican could appear to be the same thing. Seneca had urged Rome's elite to rule themselves with unflinching integrity before they ruled others. America's elite was now saying that the same thing had to apply to everybody.

With this move, all sides could be drawn to a "practical" view of Christianity as being more about morality than about particular theological doctrines. Even Jefferson, never one to shun an intellectual debate, was much less interested in attacking the irrationality of his Trinitarian opponents than in strongly affirming their common capacity with Unitarians to uphold social morality and produce upright citizens.[40] Despite the poisonous politics of the day, the moral calculus could help defuse not only doctrinal disputes among Christian denominations but also political hostility between those more and less favorable to popular government. In most cases, those who resisted the democratizing impulse were defeated. In the long run, however, these defeats were made more bearable by the widespread commitment of all sides to the moral calculus and its underlying doctrine of religious liberty. Since Americans had reason to trust each other's commitment to religious liberty, talk of a popular government with Christian-based morality could be seen as a unifying theme rather than the threat of a divisive sectarian agenda.

Thus it came to be accepted that what mattered for a workable republic was a shared morality rather than the details of a shared theology. This moralization of Christianity meant that specific doctrines revealed through Scripture could recede into the public background in favor of the general revelation of right and wrong open to all men. Energized by individual liberty of religious conscience and protected from any politically established church, American civil society could be a "sanctified ground" for citizens to be good and to do good.[41] Teaching the "moral sciences" to awaken citizens' inner moral gyroscopes became established and went on to become a prominent part of educational curricula throughout the country in the nineteenth century.[42]

Without over-generalizations there can be no lectures, not even bad lectures. There is ample evidence to show that the early generations of Americans I have been generalizing about had a complex, highly sophisticated view of the likely conflicts between human reason and divine revelation. Theirs was no naïve view of sweet harmony on this side of Paradise. But I think we do these ancestors no injustice to say that with all the caveats that might be offered, there was a general consensus that reason and revelation overlapped sufficiently—not just for philosophers but for ordinary citizens trying to live decent lives—to make self-government a hopeful, going concern.[43] This consensus assumed that reason in the political realm and revelation in the autonomous religious realm would by and large agree on basic moral standards guiding political action. This mostly unspoken belief was greatly facilitated, and could remain mostly unspoken, because the areas of life subject to national and state governments' policy activity were extremely limited. Of course local government was a much greater presence in people's lives, but then the towns, villages, and counties in agrarian America also constituted more or less cohesive moral communities (even if more socially stratified than pure republican theory or Gospel teachings would endorse).[44]

So in the end—not a final end but an ending of substantial scope—there was a denouement to the puzzle of reconciling Christian religion and civil authority. It was "great" because it found a way out of centuries of argument, mutual recrimination, and suffering. Because it was an end of sorts, the Great Denouement in the young American republic could also be a beginning. Instead of contraries there was a contrapositioning, not something univocal but an equivocal coexistence of reciprocal influences. While the Christian gospel certainly was a key long-term force shaping the democratic vision, organized Christianity and democracy had had an ambiguous relationship throughout their respective histories.[45] In America, for the first time, Christianity and democratic self-government launched themselves together in a kind of double-stranded helix spiraling through time. Christianity and civil government were both now freed from the old dialectic of yes/no, unity or chaos, and became two maybes, moving together, each affecting the other.

A Christian Democracy / A Democratic Christianity

The Great Denouement meant that government (beginning at the national level and eventually extending to state and local governments) would have "no cognizance" of its citizens' religious beliefs. In this context of religious liberty, there was also an open invitation for the nation's overwhelmingly Christian religious groups to enter politics as sanctified defenders of the morality underpinning republican government. Implementing this moral calculus would not violate the Constitution as it was then understood, but failing to implement it would violate Christianity's "prophetic stance" toward the worldly powers-that-be.

In the years after Tocqueville returned to Europe, Christianity helped make a certain kind of democracy and democracy helped make a certain kind of Christianity in America. Space not does permit a complete chronicle of this twisting helix of reciprocal influences; the best I can do is to dip into the stream of events and hold up for examination some specimens of this interaction. Snatched out of a flowing historical context, they unfortunately become rather lifeless, but I think they are three specimens of enduring importance. I will call each of these an "idea" in the philosophical sense of the term, that is, a guiding principle of interpretation that can improve our understanding of the facts we see. These three ideas direct our attention to the meanings given to American life in its historical, individual, and societal dimensions. Using the ideas of history, personhood, and political society, we can consider the mutual influences of American democracy and American Christianity on each other.

AN IDEA OF HISTORY

Christianity helped imbue American democracy with a particular historical outlook that is especially bewildering to foreigners. It is summed up in the unnecessarily exaggerated phrase of William McLoughlin that "American history is thus best understood as a millenarian movement."[46] We can appreciate what this might mean by starting at the level of Christianity's general view of history and then moving to the more specific case of America's millenarian strangeness.

Like its two kindred "historical" world religions (Judaism and Islam), Christianity imparts a linear, content-rich view to time. Time is not mere duration. Other major worldviews from classical antiquity and elsewhere have seen the cosmos and man's existence on earth as either a timeless unchanging order or a cyclical eternal recurrence of birth, growth, maturity, decay, rebirth, growth, and so on.[47] By contrast, in the three Abrahamic religions, history—like Abram—is being called by God to go somewhere. In theological language, they are eschatological religions in that they look forward to the great consummation of a magnificent promise. Impelled by the Word of God, the world is moving toward the fulfillment of God's plan for ending history as we know it. In playing out their part in this plan, the origin and development of each of these religions are denominated in terms of dates and events in a particular temporal order, known through written records.

Over the past two centuries, people in Europe as well as America have translated such a theology of history into secular terms and created this or that philosophy of history.[48] For theology the promise for the fulfillment of all things comes externally, through God's plan for man. For secularized versions, the fulfillment of promise comes through the unfolding of forces within history itself. Examples of such secular philosophies of history are ideologies of progress through science and technology, Marxist class conflict, human enlightenment, and the racial struggle for *Lebensraum*.

Christianity adds something radically historical to this general picture. In fact, this is the radical something that makes it Christianity. The Christian claim is that God invaded historical time by taking on the form and substance of a living human being in a particular place and time. None of the other historical religions even remotely claim such a thing. Given this specifically Christian view, thinking about history now becomes a more ambiguous task. In a sense, the centerpiece of God's plan for history has already occurred in those few years at a marginal province of the Roman Empire. Christianity presents a "realized" eschatology in the coming of the promised Messiah, a man named Jesus, a Jew from an utterly insignificant town called Nazareth in the time of the great Herod dynasty. And yet the Christianity founded on this person also presents an unrealized eschatology, since the end of historical time has obviously not come and is somewhere off in the future. Indeed, this final fulfillment of history awaits the return of Messiah Jesus. The Messiah has come and will come again; the Kingdom of God is already here, and is not yet fully here. A space of special expectancy is opened in history. It is like waiting for the end of a war after the decisive battle assuring victory has already been won. "The time is already fulfilled but not yet consummated."[49]

All this sounds, and is, terribly abstract until we start putting it into the English/American context. The Protestant Reformation taught a return to God and his Scriptural Word, lived out in this world and unmediated by human authorities. Among the most prominent of these newly disputed texts was the Book of Revelation, and especially the lone place in that book where one encounters the insistent prophetic vision of a "thousand year" reign of Christ's kingdom on earth—that is to say, a millennium (Revelation, chapter 20).[50] For an English society thrown into decades of turmoil before, during, and after the Puritan Civil War, interest in the biblical end-time prophecies blossomed. The Puritans coming to America were part of this climate, seeking and defending various interpretations of biblical prophecy about the end-times of history as these applied to all sorts of political events in their world.

It was in this theological-hermeneutic-political context that the early American republic was self-consciously casting aside the traditions of the old world and trying to make sense of itself. Here Tocqueville's focus on the early Puritans as an ideological template for the new democracy misses a crucial development. To put it briefly, the early colonial Puritans were strong providentialists and mild millennialists. However, as they and subsequent generations of Americans tried to make sense of their experiment in self-government, and necessarily did so in a cultural context of Protestant thinking, the struggle to define their political identity pulled Americans' outlook on history in a more thoroughly "progressive" millenarian direction.

The earliest Puritans coming to America were providentialists in that their self-understanding was one of essentially casting themselves and their efforts onto God's sovereign power to make things come right. A highly favored Puritan biblical text finds God's people wandering, heaving up and down on the seas, crying out, comforted, thrown about, oppressed, but in the end brought to "understand the loving-kindness of the LORD" (Psalm 107:4). Likewise, Governor John Winthrop's characterization of the Massachusetts Bay colonists as a "city on a hill"—rhetoric so beloved and so thoroughly misrepresented by later American politicians—was a warning about Providence's judgment. Coming as the concluding application of his main message that the colonists must live together in love, the Governor's biblical metaphor pictured a world watching the call and response between God and these colonists. As Winthrop put it:

For we must consider that we shall be as a city upon a hill, the eyes of all people are upon us. So that if we shall deal falsely

38

with our God in this work we have undertaken, and so cause
Him to withdraw His present help from us, we shall be made
a story and a by-word through the world.[51]

To understand what Winthrop is saying, we need to realize that
this is not an American talking to us, but an Englishman speaking
to compatriots out of the depths of the English Christian tradition. Nine hundred years earlier, Baeda (later known as the Venerable Bede) had cast the Saxon military adventurers as a single
"English" people united by their Christian religion if by nothing
else. Bede's biblical analogues held immense imaginative power,
and they became a story of nationhood which no educated Englishman could escape. Like the people of Israel established in their
promised land, these island English people were especially held up
by God as responsible to God. They were to be blessed for obedience and punished for sin, usually following the Old Testament
formula of good and bad times corresponding with good and bad
kings.[52] Out of this deep cultural context, Winthrop and the thoroughly English and Puritan colonists of seventeenth-century New
England could see themselves as a chosen people but not yet a millennial people. For that, they needed to become more "American."

All millennial views are providential, but not all providential
views are millennial. On this subject it is useful to think of a continuum. At the extreme providential end are those who see man as
having no role in his God-ordained destiny. This suggests a fatal-
ism and quietism little-favored by Protestants, much less the Puritans. Next would be a view of being used by Providence as something like a test-case or an example for better or worse to others, a
model that Winthrop clearly had in mind. From here one might
imagine a more positively active role as an exemplar of Providence's work, the city on the hill now "shining" (as it did not for
Winthrop) to witness and light the way for others. Closing in on
the millennial end, we would come to a still greater engagement in
the plans of Providence by securing its possibilities, the rock in the

sea and the Promised Land for pilgrim refugees. Finally there is the full-blown millennial view of being the active instrument of Providence's plan for history. Here we come to being not just one of God's chosen instruments but to being *the* chosen instrument to lead the divine scheme of things. The image is nothing less than a first-born redeemer leading the way for others in God's ordained procession into the future. It is straight, 100-proof millennialism.

Obviously these conceptions overlap, and the accompanying images of beacon, rock, promised land, redeemer, and so on have varied throughout American history.[53] However, from early in the republic the dominant tendency that developed in American democracy was to lean into the millennial end of the continuum.[54]

If this millennial vision was not always there, when and how did it appear? According to one author, we must look to the later-generation New England Puritans: "The myth of a divine *telos* for New England did not emerge until the middle years of the seventeenth century, and it did not appear spontaneously. It emerged as the centerpiece of a deliberate effort to reassure and reinvigorate the faithful during a period of doubt and anxiety." On this telling, people who were vexed and troubled by the failure of their own lives to live up to the spiritual hopes of their Pilgrim forefathers (1620–1630) found comfort in identifying themselves with a community that had collectively been sent forth by God and would share its grace as long as the community kept faith with Christ.[55]

Another account finds the time "when destiny became manifest" to be a hundred years later, following the religious upheaval of the Great Awakening and the unexpected terrors of frontier warfare. "It seems that in the 1760's, in the nascent nationalism that followed the French and Indian War, there began to emerge a conception of the colonies as a separate chosen people, destined to complete the Reformation and to inaugurate world regeneration."[56]

A third view emphasizes the millennial move in American political thinking amid the fears of national disunity and a second religious awakening at the end of the eighteenth and beginning of the nineteenth century. These mounting anxieties about the meaning of America were eventually resolved in a new consensus of Christian evangelical patriotism that "included the belief that Americans are a peculiar race, chosen by God to perfect the world. That was clearly the nation's manifest destiny, and it was unique."[57]

Drawing these threads together, it makes sense to conclude that there have been multiple beats in the millennial pulse. These pulsations have found religious awakenings—revitalizing calls for God's kingdom to come into men's hearts—to be simultaneous with Americans' awakening to a national political self-consciousness. America existed in order that political principles of equal rights, self-government, and personal freedom might come into the world. Americans became a people constituted by discovering their faith in those political principles that now seem commonplace. In the ongoing struggles to define their national identity, Americans fitted a political reading of the democratic faith into the millennial framework supplied by certain Protestant versions of the Christian faith. This melding of the sacred and mundane, the religious and political, grew into America's sanctified vision of itself. The sacrality consists in understanding the American experience as something set apart for transcendent purposes in at least three senses.

Turned at one angle, this vision reflected the idea of divine election: God chose America as the agent of his special purposes in history. By superintending the first political revolution that did not simply exchange one set of rulers for another but instead produced a government by the people, Providence intended for America to be something special in the larger scheme of things.

Seen from a second angle, this vision of consecration claims that the nation is not sanctified simply for its own sake. America is charged with a mission in political freedom that has significance for mankind as a whole. There is a story for all people in the heart of America's history, a story that Americans did not put there but are living out. To take only the most recent illustration, one can hear the old theme played at the beginning of George W. Bush's presidency in 2000 and then later given its full-throated declaration in the crisis after 9/11.[58]

It is not just people but time itself that is to be redeemed. Viewed from this third angle, the sanctified vision sees an end to the wreck of history and the beginning of a new time. The claim is that the hold of recurrent time on republics—a political life cycle of birth, maturity, and decay—has been decisively broken in America. A new era has come to renew the world. To take two utter extremes from the religious-political spectrum, the "new light" theologian Jonathan Edwards saw America's spiritual awakening in 1740 and reasoned that "it is not unlikely that this work of God's Spirit . . . is the dawning, or at least a prelude, of that glorious work of God so often foretold in Scripture, which in the progress and issue of it shall renew the world of mankind. . . . And there are many things that make it probable that this work will begin in America." In *Common Sense,* anti-Christian rationalist Thomas Paine urged America's revolutionaries of 1776 to realize that they had it in their power "to begin the world over again. A situation, similar to the present, hath not happened since the days of Noah until now." Although Paine was certainly no believer in revealed religion, much of the public power in his secular-rationalist ideas and rhetoric came from their correspondence with Calvinist and other Protestant ideas in the general cultural atmosphere of the time.[59]

Americans' historical outlook is strange to foreigners because the millennial model of Christian time-reckoning has been brought down to earth in one nation's sense of destiny as a permanent new beginning. The sanctified vision reveals a divinely-purposed nation, on a world-redeeming mission, breaking through historical time with the expectation of a coming kingdom of democracy and freedom across the earth. It would be naïve to think that a great many Americans did not really mean it when they stamped their national seal and, even more significantly, their money with a self-description as the "new order for the ages."

Not only foreigners but many Americans, Christian and secular alike, have criticized the abuses of power that have often accompanied America's sanctified vision. Even in the nineteenth century heyday of evangelical patriotism, critical voices loudly opposed Cherokee removal, war with Mexico, and colonial expansion in the wake of the Spanish-American War.[60] And so it remains today with the Bush doctrine of war on terrorism.[61] But while the exercise of power has always been subject to criticism, it is much rarer to find American voices criticizing the sacral vision itself. Indeed, all the criticisms generally presuppose the vision. Why else imagine that the United States *should* be any different from any other country in ruthlessly exercising its power?

Viewed over the long term, America's sanctified vision has always been Janus-like. One face sees America's hope for the world to lie in the nation's special separateness, a holding back to protect its innocence from contamination in a corrupt world. Over against isolation and non-involvement is the other face, calling for robust leadership to save the world from itself. Each side presumes a final apocalyptic answer to the grayness of things. Each side gives the moral critics of America—criticism that itself presumes the sanctified vision—ample room for maneuver. That space invites alternating critiques between sins of commission and sins of omission. Seen together, these opposing tensions present an idea of history in American political development that is a tortured rather than triumphant millennialism. The image is less a shining city on a granite hill and more a narrow ridge of hard passage, one situated between the pride of withdrawal and the pride of control. Not surprisingly, that walk on the narrow ridge begins to resemble the story of the individual pilgrim Christian journey. It is a very Christian story through which Americans have come to understand their nation as a historical phenomenon.

What then can we say about the other strand of the helix—the reciprocal influence of American democracy on American Christianity's understanding of history? Three points stand out.

43

First, the religious pluralism embodied in Protestant America meant the loss of control over any authoritative interpretation of Christian Scripture. Unlike the situation for Catholics, diverse views of biblical millennialism could flourish across the Protestant landscape and attach themselves to politics with a wholehearted frontier abandon.

Second, this open-market religious competition, operating in an environment of democratic faith in the common man, pushed Christianity toward popularly appealing versions of millennial doctrine. Pre-millennialism had its appeal—Christ returns to usher in a wonderful earthly kingdom for all true believers regardless of worldly economic, educational, or social distinctions. Even more appealing in the American setting has been the post-millennial view—Christ returns after a millennium that has been prepared for him by a people empowered and made hopeful through the ethos of democracy. The politically pro-activist message for a free people is: get busy! There is much preparation and work to be done in bringing in the kingdom.

Finally, there is the main implication for American Christianity. The thrust of these religious-political developments in America was to supplant, if not obliterate, any orthodox Christian view concerning the meaning of history. After debate in its earliest years, the young Christian church decisively rejected "millennialism," that is to say, the doctrine affirming Christ's 1000-year reign in a coming earthly kingdom. It rejected millennialism as a "Jewish error"—not because early Christians were anti-Semitic (for over a hundred years Christian believers were mostly Jews), but because the idea of an earthly millennium was repeating the Jewish authorities' mistake of expecting the Messiah to re-establish the earthly kingdom of national Israel. For the following 1500 years Catholic teaching and, after the Reformation, all leading Protestant authorities (Luther, Calvin, Knox, and so on) interpreted Scripture to mean something quite different than what came to be accepted as the optimistic American view.[62]

The Christian teaching regarded as authoritative was not premillennial, nor post-millennial. It was "amillennial." With Christ's first coming, the millennium had already arrived.[63] It was understood as a spiritual kingdom populated by those who had been spiritually reborn (the "first resurrection") through faith in Christ. Its thousand years were not calendar years but a poetic expression for the perfect fullness of its duration. Essentially, human history since its culmination with Christ's first coming was not a story or progress, or a regress, or alternations between the two. It was a parenthesis during which two kingdoms, wheat and tares (or in Augustine's metaphor, the City of God and the city of man), existed together awaiting Christ's second coming and last judgment. The fact that the thousand-year reign of Christ with his believers was already here was not a call to quietism (though some took it that way). As noted earlier, the people of the City of God were not meant to be indifferent to matters of righteousness and godly living in the city of man. The remaining period of human history called believers to a watchful, active "waiting" through lives that would bear witness to the world about the true meaning of human existence. In this sense America's Puritan forebears stood four-square with the early Christians. If there was an idea of progress, it was not the positive forward movement seen in the world's affairs. Progress was measured in terms of one's attention paid to the things of God while living in his good, though fallen, world.

With development of the nation's sanctified vision, a quite un-Christian idea of historical progress was gradually imported into American Christianity. It came in sideways, so to speak, not by directly challenging Christian orthodox doctrine but by nudging Christianity's ambiguity about time into a more "optimistic" and can-do attitude that American democracy found appealing. In the older, more "pessimistic," or (let us rightly call it) Christian view of things, any future coming of God's kingdom must necessarily mean the final crisis, judgment, and destruction of what worldly men prize. This historical consummation would mean not only the wheat being gathered but the chaff being burned. The twentieth century's leading scholar of American Protestantism, Richard Niebuhr, looked back on what had become of the once-Christian idea of a coming kingdom and despaired: "It was all fulfillment of promise without judgment. It was thought to be growing out of the present so that no great crisis needed to intervene between the order of grace and order of glory."[64]

In terms of an outlook on history, everything in America became more or less Christian as measured by the cyclical standard of pagan antiquity and at the same time more or less un-Christian as measured from the perspective of orthodox Christianity. From that latter perspective, if America is the redeemer of nations and time, then America is the Christ of history. This notion may be inadvertent, but it is blasphemy all the same.

AN IDEA OF THE PERSON

I have introduced the image of a double helix of mutual influence between American Christianity and American democracy. If we apply this image to understandings of democracy's basic unit of analysis, there may be much that seems commonplace. There is a good reason, however, why certain notions become commonplace: it is because they are regarded as true place-markers worth holding in common.

The basic unit of analysis in democracy is a singularity—the citizen, individual, person, community member, or what have you. But what is the nature of this singularity? Since Christians have historically been a strong presence in America, there has been a general seepage of Christian ideas into understandings of the human material that makes up democracy. The task here is to try to be more specific about how Christianity in general and Protestantism in particular helped shape American understandings of democratic man.

But first a caveat is necessary. It is abundantly clear from the historical record that Christians have violated all of the principles that will be discussed. They have done so actively, especially when their religion has been allied with privileged groups in society.

They have done so passively, by failing to act against evils they verbally condemn. Either way, there is no doubt that Christians at times have helped oppressors preserve and extend their power and privileges. But it is also the eye of religion that identifies such behavior as transgressive "violations" of transcendent norms, and not just unattractive preferences or mistakes in opinion. And it is the voice of religion that demands, not just suggests, the mending of one's wrong ways. Without this religious eye and voice there would be no sense in speaking of the violation or correction of anything. Without the standards, no one would know or care that something being done or left undone was un-Christian.

From its first days, Christianity proclaimed a radical equality before God and, through Jesus, of all men and women everywhere. The God who is "no respecter of persons" acknowledges none of the world's distinctions of rank, station, or anything else. The earliest congregations of Jewish Christians clearly anguished over the obvious implications for Judaism of this radical equality. And they came to a conclusion. The Lord of history had used the nation of Israel for his purposes. But one did not have to become a Jew to be a Christian. There was now a new Israel for all men and women (Acts, chapter 15; Galatians, chapter 3).

Every effort to ally Christianity with human structures of rank and privilege has had to fight against the religion's insistence on a thoroughgoing equality among human beings. On the one hand, there is the formal, or positional, equality before a Creator-God. Placed next to the infinity of their Maker, every finite member of humanity is the equal of every other. On the other hand, Christianity also insists on a conditional equality among humans, and this is understood in two respects. First is the equality grounded through each person being made in the image of God. Dignity is inherent to man because it is derivative from God. Each human being is a God-breathed-in eternal soul that, unlike other earthly creatures, is made capable of knowing and loving its Creator. There is also a second, less flattering version of conditional equality: All are also equal in their fallenness from communion with their Maker. "There is none that understands, there is none that seeks after God . . . For all have sinned and come short of the glory of God" (Romans 3:11, 13). Human beings are not divided between the sinning and the righteous; they are all sinners saved by grace. The aim of these Christian accounts is not to exalt or debase man but to call him to recognize himself and his condition for what it is.

This is an impressive arsenal of egalitarian claims, and American advocates of democratic equality have repeatedly returned to it for sustenance. At least equally impressive is the concept of individuation. Throughout the Bible God calls to humans by their personal names, often bypassing their tribal or other identities. In the New Testament this is radically reaffirmed with the poetic but still extraordinary claim that the hairs on each person's head are "numbered"—known to God not just in their collective sum, but each bar-coded, so to speak. Humans have inherent dignity and worth as individual, personally distinct beings.

The importance of this individuation is overlooked in a common political science claim, generally to the effect that democracy assumes "the essential dignity of man."[65] For whatever portion of American democracy has been influenced by Christianity, this is not true. Pagan philosophers, Enlightenment monarchs, aristocrats, and elites of all sorts have often espoused the essential dignity of man. In America democracy assumes, as Christianity declares, the essential dignity of each person, one at a time.

Amid this equality and individuation of persons, Christianity also seems to make a special point of overturning man's preferred order of nobility and exalting the lowly common person. The second, not the first-born, son is honored. Biblical stories of drama and tragedy are told about common people whose only way into a Greek or Roman play would have been as comic characters to be mocked by the audience. For Jews, the Messiah's earthly line of descent is shown to pass through a sequence of women specifically identified as a liar who sleeps with her father-in-law, a Gentile whore, a servant girl from a foreign nation specially cursed by God, a flagrant adulteress, and an unmarried peasant girl from a widely despised village. The royal purple is laid in an animal feeding trough.[66] For Greek philosophers, from their first encounter with Christianity in the second century, there was no difficulty in pointing out the absurdity and inherent contradiction in this new religion. Philosophical wisdom taught that the divine lies in the eternal realm of perfection of every kind, and true knowledge comes from turning the mind's eye away from the changing sensations of this world. Hence it is patently contrary to divine nature that it should be revealed in a flesh-and-blood historical person.[67]

The Christian affirmations of human equality, individuation, and ordinary life have been critically important grounding influences for thinking about democratic man, but they are not the whole story. Under the pressure of wartime, some Christian thinkers such as Jacques Maritain have wanted to claim that the secular democratic conscience as it developed in the West was wholly and simply the slow absorption of "truths evangelical in origin." With less justification, other Christian writers in recent years have felt a need to credit their religion with every good thing the world might seem to value, from freedom and capitalism to western civilization itself. Besides betraying an unseemly desire to fit into non-believers' idea of progress, such exaggeration hurts a very solid case that can be made for seeing biblical Christian values as one root source in the evolution of the modern democratic self.[68] Such a self could not help bearing the marks of Christianity's radical view of humanity—as equals; as universally exalted, God-breathed-in souls; and as individual persons helplessly fallen into the sin of exalting themselves.

A particular (Catholics would say distorted) view of these concepts followed from the fact that the vast majority of Americans were not just Christians but Protestants. Catholic social thought has traditionally drawn an important distinction between the person and the individual. A person is a spiritual whole endowed with freedom of choice, but also an open whole that demands relationships with others. Not just the heart requires these attachments, but human reason itself "needs to be sustained in all its searching by trusting dialogue and sincere friendship."[69] The self becomes a self in "webs of interlocution" and attachments among family, friends, community associations, and so on. By contrast, the Protestant individual stands as a lone figure on a socially barren landscape of other such figures—the lonely crowd of liberal democracy. If one accepts this distinction, then being Protestant sharpened Americans' understanding of democratic man as an autonomous individual. It was precisely this notion of the autonomy and liberty of individual conscience in the Great Denouement that contrasted so sharply with the Catholic tradition of a guided conscience within the community of the one true Church.[70]

It is often said that "belief in the common man is the core of the democratic creed."[71] This sounds good until one realizes it leaves up in the air what it is that is to be believed about the common man. For centuries, thinking persons claimed that what you could believe about the common person was that he was ignorant, emotion-driven, and capricious. The Protestant Reformation helped to overturn this view and set the democratic faith in fast motion. Through a religious affirmation of the common man's capacities, democracy could be reconceptualized—from the "mass rule" feared by philosophers to the "self government" championed by all right-thinking Christians and republicans. In light of what has followed in our own time regarding the sovereignty of individual choice, we need to be careful here. The Reformation did not assert that what any individual judged to be right doctrine was in fact right doctrine. It did assert the perspicuity of Scripture, through which individuals of every sort (thanks first to God's saving grace) could come to a common and right understanding of the things of God. Hence the massive Protestant emphasis on Bible translations into national vernaculars and literacy for the masses.[72] And hence too the intense, fine-grained emphasis on creedal statements expressing the common understandings in the Reformation era, producing of course different creedal statements that today seem hardly distinguishable. It was not the responsibility of the individual to choose his own version of doctrine; it was his, and her, responsibility to know right doctrine.

To grasp the significance of what Protestantism did, and then redid as it immigrated to America, we might return to the Protestant Reformation while it was still Catholic. In August 1513 a young Catholic professor distributed the readings for his 6:00 A.M. lectures. Twice weekly for over a year, the young Martin Luther taught his students from a specially printed text of the Psalms whose wide margins had eliminated all of the centuries-old commentaries by Church authorities on the texts. Instead, each student was presented with the words of the Bible and the blank space on which to write his own commentaries and observations on each Psalm.[73] This was not heresy but something more radical: it was a different way to think about heresy.

Foreshadowed here was the master idea that exploded into a "reformation" of not only religious but also political thinking. Generations of people would be taught that in searching for truth, a person has to go to the scriptural source for himself, decide for himself, and believe for himself. This was more than just an exalting of the lowly; it was an affirmation of the competence of the common man. There was to be no churchmen's *Regula Pastoralis* for the "care and governing" of parishioners' souls. You care for and govern your own soul. There was to be no more doctrine of "implicit faith," that is, the conception of faith by which individuals in the Church need not fully understand what it is they are to believe. The contrast with the older ways—ways that submerged individual judgment into a community and tradition—could not have been starker. Catholic authorities rightly complained that the Reformers made "individual persons the judges in matters of faith, not only of the Fathers but also of the councils," leaving "almost nothing to the common judgment of the Church."[74]

This religious dispute was also a contest about the presumptions for democracy. The individual's capacity to read and understand Scripture inescapably pointed to the common person's capacity for self-government. If the ordinary person was up to such momentous and eternally important things of the spirit, how could he not be capable of participating in the lesser political things of this world? It is misleading to say that democratic thinking in the West adopted these ideas from Protestant Christianity. Unless one counts the bulky philosophical writings on why democracy is a bad idea, there was no substantial body of democratic thinking preexistent to the Protestant Reformation to do the adopting.

However, we can leave aside the general issue of whether or not Protestantism promotes democracy.[75] The point here is that in the United States, conditions were generally favorable for it to do so. And in doing so, there was a favored understanding of the democratic personality. Protestantism in America carved distinct features into the profile of that individual.

In the first place, the consensus forged in America's Great Denouement established the presumption that all religious sects should be free of government entanglements; to be true to godly worship, everyone should worship God as his or her conscience dictated. In this American setting, the individual was not a philosophical abstraction but a living, breathing human being who could plausibly be recognized as a voluntary figure to himself—not self-sufficient but self-activating and in that sense independent. Likewise, the abstract idea of the church as a voluntary body of believers came to exist as a reality of churches in a religious marketplace, all competing to secure the voluntary attachments of those living, breathing individuals.

Second, while Protestantism emphasized the individuation of religious experience, with each human being standing alone so as to experience divinity authentically and deeply, that individual was a work in progress. Especially in the evangelical version that filled the New England template and spread from there, Protestantism stressed the second, spiritual birth of the individual, the born-again conversion experience. Here religion lined up in America with the reality of a remarkably open society, a place of second and third chances to take up again the opportunities offered by such a "new world."

Third, the American individual as a work in progress could be uniquely unencumbered. Protestant reformers in Europe had taken up the stern Gospel teaching that one must be willing to leave all—to be told that your mother and brothers are standing outside the door seeking you, and respond that only fellow believers are your mother, brothers—and sisters (Mark 3:33; Matthew 12:48). In this sense, the real-life condition in America was very Protestant. It was a setting for continually making and remaking attachments to a changing array of kith and kin. In the vast open spaces, waves of immigrants, and social churning of its cities, America was a solvent that continuously disrupted inherited social status and put into ordinary people's hands the opportunity to challenge authority and make their own way.

Fourth, each of these unencumbered individuals was a rough-hewn equal, as good as any other. The practical necessities of surviving in America shredded pretensions of superior and subordinate status in a way that was fully in line with Protestant conceptions of natural, democratic equality. As Tocqueville reported, a European aristocrat could come to America to set himself up as a proprietary landlord; in short time, the facts of the situation would leave him a supplicant for labor—seeking "free hands," as they knew themselves to be. Moreover, every would-be proprietor was likely to find himself and his family lending a democratic hand to cope with the facts of existence in agrarian America. These facts of American life fit well with a Protestant indifference to "religion" as a matter of holy days, holy sites, relics, ritual, or sanctified ornamentation. Worship was expected to be coexistent with everyday life, and this affirmed a dignity in ordinary working people's lives, which as a practical matter also had to be lives of substantial drudgery.

Finally, the Protestant movement did not see the individual as simply standing in contemplation of the divine. Its "beatific vision" was about movement—the pilgrim on a journey through the alien land of this fallen world. That helps explain why *Pilgrim's Progress* had such a massive cultural resonance throughout most of America during at least the first half of the nation's history. Pilgrim's journey is an individual journey, which begins by breaking family ties and on its way encounters only a few temporary companions. All the trials, despair, and waywardness in Pilgrim's trek are not about making his way to salvation. America's Puritans clung to nothing more fiercely than the orthodox Christian view that personal salvation came from unmerited grace through faith and had no part of "works" or making "your own" way to it. Pilgrim's troubles in his progress are *after* his salvation as a believer, as he travels in this world to his heavenly destination. Hope—optimism, if you will—was a firm conviction, not just a wishful fantasy. But the fulfillment of forward-looking hope was a tough, hard slog requiring immense individual effort. The opportunities for upward mobility in America confirmed both the necessity of individual effort to get anywhere and the real possibility of the individual sojourner's dreams coming true.

In short, a Protestant view of forward-leaning, unencumbered, ordinary, and equal individuals was repeatedly reinforced amid the realities of life in America. Whether or not one was a good Protestant and read the Bible and the Puritan Fathers, daily life in America could seem a material version of Pilgrim's progress. Moreover, all of these ideas were revitalized by recurring periods of Protestant revivalism in both rural and urban parts of the nation, and these continued into the twentieth century.

As all of this was going on in America, there obviously continued to be oppressed groups in all the familiar categories of race, class, and gender. The issue here is how people in such oppressive situations were being taught over time to think of themselves in America. I think the historical record shows that when you listen to the voices in any such group at almost any time in American history, you hear talk of disadvantage and exploitation but not of defeat and submission. It is generally true that in America the oppressed were taught to think of themselves as free-standing selves, individuals pushing into the future with legitimate, equal claims to freedom, opportunity, and a better life—pilgrims with a promissory note for the American Dream.

While these Christian and largely Protestant influences were at work on democratic ideas of the person, America was also democratizing the Christian mind. The general effect, as with millennialism, was to push Christian doctrine in a series of popularly appealing directions.

The vast majority of Americans have probably always considered themselves Christians. Today upwards of 85 percent of all adult Americans identify themselves as Christians,[76] and it seems unlikely that earlier historical periods would have had significantly smaller proportions of self-professed adherents. What Americans historically have meant by calling themselves Christians is of course another matter. Here we have to rely mostly on what historians of religion have had to say about any changing understandings of the faith. In this complicated mix of developments, there are some general tendencies that can be sketched regarding ideas of the person in American Christianity.

Despite the plurality of Protestant sects, Christianity seems to have come to America with a core of orthodox doctrines distilled out of the fiery disputes of the Protestant Reformation. As noted earlier, Christianity is centered on faith in a person, not doctrines, but doctrines were important for spelling out what it is that a believer believes about that person and his meaning for the world. Of course, since Protestantism was the point of departure for America, this did favor the Lutheran-Calvinist tradition as against, say, the Thomistic tradition in the Catholic Church. Even so, the differences between Protestants and Catholics, overheated on so many things, were less than might be expected on central points. Nor is this surprising, since both Catholic teachings and

Protestant Reformed theology traced a central line of interpretation on these essentials back to Augustine, and through him to the statements of doctrine in Paul's letters.

One body of such principles dealt with the easily misunderstood view of individuals as "elected" and "predestinated." The very terms summon up images of self-righteous prigs preening themselves in New England churches before going out to look down their noses at their neighbors. In fact, this is exactly the pride of the Pharisee that Puritans believed condemned people to hell and wanted no part of.[77] As doctrine, the election and predestination of individuals had to do with the sovereignty of God in choosing those he would save or not save, and his sovereign power in seeing to it that nothing through all time could prevent that choice from being efficacious.

Another body of fundamental doctrine had to do with original sin and the limitations of free will. Here too the scope for modern misunderstandings is immense. The doctrine of original sin ("the total depravity of man" in Protestant Reformation language) is not a claim that human beings never do anything good. It is that even an individual's best actions are tainted by a prideful rebellion against God's rightful rule in one's life, a fall into the yearning to play God. The bent of every person's willful heart toward this rebellion, known as sin, means that no one in such a spiritual state has the goodness that God's holiness requires for fellowship with him. Individuals do have the capacity in their free will to make choices, but not to love and thus obey God as they should. Thus every human being is born without the ability to be in what should be a natural state of communion with his Creator. During the centuries after 400 A.D., major chunks of Catholic and Protestant Reformed theology were devoted to denouncing as heretical the claim of the Irish monk Pelagius that humans have the capacity to initiate or earn their own salvation. By contrast, the orthodox Christian view has been that unsaved man, being spiritually dead, has no capacity to help God do what only God can do for sinners.

My aim here is not to argue the many intricacies of these doctrines one way or the other. It is to point out that the prevailing tendency was for democratic thinking in America to sweep aside all these views of the individual. The theme is a Christianity that became more aligned with the desires of the people, more democratic or, as we would say today, "market-driven." (This is also to say, less Christian.)

I noted earlier that the Founding Fathers' generation had good political reasons to de-emphasize differences in religious doctrine in favor of a common Christian morality. After 1800 the upsurge of "democratic evangelicalism" gave a much more powerful and sustained push in that same direction.[78] The doctrine of election—some saved and others not—appeared undemocratic in its inegalitarian overtones. Predestination could just as easily be recognized as undemocratic in what it seems to deny about an open future of hope for individuals unencumbered by the past. With little effort, the doctrine of original sin could be perceived as a slam on an American faith in the common man's goodness. The doctrine of limited free will seemed an even worse violation of faith in the common man's capacity to govern himself and work at achieving his full God-given potential. By contrast, traditional Christian doctrine offered hope for, but no faith in, the common man or any other man. Apart from God's grace, each person had all the spiritual potential of a corpse.

Traditional Christian doctrine clearly did grate on what was becoming the American democratic creed. The result was that, over time, such doctrine had its undemocratic rough edges smoothed off, even though substantively speaking these ideas were more the core than the edges of Christian teaching. This smoothing work was done not by secularists and unbelievers but by Christian leaders of the various democratic flocks proliferating in nineteenth-century America. There was no overt design to deny traditional Christian doctrine, but there was an overt incentive and desire to keep the flocks from deserting the shepherds for preaching unpopular, democratically incorrect things. Within the ever-recurring divisions and subdivisions of American Protestantism, the competitive advantage over time—even among American theologians—consistently lay with those preaching more popular views and not with the learned clergy suspicious of a merely emotional religion, sentimentalism, and a Gospel bound to American political values.[79] At any one time one could say that there was simply a question of emphasis, say using Jonathan Edwards' or some other learned distinctions, to offer a more popularly palatable message. Do that long enough and carelessly enough, and one has changed the traditional teaching of the religion—and the theological populists did so.

Usually the first move from the pulpits was to temper public presentations of unpopular aspects of orthodox Christian doctrine, such as God's wrath against sin and the damnation of sinners. The next step, encouraged by and well under way during the Protestant revivals in nineteenth-century America, was to accept outright self-contradiction and embrace popular opportunism. Lyman Beecher, the North's leading revivalist and moral reformer in the first half of the nineteenth century, declared: "I believe that both the doctrines of dependence [man's total dependence on God for salvation] and moral accountability [man's ability and free agency in choosing to be saved] must be admitted. . . . I also believe that greater or less prominence should be given to the one or the other of these doctrines according to the prevailing state of public opinion."[80] The next step was simply to assert the opposite of traditional Christian doctrine as if nothing was happening. By the mid-nineteenth century the nation's revivalist superstar, Charles Grandison Finney, was brushing aside 1500 years of anti-Pelagian doctrine: "The moral government of God everywhere assumes and implies the liberty of the human will, and the natural ability to obey God." By the Civil War era, Lyman's son, Henry Ward Beecher, was achieving an immense public following by concentrating on the pleasures of God's love in popular sentiment and preaching little or nothing about God's judgment.[81]

A careful study of America's leading antebellum theologians

describes how easily they equated America's political morality with Christianity itself. The author, Mark Noll, concludes: "Their tragedy—and the greater the theologian the greater the tragedy—was to rest content with a God defined by the American conventions God's own loyal servants had exploited so well."[82] If this is what was happening in the higher, elite realms of American theology, it is not difficult to imagine what was going on in the free-range, hardscrabble locales of American preaching. Hierarchy and deference to authority or tradition were all but nonexistent in the competitive marketplace of American Protestantism. In this setting, any serious discussion of doctrine would invite only unending debate, confusion, and the threat of driving people to competing churches of a less "highbrow" nature. Thus there was a strong incentive to avoid what ordinary church people considered intellectual speculations (that is, careful efforts to clarify, correct, and responsibly expound doctrine) in favor of the "primitive simplicity" of Gospel truth.[83] And there was this all-important point as well: Appeals to a popular religion of the heart made much more sense than doctrinal expositions because such appeals could be presented to the common man as more authentic. Heartfelt religion seemed truer than a mere intellectual understanding of Christianity, action more useful than contemplation in America's kinetic society.

If theological populism was a constant temptation in the routine weekly sermonizing of American clergy, it was omnipresent amid the excitement of recurring Protestant revivals led by populist preachers across the land. During the nineteenth century, periodic surges of revivalism produced changes in Christian understandings of the individual that made perfect democratic sense. Something seemed to be amiss if Christian faith denied the individual's free will (that is, his or her capacity to choose, to work, and to deserve his salvation), while at the same time America's democratic faith was affirming every person's capacity for self-government in the political realm.

In the early twentieth century, new and much more thoroughly secular forces emerged to push in the same direction. A sense of guilt before God and feelings of shame for sinning were now understood to be unhealthy, psychologically damaging self-conceptions. "The old-time religion" was another name for such conceptions, and in educated circles this was coming to be seen as narrow, illiberal, and judgmental. Despite their importance among intellectuals, however, these new psychoanalytic-therapeutic ideas of the twentieth century were only overlaying influences; they served to reinforce what had already been under way for some decades in the pulpits and revival tents of America's ever more democratic Christianity. In the nineteenth century, Unitarians and other opponents of traditional Christianity had taken special delight in publicizing the doctrinal prevarications of Protestant revivalists as they sought to appeal to mass audiences. By the twentieth century fewer people seemed to notice or care, apart from an outraged subset of Protestant intellectuals who would become known as "fundamentalists." In the main body of American Protestantism, centuries-old articles of faith were becoming an empty shell. As Richard Niebuhr described it, "A God without wrath brought men without sin into a kingdom without judgment through the ministrations of a Christ without a cross."[84] In this more modern, liberal view, to become focused on creedal issues of doctrine was to risk being doctrinaire—an odd worry since there was so little doctrine to be doctrinaire about.

Beyond any particular issues of doctrine, the overall effect was to shove doctrine itself to the sidelines of American Christianity. What prospered instead was an "emotional, legalistic, and superficial folk-theology" that had literally uprooted "large sections of American Christianity . . . from the Church's great tradition." The individual American Christian could be portrayed as a feeling person but not especially a thinking person. By the mid-twentieth century, America's leading religious historian described the modern result as "a kind of 'Christianity of Main Street' . . . and with it an implicit theology—a farrago of sentimentality, moralism, democracy, free enterprise, laicism, 'confident living,' and utilitarian concern for success . . . It has reduced the number of theologically responsive and responsible people, lay and clerical."[85]

Since Sydney Ahlstrom wrote those words almost fifty years ago, the democratizing of the Christian mind has continued to push American Christianity toward a simple fideism with scant regard for doctrinal reasoning. A person is sure of what he believes because he believes it. According to a leading sociologist, since World War II the approach governing religious obligations is modern Americans' strongly held belief in "quiet faith" and "morality writ small":

> People who adhere to such a creed think the best way to fulfill our obligations to others is not by lecturing them about right and wrong, but rather by personal example. They do not believe in absolutes but in balancing what is right with what is practical. They distrust extremes, even those views they consider correct but that are asserted with too much finality. And they feel that one has to do one's best to understand, even when one does not agree with, those who think otherwise.[86]

It appears that in the last half-century many Americans have arrived at a self-understanding that is religious in tone and intent but also nonabsolutist, inclusive, modest and, above all, nonjudgmental of others. Scholars have sought various ways to describe this overall trend. One speaks of a "spirituality of seeking" replacing the "spirituality of dwelling" provided by traditional religion. Another sees competition in America's religious marketplace as being won by self-expression values—"the pursuit of self-realization through personal quests for spiritual insight and fulfillment." A third describes the general trend of "shrinking transcendence." In this process, the "little transcendences" experienced by seekers of spirituality displace the "great transcendences" of salvational religion and its promise to bridge the divide between God and man.[87]

Although none of this represents traditional Christian doctrine, by any normal understanding of the meaning of words this non-judgmental spiritual quest for self-realization is in fact doctrine. It cannot be anything else, since it is self-evidentially a thoroughgoing claim of what is right and wrong to believe. It is right to believe that all religions teach the same truths; it is wrong to believe that they do not. It is wrong to believe in absolutes without balancing them with what is practical. It is right to seek to understand those with whom you disagree but wrong to seek to tell them why you think they are wrong. It is right to distrust extremes and wrong to trust extremes you think are correct if they have too much finality in being correct.

Nonjudgmentalism, which holds that it is right not to judge others, amounts to a kind of judging without criteria. To assert the non-judgment of others can mean judging others to be worthy of respect, or to be a matter of indifference to you, or to be innocent of anything deserving judgment, or anything else one chooses it to mean. But for those who are not interested in doctrine, it does have the superficial appearance of virtue. The person of nonjudgmental faith in faith appears to be humble and open-minded. But in fact, he is just the opposite. He disdains any need to give reasons to others. He refuses others the respect of engaging in serious disagreement. He holds that to judge is to exclude and to condemn, and so he excludes and condemns anyone who does it.

But in addition to being able to claim the virtue of tolerance, not judging others also opens up a comfort zone for having a relaxed attitude about judging oneself. In this open and tolerant democratic ethos, it is far more desirable to be seen as a seeker than as a true believer (read "fanatic"). In the older Christian tradition, Pilgrim, as a true believer in the revealed Word, is racked in this world by the tribulations of faith, including the doubts and honest questioning that accompany faith on its journey. Today's Seeker is on a more open-ended and wholly self-referential journey to find what satisfies him, the place in a world of unanswerable questions where he can come to psychological rest. The odds are good that Seeker will find the Church of Don't-Be-Too-Hard-on-Yourself. Self-realization does not fit well with the ancient Judeo-Christian precept of self-mortification before God. Thus it is not surprising that among Christians and non-Christians alike, more Americans than ever before are engaged in "new" forms of an eclectic spirituality that has little or nothing to do with the Christian religious tradition.[88] On the contrary, much of this spiritual seeking resembles the pantheism that Tocqueville foresaw in America's future.

The fact is that orthodox Christianity has long rejected fideism. It has been regarded as an error, which mainstream Christianity began attacking in the third century during the days of the first Christian apologists. "It is far better to accept teachings with reason and wisdom than with mere faith," said Origen. According to this ancient view, reaffirmed by Pope John Paul II in 1998, doctrine is the product of reason applied to faith. If believers see only through the eyes of faith and neglect reason, they won't understand what they are seeing. The fideist, who considers religion as an expression of "blind faith," denies the need to give reasons for believing and thereby denies the individual's responsibility for understanding his or her faith. In the third century this opened the door to all sorts of Gnostic cults; in twentieth-century America it opened an even wider door to all sorts of "new spirituality." As John Paul put it, "It is an illusion to think that faith, tied to weak reasoning, might be more penetrating; on the contrary, faith then runs the grave risk of withering into myth or superstition."[89]

In the democratizing process that I have been describing, the exalted individual of Christianity has become exalted indeed. One might say that in the spiritual courtroom for judging righteousness, the individual has been slowly transformed from defendant to prosecutor. In what Ahlstrom called Christianity's "great tradition," God is praiseworthy whether or not He saves any sinner (grace is "amazing" in that any individual in His dock should be let off). The modern democratized Christian appears to offer praise and worship to God for having the good character to save him, with God now implicitly in the dock to explain why He does not save everybody.

Assuming that one is allowed to judge, how should we view this democratized Christianity regarding the idea of the person? Tocqueville, we recall, in considering the characteristics needed if religion was to survive well in the democratic future, put high importance on the issue of doctrine. In his view religion could do well in a democracy only if it gave up external formalities to hold onto its core articles of faith. By that standard, it would not seem that Christianity has survived very well.

There are important reasons for thinking that the demise of doctrine and the rise of nonjudgmental, quiet faith have been a very good thing. By abandoning claims of absolute truth by which the social order and individual behavior can be judged, Christianity has been made safe for democracy. It has helped produce moral citizens who are moderate in asserting any claims to truth and willing to compromise with others to produce practical results. Americans have been able to remain religious in their self-understanding as well as generally tolerant, constructively engaged democrats. Especially in light of the domestic turmoil in other religious societies, these are immense accomplishments.

But to leave the matter there is to be unfaithful to the subject. There is also the claim that religion is not something to be valued simply by the criterion of how well it serves the interests of the state and society. Seeing religion merely as something in service to earthly powers is what Christians in the Great Denouement totally rejected, as did the early Christians in the Roman Empire. This rejection was based on the very religious reason that what is absolute must not be subordinated to what is relative and human. Limiting the power of the state and the organized church over each other was a matter of keeping relative things relative. Over, under, and around all that was the superior matter of man's relation to his sovereign Creator. Christianity did much to shape the idea of the individual in American democracy, mainly it would seem for the better. America drew Christian thinking on that subject in its own democratic direction, mainly for the worse in terms of anything like traditional Christian doctrine.

How did Christianity help build a particular kind of political society in America, and how was the religion shaped in turn by that society? I have already discussed one of the chief influences of Christianity on the idea of political society. The Great Denouement was explicitly about individual religious liberty, but implicitly it presented a more general vision of a political society that could be pluralistic, non-hierarchical, and yet unified, or at least in a very important sense at one with itself. In philosophical terms, evoking such a possible vision was a very Big Deal. From the origins of Greek philosophy, one of the most enduring problems in thinking about political society has been the conundrum of the one and the many. If society is only a many, there can be no unity and chaos must result. If society is unity, there can be no many and the vibrant hues of humanity must be crushed. Christianity entered this intellectual puzzle palace and in effect said, no, unity and plurality can be compatible. Christian theology gave warrant for this seemingly illogical claim: there is one God in three persons. So too did ecclesiology: the Christian community is one body of different, mutually dependent members.

Of course these abstractions could be and were consistent with a medieval hierarchy of such differentiated members, in one great Chain of Being, as it was called. The advent of Protestantism, and the practical experiences of such people in America, flattened pluralism, so to speak, into a horizontal vision of differentiated unity. The one church of Christ, to be the true church of Christ, must exist as a multiple and voluntary body of believers. So said Protestants. Moreover, as noted earlier, America was born religiously pluralistic, and colonial thinking gradually moved to accommodate itself to that inescapable fact on the ground. A singularity could be plural—varied flowers, one bouquet. These were not just poetic metaphors but new conceptualizations introduced into antiquity's debate. As such, they had the capacity to make what was unthinkable into something thinkable. And until a pluralistic society of oneness, an "E Pluribus Unum," became thinkable, there was no intellectually defensible way to work for it. In many ways worth discussing but beyond the scope of this essay, Protestants and Catholics in America brought such intellectual conceptions down to earth as religious associations in civil society that insisted on holding together the seemingly contradictory commitments to human individuality and social solidarity.[90]

Given the actual religious and social conditions in America, this structural puzzle about political society was relatively easy to address (though always difficult in practice to resolve). The problem of stability and change in the new political society was another matter. For classical republican thinking, change meant ultimate decay and collapse, as republics were born, matured, and aged. But the idea of stability could be no less threatening; it seemed to endorse the entrenched powers of every status quo fixed in place against republican liberty. Christianity in America did not really debate this philosophical problem of stability and change. It simply went into action and helped solve it.

At first glance it might seem an absurd idea for religious "pilgrims"—literally, foreigners passing through—to be building anything in their field of transit. In this common view of religion, a truly spiritual person must regard this world as "fly-over" territory that is not worth bothering about. But orthodox Christian dogma has always rejected any idea of believers living a spiritual existence apart from the world. As Christians and particularly as Protestants, many Americans saw themselves called to act in their local world, and their particular ways of acting helped shape distinctive features of American political society.

It might be said that by definition, Protestants are protestors. And there has certainly never been any lack of people in America who are willing to protest. However, it is important to understand that before Protestantism is a "protest," it is an affirmation. Otherwise there would be no basis for protesting. The Protestant political influence in America has not come from people who have primarily thought of themselves as protestors against authority; rather, it has come from people who have seen themselves as affirming the original values that existing authorities have forgotten or corrupted. Authenticity had to trump authority. This has important implications for the kind of "protesting" presence these people have been in American society. As Richard Niebuhr put it:

> The protests of Protestantism—always allowing for the presence in them of rebellious self-assertions—have been secondary, for the most part, to revivals. The movement of protest from generation to generation has followed, not preceded, a movement of reformation, regeneration, awakening, and renewal. And the protest was raised not against the authority of the old, but against its acceptance and establishment of a mediocre form of men's moral and religious existence.[91]

A political society of affirmation and protest not only called people to act in the world; it also continually re-called them to revive from their slacking off. Protestant revival and political renewal fed off each other. In democratic America, the Old Testament's easy way out of blaming bad kings for moral decline was no longer available. One had to dwell on the shortcomings of an entire people, and Protestant democracy could do so in the confident hope of striving for spiritual and moral renewal. Just as the Puritans' godly covenant had the jeremiad as its inevitable accompaniment, so post-revolutionary American political society became accustomed to develop through pulsations of Protestant revivalism. Puritans saw themselves as a chosen people continually on the verge of becoming Babylonians. Revivalists saw America as a Christian nation in repeated grave need of being Christianized.

Thus any simple idea of liberal/conservative, pro- or anti-change, wholly misses the point—which is that "revival" can mean any or all of those things. Protestantism was both a stabilizing and a destabilizing force in American political society. In implementing the moral calculus of republicanism, such religion helped produce stable citizens with at least an expectation (if not always the fact) of responsible moral conduct. Acting under the affirmative impulse to help purify society, these same citizens could be counted on to be destabilizing agents of change. Likewise, their religious energy meant that Protestants were both a dividing force, as they followed a penchant for sticking their noses into other people's business, and a uniting force, as they called all Americans back to widely shared ideals. America has many political stories, but squarely in the center of them is a procession of recurring Protestant revivals, personal awakenings, and religious-political reform movements pressing for institutional change.

These themes began appearing with the first of the noteworthy Protestant revivals to occur in the nation, the Great Awakening in the 1730s and 1740s. For reasons that are not clear, these years witnessed an outbreak of religious fervor across the colonies. Although it varied in different regions, the common experience reported was an awakening to God's call in one's life. Dullness and despair, often superintended by a spiritually dead clergy, were transformed into hope and joy through regenerated hearts.

The spreading revival cut across traditional lines of occupation, region, gender, and race. It overturned churches of unregenerated clergymen and created new congregations and new preachers (including, in the North at least, blacks, Indians, and women) who were "alive to the word of God." The revivals mobilized ordinary people to assemble as they never had before and helped promote a shared identity, the first to actually spread across colonial boundaries. Among the many important implications for political society, perhaps the most significant for our purposes is that the Great Awakening endorsed personal commitments to living in truth even at the price of challenging and rejecting traditional authority. It was the "old lights" of paternal authority who had betrayed the experiential truth of Christianity. Rebellion by the "new lights" was not in the name of new values or the work of a rebellious heart; rather, rebellion was in the name of old, eternally true values, and thus a duty. There is good reason to see the years following the 1740s as an extension of this awakening. Political republicanism and spiritual regeneration were blended to make the independence claimed in 1776 a moral as well as a merely political concept.[92]

Subsequent revivals lacked such revolutionary implications, but they nonetheless had great political importance. For millions of ordinary people, over many time periods, this line of movement from personal regeneration to social regeneration infused American political society with a penchant for moralization, voluntary organization, and popular inclusiveness that would otherwise not have been there. These are precisely the features of American public life that have always evoked knowing smirks from Old World sophisticates amused by Americans' puritanical and innocent approach to public affairs. I will consider each of these three features in turn.

First, revivalism has served to continually re-moralize American politics, a point that is easily caricatured and misunderstood. Europeans have always found it amusing, even touching, to observe Americans' earnest efforts to "clean up politics" and produce "good," rather than merely effective, government. And it is surely true that over the years there have more than enough examples of American reformers' naïveté to keep the snickering going. Abandoning doctrines of original sin in the nineteenth century helped produce a far too rosy view of what could be expected from human beings and their institutions—a foolishness which eighteenth-century Calvinism saw through and to which liberal Protestantism was especially prone.[93]

However, the continual efforts to re-moralize politics did more than just reveal reformers' naïveté. Revivalism imparted a distinctively Protestant tone (now commonly labeled as "puritanical") to American politics. As revivalists viewed the world, a base and unreformed politics interfered with the moral duty to try to correct the failings one saw in society. Such a politics corrupted the benevolent purposes that should guide public action. This way of thinking helped teach Americans to view political action in a particular way, as a kind of benevolent problem-solving aimed at purifying and restoring society. Obviously this is not the whole story on political thinking in America, but it needs to be understood as an important and distinctive element of the story that Protestantism contributed.

The Protestants' impulse to moralize politics has deep roots. In this tradition every believer is to be viewed as "his own priest," with no need for churchly human intermediaries between himself and God. And with no confession booth for confiding to a priest, no penance imposed by church authorities, no earthly apparatus of indulgences to get him off the hook with God, every Protestant believer is in a way his own moralist. A proactive stance toward judging what is right and wrong comes with the Protestant territory. At the same time, the individual is not left on his or her own without standards. There is of course the Bible, the Word which each person is to encounter directly. Some efforts to re-moralize politics have found Protestants trying to place the Bible's dos and don'ts more or less directly into legislative enactments. At the same time, there has also been a Protestant moralism that has continuously challenged such "legalism" in the name of a larger Christian calling to benevolence and following the Word that took the form of a person.

The messy historical fact is that both these views of Protestant moralism have been operating during every effort at spiritual and political regeneration. But especially with the nineteenth-century evangelical explosion in America, the dominant emphasis in moral standards was put on "knowing Jesus." This in turn had a very definite meaning for Protestant reformers. While all religions offer their followers enduring rules and positive ideals to be sought, Christianity offers an ideal person. For believers, this person offers (among other things) a perfect model of human existence, a God-man who fully reveals man to himself. By this standard the mark of *agape* love is what it means to be fully human—in other words, to love others selflessly without judging their merits or thinking of one's own needs. Protestant reformers saw such benevolence as wholly consistent with telling those same people that they were doing something wrong and should stop it.

Since evangelical Christianity focused on the individual and his or her moral behavior in society, political reform efforts were often heavily tilted toward public measures against drinking, gambling, prostitution, Sabbath-breaking, and other "vice" issues. The moralization of politics became more confused as industrial development transformed America after the Civil War. Some looked at the joblessness and other urban problems and saw a need to redouble efforts at anti-vice legislation to enforce middle-class propriety and personal responsibility. Others sought new ways of uplifting urban lives with "scientific charity," orphanages, settlement houses, and education. Yet others saw the social evils as something more than the result of individual acts of sinfulness. For them, the need was to apply the "social gospel" to the new large-scale structures of commerce and affirm the moral quality of economic relations with new forms of labor legislation and social insurance.[94] And still others launched the "godly insurgencies" of Populism to try and make the economic and political regime responsive to the interests of the common man.[95] Over the decades, Protestant reformers in conjunction with others pursued all of these causes and many more. If their Christian commitment did not provide all or even most of the answers, it did supply the unmistakable moral energy for social and political reform in America well into the twentieth century.

Protestantism's revivals and reform movements were not about legislating evangelical theology, which as we have seen was in a general state of doctrinal decline. They were mainly about Protestant moralists working out the model of Benevolence, the religious duty of seeking the good of others. To modern eyes they were, of course, committing the ultimate sin of thinking you know what is best for other people. But they did think that, and they busied themselves in the public arena trying to be faithful to that belief. They were rightly dubbed do-gooders, although they prob-

71

ably would have rather been called "those who hunger and thirst after righteousness." In any case, the issue was not whether a person can be good without God. It was more basic than that. Protestant revivalism helped instill in public life the expectation that in the first place one ought to be good—rather than merely powerful, smart, effective, and all the other attributes the world expects.

The second effect of revivalism on political society is easier to identify and briefly describe. It has to do with learning the politics of voluntary organization in a democracy. Protestant revivals were not identified with particular churches, and they did not aim at strengthening institutional religion. They were mobilizations of ordinary people—a religious populism. Their leaders were entrepreneurs with the common touch rather than representatives of the learned clergy in established church orders. Their expertise was in reaching people, organizing them, and moving everyone forward with a common purpose.[96] Protestantism, which had always been more of a movement than a structure, became in America a way of doing religion and then organizing the same way to do good in politics.

In the early revivals and awakenings, Protestant elders often expressed concern that such occurrences should be spontaneous—the independent workings of the Holy Spirit rather than something "gotten up" by preachers who were skillful in appealing to common people's emotions. In this way, America's religious founders matched the political founders' concern for a virtuous republicanism in which one stood and was drafted rather than "ran" for office by courting the people. And in both cases, the realities of democratic life in the nineteenth century swept aside such views. Soon it was difficult to distinguish the preparations and machinery of mass evangelism from the mass politics of political parties. The conversion of a sinner could be seen as nothing miraculous but rather as the natural result of a properly planned and effectively implemented set of organizational techniques. As one of the greatest of the nineteenth-century revivalists put it, conversion "is not a miracle or dependent on a miracle in any sense. . . . It is purely a philosophical result of the right use of con-stituted means."[97] As the campaigns for moral reform grew more sophisticated, the same pattern repeated itself. Between 1865 and 1920 it was overwhelmingly religious groups who invented and applied the lobbying techniques that later became standard oper-ating procedure for interest groups of all kinds.[98]

In helping Americans learn how to organize politics, Protestant revival and reform contributed something very mundane yet very important to political society: it taught people still experimenting in self-government a practical way to domesticate the question of political power. Political power could be, and was, domesticated by people organizing within a free democratic process to push for needed change. The practical political effect was to house-train an issue drenched in centuries of blood and turn it into something or-dinary people could live with—indeed, participate in—amid rela-tive peace.

Finally, the Protestants' revival and reform movements, by their very nature, introduced a pluralist politics of inclusion into the American scene. It was a paradoxical, Protestant kind of inclu-siveness in that it was achieved by ever more denominational divi-sions accommodating differences of race, class, region, and con-gregational opinion. This conflict within pluralism itself could be portrayed and then celebrated as a series of successes of the Amer-ican pluralist ideal.[99] In this welter of denominations and moral-ized politics, it was always difficult for Christian reformers to get around their religion's commitment to human equality. It was this problem—taking form in the early abolition movement's de-bate over women speakers and "mixed" (that is, male and female) audiences—that almost immediately set in motion the forces that led to the women's movement of the 1840s. If notions of Chris-tian equality did not suffice to produce inclusion, then the prac-ticalities of movement politics in a democracy did: more people meant more influence.

In either case, the revivals and reform movements of Protes-tant do-gooders opened up new spaces in political society that women and other oppressed groups had never had access to before. Among the earliest and latest beneficiaries were blacks and women. After the abolition and early women's suffrage movements, the coming of industrialization and its attendant social problems gave even more prominence to the "feminization" of Christian social activism. Americans still believed that women's place was in the Christian home, but many American women also believed it was women's place to protect the Christian home. The result was many new mobilizations around measures that would safeguard women and families amid the pressures of urban factory life, as well as against the temptations of bars, gamblers, and low women that were leading men astray. None of these religious-political movements was more formidable than the Women's Christian Temperance Union of Frances Willard and her mass of associates spread throughout the federal political system.[100] From this feminization one could track a corresponding reform movement to reaffirm a "masculine Christianity," especially among disadvantaged young urban males through scouting, the YMCA, and other manly sports associations.[101] And still to come was the much bigger story of the twentieth-century civil rights movement and the pivotal role of black Protestant churches.

For a time moral reform movements succeeded in the legislatures, with laws prohibiting or regulating Sabbath-breaking, alcohol, lotteries, and distribution of immoral literature and birth control through the mail. Ultimately almost all of this anti-vice legislation failed in the first half of the twentieth century, none more spectacularly than Prohibition. By contrast, economic and human rights legislation produced through such efforts—maximum work hours and minimum wage laws, worker safety and sanitation, Mothers' Pensions, child protection laws, civil rights initiatives—served as the basis for permanent reforms in American institutions. The point here is not to list the successes and failures of Protestant reformers in producing new policies, but to point to the kind of political society they tended to produce. And on that score, Protestantism was a powerful civics school. It helped produce a lively, kinetic political society of joiners. It mobilized people who often disagreed with and annoyed others, but also pushed everyone to keep talking. It taught people to pay attention to what is right or wrong in the way American society is behaving itself. In doing that, it taught people to see the social world not as a set of permanent conditions but as a series of problems that need to be "fixed" (itself a uniquely American term). It schooled ordinary people in the confidence that, if there "ought'a be a law" to fix things, then people like you and me have the capacity to make or unmake such a law and set things right. It taught citizens that, whatever you might personally stand to gain, you had better be able to argue that what you want is for the larger good of a moral republic. In short, it taught Americans how to be responsibly democratic.

How then did such a political society affect Christianity? Although the reforming evangelicalism of the nineteenth century taught Americans to equate the Christian gospel with their democratic political society, there were always some Christian voices worried that such political engagements were a distraction from the true purpose of their religion. That purpose, they said, is to fulfill the Great Commission to spread the good news of God's salvation, given through Christ's atonement for human sin. And as these critics pointed out, the early church of believers who knew the flesh-and-blood Jesus left no record of trying to reform the inhumane politics and policies of the Roman Empire.

The ambivalent relationship between Protestant revival and political reform was embodied in Charles Grandison Finney, the leading antebellum evangelist. To old-style Protestant revivalists, Finney was the incarnation of suspicious "new measures" for getting up a revival movement. He mastered the arts of publicity—holding all-night prayer sessions and week-long meetings, praying about sinners by name, including women to pray and exhort in mixed company, attacking unregenerated clergy as spiritually cold and dead, designating the "anxious seat" at the front of a revival meeting to publicly acknowledge the sinner's repentance. In short, he was a master entrepreneur in mass evangelism. And yet Finney and some Protestant revivalists after him were skeptical about using laws to deal with social evils. Slavery, for example, was a spiritual sin that needed to be confronted by converting slave holders, not by joining the abolition movement. From Finney's antebellum doubts to the mid-twentieth-century opponents of Martin Luther King Jr. in some black churches, the claim has been that Christians do their duty by changing hearts, not laws.

Despite misgivings about marrying Christianity to various worldly projects to do good, there have been few doubts about a larger bond that has grown over the centuries. It is the bond uniting Christianity and the democratic faith in the political society that is America. This general outlook is so pervasive and taken for granted that no single term, such as the old standbys "civil religion" or Americanism, really does it justice.[102] The outlook is philosophical in that it is devoted to democracy as the sole legitimate form of government. It is historical in that it upholds the sanctified vision of the Nation's mission. It is sociological in that it is committed to the American way of life. It is political in that it champions self-government by free individuals. It is all but mystical in invoking "the promise of American life." Theologically, it is possible to imagine a person being a Christian and not believing any of those things, but it is almost unthinkable that one could be an American Christian and not believe those things. To be un-American is to be un-Christian.

None of this is to imply that Americans developed an outlook asserting the converse: that to be un-Christian was to be un-American. The Great Denouement and its long-established results inoculated Americans against any such theocratic intolerance. The question here is how American political society affected Christianity, and the answer is that it more or less absorbed Christianity into a political identity.

Pushing for this fusion were all the convergences we have seen between American democracy and Christianity in the ideas of history, the person, and political society. More than anything else, however, it was war that helped Americans to understand the Christian faith and the democratic faith as virtually indistinguishable. The antecedents for this merging went back to the American Revolutionary War and then, with even greater public force, to the Civil War.[103]

Even so, at the beginning of the twentieth century a significant body of Protestant opinion held itself fairly indifferent to public affairs, and implicitly to America's political fortunes. In the words of the leading revivalist Dwight L. Moody, "I look upon this world as a wrecked vessel. God has given me a lifeboat and said to me, 'Moody, save all you can.'"[104] Beyond that, a growing body of pre-millennialist Protestants found the events surrounding World War I significant only insofar as they might usher in the prophesied second coming of Christ before the millennium. With American entry into the war in 1917, these "fundamentalists" (the term had just been coined) found themselves under devastating attacks from more moderate, mainstream Protestants for being unpatriotic and a threat to national security, possibly with the help of German money.[105] Such incidents gave only a small indication of the larger tendency, under the pressure of events, to merge political and religious identities. Whether one went on to be for or against the League of Nations, the underlying premise took root: America's democratic cause in the world was also the Christian cause.

It was above all the two great wars of the rest of the century—World War II and the Cold War—that seemed to cement the union of democratic faith and Christian faith for America. Writing from the depths of World War II's darkness, Jacques Maritain as a European Catholic expressed the idea that many Americans had already come to understand in their bones: "The democratic impulse has arisen in human history as a temporal manifestation of the inspiration of the Gospel." Maritain went on to quote President Roosevelt about the war coalition's aim to establish "an international order in which the spirit of Christ shall rule the hearts of men and of nations," as well as Vice President Henry Wallace's claim that "Democracy is the only true political expression of Christianity."[106] If some harbored doubts about America's redeemer role as a Christian nation, fascism helped remove them.

Immediately on the heels of defeating anti-democratic paganism, Americans found themselves turning to lead the worldwide fight against anti-democratic atheism. One did not have to be either a right-wing anti-communist or a Christian to see that once again, America faced a foe devoted to liquidating at the same stroke both Christianity and democracy. As much as anything else, it was their enemies that taught Americans to merge the Christian into the democratic identity. It made perfect sense to see Christian democratic liberty fighting against anti-Christian totalitarian slavery. It was not an illusion to see that freedom's chances might coincide with those of the evangelical message.

Amid these storms, Augustine's image of two cities now became the patriot's assertion of one city. What had been an equivocal relationship was becoming univocal. There was, to say the least, a downside for Christianity in all this. Missing from the view of America as the shining city was Winthrop's understanding that the brightness meant simply exposure; it could be for good or ill in the eyes of both God and the world. And if faithless, it would have been better to stay an unchosen people in history's shadows. That was not just Puritan doctrine and but solid Christian doctrine. However, it was not America's doctrine. By the middle of the twentieth century that doctrine amounted to a generally unqualified assertion of American goodness, especially in light of its enemies, with only the barest sense of judgment looming in the background. America, the carrier of the sanctified cause of freedom and democracy, acquired a purity and ultimacy of meaning that was all but indistinguishable from worship. Christian Patriotism could become a way of kneeling before the world while telling yourself you are not committing idolatry.

In the mid-twentieth century the sociologist Will Herberg surveyed the American scene and famously concluded that "to be a

Protestant, a Catholic, or a Jew are today the alternative ways of being an American." Generally overlooked is what Herberg saw as the result of this political absorption of religious identity: a religiousness with almost any kind of content or none, a way of sociability or belonging rather than a way of reorienting life to God.[107] Herberg was ahead of his time in catching the drift of things. He just had not yet come up with the terms "spirituality" and "self-realization."

With these results in mind—a generally unchristian view of history, the submergence of recognizably Christian doctrine in favor of a popular religion, the elevation of a political identity at the expense of Christianity's critical and hesitant stance toward even the best of human intentions and claims—what then should we conclude? Tocqueville took as his point of departure the New England Puritans, an admittedly hard act to follow. But if we take that same baseline and look at the span of almost 400 years since then, it is reasonable to conclude that Christianity has probably been better for American democracy than American democracy has been for Christianity.

Coming Apart

Writing from a Birmingham jail in April 1963, Martin Luther King Jr. grieved over the Christian church in America:

> So often it is an arch-defender of the status quo. Far from being disturbed by the presence of the church, the power structure of the average community is consoled by the church's silent and often even vocal sanction of things as they are. . . . If today's church does not recapture the sacrificial spirit of the early church, it will lose its authenticity, forfeit the loyalty of millions, and be dismissed as an irrelevant social club with no meaning for the 20th century.[108]

King's words repeated the time-honored call. Americans must turn revived, more authentic Christian hearts toward political action that will reform society and institutionalize God's call to righteousness and justice. However, his words were also a lament that indicated how, by the middle of the twentieth century, the easy conjoining of American Christianity and American patriotism had produced a fundamental complacency. That self-righteous complacency of a "Christian nation"—long and quietly being eroded by even deeper forces—set the stage for what happened next. That next big thing was, of course, the Sixties. The Sixties were a broad, political-cultural phenomenon that amounted to something much more than just a ten-year span on the century's calendar. With the crucial exception of the early civil rights movement, the reform demands in this period did not come from politically engaged Christians. The push to overturn the prevailing complacency came mainly from secular moralists, for whom the patriotic/Christian worldview was overwhelming evidence for the charge of hypocrisy.

Despite the hoopla of the time, the Sixties were not a sudden breakdown or fork in the road concerning democracy and Christianity in America. To recall the metaphor I invoked earlier, the Sixties were a dramatic confirmation that the two strands in the double helix had been winding away from each other for some time. And if the Sixties were a marker about what had already been happening—a story of America's democratic faith and its Christian faith coming apart—they were also a marker for the future, pointing to the development of two antagonistic stories between those two faiths. That is the subject of this section.

I do not wish to exaggerate the growing antagonism; and here, as usual, Tocqueville offers good advice. Although he was referring to his French peers, Tocqueville might as well have been writing about some of today's Christian activists campaigning to "reclaim America." As he put it, "Imagining unbelief to be something new, they comprise all that is new in one indiscriminate animosity. They are at war with the age and country" (275–276). The coming apart being discussed here does not mean that Christians have been turning their backs on the country. On the contrary, they, like Americans in general, have continued to endorse values of family, piety, and patriotism as a united whole. The current evidence is that conservative Protestants, when compared to Americans of other religious affiliations or no religion, actually have more national pride and feel more strongly that the rest of the world should imitate the United States.[109] But by the beginning of the twenty-first century one could also hear a new separatist theme in respected Christian circles, telling believers not to be unequally yoked to a secularized America. By the same token, coming apart does not mean that actively anti-Christian attitudes have developed among large numbers of Americans, four out of five of whom still identify themselves as Christians. But by the beginning of the twenty-first century, there was a newly articulated view in many quarters that zealous Christians who were politically active posed a threat to the ways of democracy. After several centuries of silence, the old Rousseauian view could now be heard that when Christians are behaving like good Christians, they make poor citizens.

We are speaking of a "Christian problem" for American democracy and a "democracy problem" for American Christians, and it is something much more than a simple, straight-line reaction to the Sixties. In moving through their life cycle, Baby Boomers have produced so many stresses in the nation that they are strongly tempted to think they are always the cause rather than the effect of things. In an important sense, however, the cultural-political-religious outburst known as the Sixties was a fulfillment of tendencies underway for decades. Alongside the convergences in American democracy and Christianity that we have seen (in the ideas of history, personhood, and political society) there were countervailing movements in the twentieth century that at first hardly seemed to be part of any pattern. Yet what was happening in the schools, the courts, and what I will call consumption arts eventually did add up to a new understanding of American public life. It was a development of doctrine that undercut the apparent harmony of American democracy and Christianity. The discord arose slowly and then came out with a crash in the Sixties. What we are likely to notice now is the noise of the crash and not the quieter prelude that occurred throughout the prior decades of the twentieth century.

PRELUDE: THE DEVELOPMENT OF PUBLIC DOCTRINE

The first thing to notice about the development of a new public doctrine is an absence. For roughly three decades leading up to the Sixties, the political voice of conservative Protestantism was barely heard in the mainstream of American public affairs, at least not in comparison with its resounding presence previously in American history. This silence was largely the result of a series of political body blows suffered by Protestant traditionalists during the first third of the twentieth century. Here again we need to gain a deeper perspective on how American political development was intertwined with the turns in American Christianity in general and Protestantism in particular.

At the beginning of the twentieth century, Protestantism in America consisted of a broad and culturally dominant coalition that was trying in various ways to respond to the challenge of "modernism." Natural science challenged any belief in miracles; Darwinian evolution denied man's special creation; and historical criticism threw into doubt the literal accuracy of biblical records. At the same time theological innovators sought to equate religion with morality and to identify the Kingdom of God with the moral progress of civilization. In these and many other ways, modernism—or, as it was also pejoratively termed, "liberalism"—challenged Christians to update their traditional religious ideas to conform to modern culture. In brief, the message was to drop the supernatural baggage.

Protestants, being Protestants, exhibited a variety of responses to this modernist challenge.[110] Some leading and lay Protestants in various denominations were almost embarrassingly eager to adapt to the new outlook. Still, it is fair to say that most of the responses being produced by America's Protestant establishment were more or less conservative—at least in the sense of resisting wholesale conversion to modernism. Within this larger conservative response, some were especially militant in confronting and taking the political offensive against the forces of religious liberalism (both within Protestantism and in the larger society). These more militant champions of traditional views gradually acquired their own identity and, in the 1920s, their own label: "fundamentalists." Lest we fall prey to subsequent caricatures, it is worth recognizing that the fundamentalist faction within conservative Protestantism was not a fringe group of uneducated, backwoods "Bible-thumpers." While remaining close to the dominant evangelical revivalism of the nineteenth century, the fundamentalists of the early twentieth century emphasized a rigorously intellectual dimension of correct doctrine as well as the "heart" dimension of conversion and personal piety. The twelve volumes called *The Fundamentals* that were published from 1910 to 1915 included contributions from over three dozen prominent American and British scholars. These books presented a thoroughgoing critique of modernists' attack on traditional Christianity, along with essays by more popular writers (the series ended with the conversion testimony of a prominent New York lawyer).[111]

By sharpening and insisting on a clear choice between modernism and the truths of Scripture, fundamentalism as a religious-political movement exposed and then widened the fissures existing within America's Protestant establishment in this first third of the twentieth century. The militancy of the fundamentalists meant confrontation.

In the early 1920s, highly publicized fights within mainline Protestant denominations found those now being called "fundamentalists" losing to the more moderate forces who could produce majorities dedicated to keeping peace within a given denomination.[112] As these intra-Protestant battles were being lost, the 1925 Scopes Trial gave national attention to the fundamentalists' crusade in the larger society to legislatively restrict teaching human evolution in the public schools. After dramatic coverage by the national press and the new medium of radio, the humiliation of the fundamentalists in the person of William Jennings Bryan was celebrated by cosmopolitan opinion leaders, who wrote retrospective and largely inaccurate interpretations of what happened.[113] But there was worse to come. In the words of Michael Kazin, "Prohibition was *the* Protestant issue of the day. It had transcendent significance—both because it would cure a social evil that ruined and corrupted millions of lives and because it satisfied, better than any other issue, the urge to purify American culture that had frustrated Christian reformers since the end of the Civil War."[114] The fiasco of trying to enforce the Eighteenth Amendment and then its almost effortless, half-comic repeal in 1933 made the defeat of old-school Protestantism in the public arena seem complete. If anything, the whole Prohibition issue had only enhanced the secularists' cause by portraying Christians as intolerant, self-righteous and, above all, hypocritical. Modernists felt sure they had girdled fundamentalism and left it to die.

The overall effect of these developments was for the defeated conservative Christian forces to retreat into the public and political background. Fundamentalists nurtured their own seminaries, Bible institutes, publications, and radio programs. On the fringes of this subculture in the 1930s and 1940s were populist preachers who railed against "modern ways," liberal conspiracies, and communist plots. Embarrassed by all this, the larger body of thoughtful conservative Protestants tended to simply disappear from publicly visible roles in mainstream universities, journals of opinion, the media, and politics. All in all, in the decades before the 1960s, America's increasingly secular intellectual elites had little trouble relegating Christian traditionalists to the category of anti-intellectual cultural laggards—people who, if not paranoid, were at least suffering status anxiety. And it is probably true to say that by the 1960s, the raucous radio evangelists and others whom the public perceived as Christian fundamentalists did lack the intellectual rigor to match or appreciate their predecessors' volumes of *The Fundamentals.*[115]

Thus it was that the once powerful Protestant conservative forces of earlier times tended to be the dog that did not bark while portentous changes were under way in America's schools, courts, and popular culture. I will briefly sketch each of these contributions to the development of a secular public doctrine.

The Schools. Secularization in public education, as in other spheres, was not some vaguely impersonal, natural process of social evolution. It was the result of an intentional struggle for cultural authority among differing elites, some of whom wished to enhance or maintain Christianity's educational significance while others wanted to reduce or eliminate that influence in favor of purely secular understandings of life.[116] Long before American courts had anything to say on the subject and before Progressive reformers systematized the movement with state-level centralization of school administration and curricula, champions of "modern" ways of thinking were attacking the anti-scientific religious orientation in American public schools. Traditionalists upheld a schoolroom culture of biblical theism as the bedrock of the moral education and social ethics that were to be taught. Modernizers attacked this culture using the new social sciences and advanced educational thinking from German research universities. Elizabeth Cady Stanton summed up the case for secularization in 1897:

> Theology covers the realm of the unknowable . . . The time has come to study religion as a science, an essential element in every human being, differing with climate and civilization . . . The Bible has been the greatest block in the way of [scientific] progress. Why then continue to read it in our public schools? . . . The religion of humanity centers the duties of the church in this life . . . Instead of spending so much time and thought over the souls of the multitude and over delusive promises of the joys to come in another life, we should make for them a

paradise here . . . If the same laws govern all parts of the universe, and are only improved by the higher development of man himself, we must begin to lay the foundation-stones of the new heaven and the new earth here and now. Equal rights for all . . . will be the triumph of true religion and such [will be] the solution of the problem of just government.[117]

John Dewey and his many fellow reformers went on to establish the crucial linkages between secularization, faith in democracy, and a progressive social and economic policy agenda. While the modernizers' project was not religious in any traditional sense of the term, neither was it thoroughly materialistic (however much biblical creationists attacked the teaching of evolution in the new curriculum). Ordinary Americans would never have countenanced philosophical materialism for their children. Instead, Dewey and allied educational reformers extracted the moral element of Christian theism and naturalized it into an ethics of democracy for this world. The reformers' habitual expropriation of religious language to describe what they were doing simply expressed the fact that democracy, embodied in a new democratic personality, was the religious faith of secular education. Thus in his 1892 essay "Christianity and Democracy," Dewey presented democracy "as the means by which the revelation of truth is carried on. It is in democracy, the community of ideas and interest through community of action, that the incarnation of God (man, that is to say as organ of universal truth) becomes a living, present thing, having its ordinary and natural sense." In the service of this proper social order for social growth, the secularized teacher was sanctified as "the prophet of the true God and the usherer in of the true kingdom of God."[118] Traditional religion could now be seen mainly as an impediment to broader values of tolerance and social inclusion, an inhibition on individual self-expression, and an enemy of free scientific inquiry—all of the things essential for continued human progress.

"Secularization" seems too tame a word for the transformation being implemented by the new professionalized machinery of public education. Traditional religion had claimed to authoritatively teach truth. Now the more authentically human religion of democracy taught an open-ended search for never-final truths. Before, a social ethic that taught all were responsible for all was derived from the higher spiritual responsibility of every human being who must finally stand in judgment before a righteous God. Now the social ethic of equality, freedom, and justice was derived from democratic society itself, with one's religious outlook a purely private appendage. Democracy was a form of government, as Dewey put it, "only because it is a form of moral and spiritual association."

Rightly understood—that is to say, in secular terms—democracy now became another name for experimental, intelligent inquiry by citizens, each equal in his or her human dignity precisely because each was equal in one's freedom to seek out and choose the personal meanings for one's life. Democracy was now taught not just as a way of governing but as a way of living, which is to say religiously. Democracy was a self-directing growth process of secular autonomy for both the society and the individual. Such a democratic society was continually learning to provide the equal conditions necessary for human thriving. Democratic individuals were always pursuing their continuous growth and expression of personality as an end in itself. With "God talk" set out of bounds, the young democrat undergoing such an education was invited to identify with America's secular democratic heroes: Emerson's "endless seeker," Thoreau's individual moving to the beat of a different drummer, Whitman's singer of songs democratic to himself: "Healthy, free, the world before me / The long brown path before me, leading wherever I choose."[119] The all but inescapable implication was that to journey toward self-discovery, one had to leave behind the religion of churches, parents, hand-me-down doctrines, and any idea of natural law.[120] Instead the individual is called to enter a liberated condition of being free to choose among the ideas and practices of any or no religion without being judged or casting judgments. Personal freedom is the ultimate root of moral obligations.

Thus in the modern doctrine of public education, the American seeker for his own truth and the moral advocate for equal rights would be one and the same democratic person. Such a person could be thoroughly skeptical about any absolute truths handed down from traditional religious authority and thoroughly confident in the absolute value of democracy—that is to say, individuals thinking on their own to collectively advance an unquestioned belief in equal rights and human freedom. In this view, traditional religion has been and is a bulwark to the status quo, while spiritually seeking individuals are now the natural allies of social and political progress.[121]

During the first half of the twentieth century, state-level efforts of Progressive reformers to modernize the public school system were reinforced by the thoroughgoing secularization of America's major universities and academic elites. In the vanguard were the new social sciences.[122] Sociologists, often it seems with a deeply anti-religious agenda, helped relativize all religious beliefs. In psychology, there was a particularly good fit with new advanced thinking on the nature of personal freedom; the traditional virtue of suppression of inner drives became the sin of repressing what was most natural and personal, thus violating human freedom. In history, speculations about the meaning or philosophy of history gave way to more scientific methods and middle-range interpretations. Interestingly enough, it was political science that lagged behind public school reformers in giving wholehearted endorsement to the democratic faith. After a good deal of equivocation about the common man's capacity for self-government (especially during the years of economic depression and fascist success), American political scientists chastened by World War II finally signed on to the general democratic faith.[123] In that faith, skepticism about any claims to final truth is the only intelligent position to hold, and only democracy allows free, equal citizens to engage in the open-ended search for personal choices to govern lives, both individually and in common. Social scientists could never quite explain why, but this secular truth of democracy was the one thing in which a person could have absolute faith.

By the mid-twentieth century, at all levels of schooling, the education experienced by any American under public instruction was highly secular. The issue here is not whether this was a good or a bad thing. The point is that this is a thing that happened, something that had important consequences for the development of a public doctrine regarding Christianity and American democracy.

The Courts. It was at this stage that developments in the federal courts legally enshrined and sealed the secularization of public education. This jurisprudence was a second major impulse in the development of public doctrine. As one legal casebook puts it, "Prior to 1940 the Supreme Court of the United States had never upheld a claim of free exercise of religion, had never found any governmental practice to be an establishment of religion, and had never applied the religious clauses of the First Amendment to the states."[124] Starting in that decade, a new and highly complex body of legal judgments developed in an attempt to refine and apply throughout the nation the brief sixteen words of the religious clauses in the First Amendment. The Great Denouement had focused on the individual's right to religious liberty, prohibiting in the process establishment of a national, government-supported church as in the British motherland. Now there gradually developed a stricter judicial call for a total separation of religion and government required by the First Amendment's rule that "Congress shall make no law respecting an establishment of religion." This judicial initiative went on to produce a bewildering array of largely incoherent Supreme Court pronouncements, suggesting to some legal scholars that there are no univocal principles of state neutrality or religious freedom in the relevant clauses, only a jurisdictional prohibition against Congress legislating to create legal privileges or penalties for religion.[125]

Fortunately, we need not try to settle that debate here. The point is that by the mid-twentieth century the Supreme Court had embarked on the creation of a new and immensely elaborate system of rules, the general thrust of which was to favor a thoroughly secular approach to public life, especially but by no means exclusively in public schools. In 1940, the First Amendment's prohibitions on Congress regarding religion were, through interpretation of the Fourteenth Amendment, extended over all state and local levels of government. From there, the Supreme Court in 1947 began splitting the anti-establishment and free exercise clauses of the First Amendment to develop a self-contained "non-establishment" jurisprudence. This jurisprudence, developed over dozens of cases after the Second World War, applied a strict separationist view, invoking Jefferson's personal metaphor of a "wall of separation" between church and state, and sought to define an absolute principle of state neutrality toward religion.

Probably for most Americans, the developing doctrine of privatized religion was experienced most dramatically in the early Sixties when the Court struck down state-sponsored prayer and devotional Bible-reading in public schools. From this plausible prohibition against government-enforced worship in the schools, subsequent decisions advanced a more thorough ban on government patronage or even acknowledgement of religion. With litigation by offended parties and lower court rulings now an ever-present threat, school administrators and government agencies responded by generally eliminating all provocations that might possibly be construed as an endorsement of religious, much less Christian, views. At the same time, religious traditionalists started to perceive such "neutrality" as the spreading establishment of a single irreligious, secular vision of public life.[126]

Court efforts to moderate the logical conclusions of absolutely strict separation and neutrality only reinforced the doctrine of marginalizing religion's public meaning. Thus even when the Supreme Court would permit public invocations of religion (Sunday closing laws, public Christmas displays, opening prayers at legislative sessions, and so on), it relegated such behavior to "ceremonial deism" and pro forma traditions—a polite way of saying it is all empty ritual.[127] Likewise, when court-enforced public indifference to religion veered into discrimination against religious groups in schools or public settings, the Court responded by requiring equal access for the religiously inclined. The by-product of this equal-seat-at-the-table doctrine has been to confirm religion's place as simply another set of private personal preferences.

The Consumption Arts. Alongside the public schools and federal courts, a third line of twentieth-century development was less "official" but no less doctrinal in uniting a secular understanding of the world and the American democratic faith. Tocqueville had observed that if religion was to continue to counteract democracy's excesses, it would have to moderate, but not try to thwart, democratic man's desire for material well-being. In the 1830s Tocqueville had no idea of how this desire for material well-being would be indulged, molded, and lifted up to form a totalizing way of life in the twentieth century.

Despite booms and busts, America's ongoing industrialization after the Civil War vastly expanded opportunities for mass consumption and opened up new spaces in ordinary life for leisure and entertainment. However, that was merely the necessary prelude. The development I am examining here is the commercial management of desire in filling those opportunities and spaces. No single term—popular culture, mass marketing, consumer society, celebrity culture—seems to do justice to the phenomenon. I will call it the "consumption arts"—an expanding zone of cultural authority created by new technologies for professionally marketing the consumption of material abundance.

Phonograph music, movies, radio, sports, advertising, public relations, market research, department stores, nationally integrated corporations for producing and selling consumer products, the commodification of "entertainment" and institutionalization of "shopping"—these were not just innovations in technology or organization. They were a whole new sphere of social and economic activities ever more professionally crafted, commercially managed, and implemented on a national scale after the beginning of the twentieth century.[128] The aim in all this commercial crafting and managing was not simply to satisfy democratic man's desires for "material well-being." Rather, it was to develop the allure of such well-being, to expand the range of its demands, and to promise the gratification of that desire with never-ending individual consumption choices. And since older, more settled temperaments were less open to such allure, the drive of the consumption arts was always toward the marketing and management of desire for a distinctive youth culture. The assumption being taught was that forward-thinking young people, restless against traditional ways, should set the ever-new standards of what is progressive and thus desirable in music, clothes, language, and relations between the sexes.

The exercise of the new consumption arts was inherently imperialistic, defining an expanding zone of cultural authority quite separate from the traditional forces of family, neighborhood, church, and small-town values. The result was pervasive. From an occasional appearance at the beginning of the twentieth century— a new piece of sheet music for the parlor piano, the annual mail-order catalogue, a half-hour visit to the nickelodeon—the consumption arts by the middle of the twentieth century had grown into an enveloping presence, coextensive with American daily life itself. Children growing up after the Second World War, when Sunday closing laws disappeared almost everywhere, could not have imagined that fifty years earlier major department stores had not only closed but covered their window displays on Sunday. As Americans at mid-century sat enthralled by the new and thoroughly commercialized medium of television, they could not have guessed that a few decades earlier there had been a serious debate as to whether the new medium of radio should be allowed to "invade" the sanctity of our homes with advertising.[129]

It is important to note that this development of the professionalized consumption arts was also irresistibly attractive to democratic politicians.[130] Talk of consumer prosperity as a solvent for public problems allowed one to sidestep difficult questions about redistribution. In a society of consumers, everyone could be a winner. Consumer choice in the competitive economic market-place was the companion of freedom of choice in the democratic marketplace, both together constituting the American way of life. Not surprisingly, it was not very long before the consumption arts (professional opinion research, marketing and management of the political "sales" campaign) were invading politics itself. By the 1960s, they were becoming the only smart way of doing political business with the public.[131]

Most important, the new cultural form that was developing gave authority to an essentially irreligious view of human exis-tence. With notable exceptions (such as Sinclair Lewis's *Elmer Gantry*, H. L. Mencken's work, or Lawrence and Lee's *Inherit the Wind*), traditional religion was not directly attacked; it was sim-ply undermined relentlessly from one day to the next. Like the preaching of old, the consumption arts gained their power as the pervasive, incessant "articulations" by which people are made aware of what is deemed good and worthwhile. The consistent and unchanging doctrine being taught was simple: in the work, play, and everything else of daily life, the things to pay attention to are those of material existence and its enjoyment. These are the choices that make for satisfaction and self-fulfillment. Other things can be pushed to the margins as matters of easygoing indif-ference or sporadic attention, or various personal ways of toying with the "big questions." To inject anything seriously religious into this scene would be outré, to say the least. Seemingly indiffer-ent to big, abstract questions, the consumption arts of modern abundance imbued daily life with an implicit philosophy of mean-ing, namely, that meaning was constructed by individuals making a myriad of wholly self-referential consumer choices. This was the tenacious background theme regarding how the living of one's life was to be understood. It was a radical declaration of freedom (through individual consumption choices) and submission to economic discipline (that is, the work effort required through one's "job" to make ever-growing consumption desires possible). The consumption arts taught a disciplined hedonism. The message was an amalgam of the old-fashioned work ethic in an impersonal economic system and the new-fashioned indulgence in a wholly personalized system of consumption choices—the combination of the two amounting to the democratic creation of one's own meaning for life.

Proponents of the older culture of restraint fought this emerging culture on many fronts. And these proponents of the old understandings lost on all those fronts.[132] What began as cosmopolitan chic among the social, artistic, and commercial elites in the 1920s became increasingly mainstream as the century wore on.[133] By the middle of the twentieth century American Christianity could muster few attempts to moderate, much less thwart, the growing power of the consumption arts.[134] The main religious critics were a few well-known Catholic leaders, like Bishop Fulton J. Sheen, who spoke out forcefully against democratic materialism. As he pointed out in 1948, "What the Western world has subscribed to in isolated and uncorrelated tidbits, communism has integrated into a complete philosophy of life."[135] Such commentary aroused little controversy, presumably because one could still expect a traditional Catholic leader to talk in such old-fashioned ways. By contrast, thirty years later in 1978 the world-renowned Russian dissident Alexander Solzhenitsyn used a Harvard commencement address to say roughly the same thing and was denounced throughout mainstream media and intellectual circles. The great dissident's mistake was to refuse the role of a "liberal" champion of human rights and instead to proclaim an orthodox Christian view that condemned liberal democracy's materialistic preoccupation as something that crushed human beings' religious spirit. This was a message too radically unmodern for late-twentieth-century America. Arthur Schlesinger Jr. observed that Harvard's founding Puritans would have agreed with much of Solzhenitsyn's address, but then quickly added that their more enlightened Cambridge descendants now realized that a workable democratic politics requires a secular view of relative truth rather than a religious view of absolute truth.[136]

Bringing these various threads together, we can see that long before the phenomenon of the Sixties dramatized the fact, and while religious conservatives mostly stood on the sidelines, a distinctive public doctrine was already at work to undermine Christianity's cultural authority for American democracy. Certainly there are variations and qualifications that one might make on each point. However, the following summary seems a fair representation of the developing public doctrine that the schools, courts, and consumption arts, taken together, were advancing. If the contentions in this summary seem obvious, that is only an indication of how deeply the doctrine has taken hold. Again, our earlier categories of history, personhood, and political society are useful in summarizing this developing public doctrine.

History is to be interpreted primarily as a struggle for political, economic, and cultural liberation. After centuries of trying to impose values on others, human beings have become progressively, if painfully, enlightened to see that the chief moral issue is equal respect for the rights of others. Once over that hurdle, the choices freely made by democratic peoples produce an open-ended process of social learning. The liberation of such equal, self-governing individuals is the supreme goal in history because freedom is the essence of man's nature. Thus the march of democracy and the march of secularization have been, are, and will be one and the same.

The *person*, when authentically aware of himself or herself, is an autonomous individual possessing rights freely exercised to express the attributes of personhood. The liberty of each equal person is fully encompassed by the idea of freely making choices.

95

Choices express one's own unique personality and journey of self-discovery. Liberated from traditional authority, a person's choices are self-justifying because any external judgment is a denial of respect for the inherent dignity of each individual. It is the high calling of each individual to strive to realize his or her own unique potential. The democratic person holds to a "self-reliant piety." Such persons take responsibility for finding their own meaning and fashioning lives worthy of the meaning so created.[137]

A consumer-centric *political society,* seeking to be ever more democratic, has inclusiveness as its central ethos, because inclusion acknowledges and validates each person's journey of self-discovery. A democratic political society is composed of liberated individuals in free association who tolerate all views as equally valid. To lack such tolerance is to be bigoted, discriminatory, and undemocratic. Like the individuals in it, a democratic political society is always open to new truths because no one makes claims to absolute truth, which would render democratic compromise impossible. Since oppression is based on claims to objective truth, it is important for tolerance and human flourishing to affirm that all truth and values amount to matters of personal opinion. Religious commitments, which do make claims to absolute truth, are a personal and private matter that does not belong in the public arena. By contrast, commitment to the democratic faith provides a unifying secular identity that transcends other identities, including religion.

The foregoing account is roughly drawn, and pre-twentieth-century precedents can certainly be found for various particular points. But viewed as an ensemble of ideas, there is a coherent doctrinal quality to what developed. And it developed only in the twentieth century. Understood in this context, the Sixties expressed and gave dramatic impulse to a public doctrine that had been incubating for decades. Traditional Christianity represented a culture of constraint. Democracy required a culture of choice. Quietly but clearly, the battle lines had been drawn. The Baby Boom generation was about to enter the fray.

THE CRASH

By most outward appearances, Christianity and democracy were doing well in the 1950s. Domestic policy had been set on a consensual path. Republicans in the White House and Congress were accepting New Deal social welfare and economic management policies that an earlier generation of Republicans had castigated as un-American socialism. Within that framework, the controversies (mainly civil in tone as the 1960s dawned) concerned whether the federal government should play a role in education, health care, urban planning, and transportation. The war-defined lines of foreign policy consensus also seemed clear enough. Even the excesses of Senator Joseph McCarthy showed that the only real issue was whether one was a hard or a soft anti-communist. Real American communists were so hard to find that politicians occasionally had to invent some. Moreover, Will Herberg and others pointed out that, even though it was religiously shallow, something like an old-fashioned American revival was under way in mid-twentieth-century America. Mainline Protestant as well as Catholic churches were filling up. The young revivalist Billy Graham, the elegant Bishop Fulton J. Sheen, and the positive thinker Norman Vincent Peale were all thriving in the new television media of these times.[138] In the wonderfully clear vision of hindsight, we can see that all this was a facade. Something called "the Sixties" was about to break forth.

With little public notice, a more genuine religious awakening was already occurring in mid-twentieth-century America. The growing civil rights movement in the 1940s and 1950s was centered in many (but by no means all) black Protestant churches, and this ferment seemed to be repeating the time-honored pattern.[139] Driven with a powerful revivalist moral energy, the young postwar movement called on a complacent America to abolish segregation and reform its social and political institutions. Change was not just a political demand. As indicated by the quotation from Martin Luther King at the beginning of this section, the civil rights movement was demanding change as a moral imperative derived from the authentic "sacrificial spirit" of the early Christian church. The movement's mainly Christian leaders combined natural law theory (the duty to disobey unjust laws through the suffering entailed in nonviolence) with an appeal to the sanctified values of both the Judeo-Christian heritage and America's democratic ideals. To be sure, many white Christian groups only passively endorsed the civil rights cause. Yet in doing so, however weakly, the white Christian establishment denied segregationist forces any moral standing comparable to that enjoyed by the leaders of the civil rights movement. Despite the growing turmoil, it seemed that the reciprocating pistons of Americans' democratic faith and Christian faith were powering ahead.

Looking back now, we can see that the mid-twentieth-century civil rights movement embodied the more general transition from an older to a newer version of awakening and reform. The movement originally gained its energy and manpower in the traditional way—a religious revival thrusting itself forward into demands for cultural revitalization and institutional reforms.[140] The African-American religious tradition drew on its deep roots to inspire hope and demand social change. In the early years of the civil rights movement, workshops on nonviolence asked participants to undertake a process of self-purification so that their nonviolent means would be as morally pure as the ends they sought. By the end of the 1960s, however, much of this original religious orientation had been displaced. A vocal and more youthful section of the movement rejected nonviolence and racial integration as capitulations to white supremacy. Especially after the urban riots following passage of the civil rights legislation of 1964 and 1965, assertions of "black power" eclipsed any public awareness of the civil rights movement as an American-Christian cause that all citizens should share. Considering these developments as a whole, it is fair to say that by the 1970s, the religious claims of moral authority in the civil rights movement had been eclipsed by a far more secular, power-based politics. There was a growing sense that "civil rights" was a slogan for one more interest-group coalition, pressing one more set of self-serving demands.[141] At the same time, opposition to the Vietnam War broke the twentieth-century pattern that had merged the American democratic and religious values in fighting foreign enemies. Two months before his assassination in 1968, Martin Luther King Jr. condemned the United States government as "the greatest purveyor of violence in the world today." Revivalism, moral reform, democratic idealism—all the grand old themes seemed to be in play, but nothing was hanging together. Fervor without coherence expressed the liberated view of cultural authority.

Except in one crucial regard, all the political causes of the Sixties modeled themselves on the civil rights movement. The exception was that the moral energy of the new causes and movements was almost wholly secular rather than anything that could be described as traditionally Christian. Despite all the confusion of the times, the Sixties essentially gave expression to the public doctrine that had been in preparation for decades. In other words, the political-cultural phenomenon known as the Sixties was America's first secular Awakening. As such, it represented not an aberration but a radical continuation.

It was a continuation because at their best, Sixties activists affirmed the traditional values of authenticity and democracy, "of faith and deeds, of civic virtue and redemptive sacrifice."[142] It was radical because the old Awakening vision of a redemptive community experiencing individual and collective rebirth was now redenominated into a thoroughly secular cultural framework. The venerable American tradition of moralizing politics was not abandoned, but the moral earnestness was now doctrinally secular rather than religious in its inspiration. The tradition of benevolent problem-solving for the good of others was carried forward, but secular moralists now defined this good as liberating others from oppressive authorities. Faith was not rejected nor, as Tocqueville said, could it be: "Faith is the only permanent state of mankind" (273). But the object of faith changed from transcendent standards that would judge a person's choices and preferences to faith in the individual and collective search for authenticity and self-expression. In earlier times the "prophetic stance" in public life—the critique of misdeeds, call to repentance, and promise of new hope—had been fundamentally Christian. Now the prophetic stance came from within the democratic faith itself. And it was fundamentally secular.

Thus, as in the earlier Protestant awakenings and revivals, the great theme was authenticity and a vigorous rejection of the "phoniness" of pretending to be something other than who you really are, either as a church or as a person. That insistence is what made Puritans Puritans. But unlike everything that had come before, authenticity in the Sixties awakening of secular moralism was entirely self-referential. The revivalists had said that who you really are is a sinner in desperate need of God's grace. Sixties moralists said that who you really are is however you freely choose to express yourself. Similarly, Sixties activists criticized contemporary America not so much for its values as for its hypocrisy. The call was to reform and live out the values of freedom, inclusion, and a never-ending search for social justice. At its best, the Sixties pushed people to face up to unpleasant realities, and it is no accident that the hospice movement had its American beginnings at this time. At its worst, the Sixties mentality became a figure like J. D. Salinger's Holden Caulfield, ridiculously idealistic about his own innocence and sentimentally cynical about everything else in the world.

Like other awakenings, the turmoil of the 1960s soon left in its wake major changes in American public life. Political institutions and public understandings were decisively altered, often in ways that no one deliberately intended. Whether or not the result deserves to be called a "new American political system," the changes were substantial and interlocking in a systematic manner.[143] Before getting to the deeper reverberations, I will mention four immediate changes that are especially important for our present topic. Taken together, they gradually undermined any presumption that there could somehow be a "wall of separation" between what government does and what citizens of any religious or non-religious persuasion think it ought to be doing.

First, previously restricted processes of government decision-making were opened up to public scrutiny and influence. This more participatory format for governing expressed both the democratic faith and the post-Sixties distrust of all authoritative structures of power. Today we take this openness for granted. At the time, it was a sea change in the way of thinking about the policy-making process.

Second, this new access was associated with a permanent mobilization of political activists concerned with issues that now went well beyond the older economic agenda of the New Deal. Instead of "meat and potatoes" material demands for economic security, post-Sixties activists sought to impact social, cultural, "quality of life" issues (as these came to be termed at the time). The new issues did indeed touch all facets of Americans' lives. Not least, these issues directly challenged traditional views of the family, women, sexual morality, and the self-validating quality of personal choice.

Third, the new access and activism revolved around the idea that the one thing of supreme importance in politics is government policy. More than just an expansion of government, it was a new way of thinking about all of political life, a "policy mindedness" that extended from the left to the right of the political spectrum.[144] After the 1960s the authority of the federal government to act became a non-issue; the question was what policy government would pursue, either by its action or by its inaction. Influence over policy choices now became the motivation and reward for political activism amid a nonstop flow of contested claims about public problems. To become more democratic was to become committed to a never-ending policy agenda of social problem-solving.

The fourth change—growing reliance on the courts for policy-making—may seem oddly out of place in an era that was demanding public participation in policy-making. The answer lies in the fact that the real aim of political activism was not public participation as such but control over policy decisions. The courts provided a domain well-fitted to give a secular reading to the rights-based claims of individuals and groups. Moreover, the courts' adversarial format and relatively black-and-white decisions could lessen policy activists' dependence on legislators' impure compromises and administrators' unreliable discretion. The only thing needed was legislation and rule changes to expand advocacy groups' access to the courts, and this too is what happened in the wake of the Sixties.

Thus the Sixties brought moral fervor to a secular doctrine that was in substantial tension with traditional Christianity. At the same time, the Sixties produced political-institutional changes that would fully exploit that tension through the now inescapable demand to frame expansive public policies in one way or the other. As this period continued, three distinguished historians of American religion tried to put the turmoil of the times into a larger perspective. Despite their panoramic views, none of the three could escape the notion that a unique dislocation had occurred.

After almost 1100 pages, Sydney Ahlstrom, writing in the mid-1970s, found that the nation had reached a turning point that quite probably ended 400 years of American history. "In summary," he said, "one may safely say that America's moral and religious tradition was tested and found wanting in the sixties."[145] The editors of an even larger multivolume series entitled "Religion in American Life" observed, "At the close of the sixth decade of the twentieth century, commentators on the American scene seem to be of two minds in regard to the status and significance of religion in our culture. . . . sophisticates seem to have given up on God altogether, while the naïve masses simply 'infinitize' their personal and social values and call the nebulous aggregate 'God.'"[146] However, it was the very short book by William McLoughlin that said it best: "Since 1960, we have been in the process of what may well be the most traumatic and drastic transformation of our ideology that has yet occurred." He concluded, "The ferment of the sixties has begun to produce a new shift in our belief-value system, a transformation of our worldview that may be the most drastic in our history as a nation."[147]

REVERBERATIONS

We have seen that Tocqueville celebrated American democratic politics as an arena where everything was contested and open for innovation, but also where a religious-cultural consensus set firm boundaries around that arena. As he put it, in their tumultuous democratic arguments, Americans' contempt for old ways and spirit of experiment "reaches the limits of the world of politics . . . it forswears doubt and renounces innovation . . . it bows respectfully before truths which it accepts without discussion" (40).

The Sixties showed that a different kind of political world had developed. The areas of life subject to public policy choices—understood mainly as government action or inaction in Washington—now had ever-fewer boundaries. And within that expanding political policy terrain, the assumption of traditional Christianity's worldview and supportive "moral calculus" no longer applied. To put the point most generally, the Sixties dramatized a new reality about the American Christian and democratic faiths. Reason in the political realm and revelation in its autonomous religious realm could no longer be counted on to share basic moral standards for guiding political action. More than ever before, cultural authority was a politically contested concept by Americans who no longer seemed to share the same moral universe. By vastly expanding the policy agenda and by making explicit a secular doctrine that was previously developing in hushed tones, the Sixties necessarily provoked important new divisions in religious and political life.

It is fruitless to try to decide whether changes in churches produced changes in political parties, or vice versa. Both were now linked by a double bind: more culturally significant public policy choices had to be made, and among the people active in politics there was a lessened consensus for making these choices. Developments in both America's Christian churches and its political parties testified to this different world that was emerging.

The Churches. It has been said that nothing changed so much in the Sixties as religion.[148] This is a true statement, but we need to be careful in understanding what is true about it. As with the "development of public doctrine" in the democratic faith, in American Christianity the Sixties also produced a fulfillment of tendencies that had been decades in the making. As we saw, conflicts within mainline Protestant denominations found the modernists triumphing over traditionalists in the first third of the twentieth century. The secular awakening of the 1960s revived this conflict and ultimately gave the traditionalist side a new and powerful political impetus. Both Protestant and Catholic versions of American Christianity developed strongly opposed modernist (or liberal) and conservative wings, at times seeming to leave very little room in the middle. However, it was especially among Protestants that the pre- and post-Sixties change in the American religious scene carried the greatest consequences for today's politics.

In 1923 the fundamentalist leader Gresham Machen had declared that "in the intellectual battle of the present day there can be no 'peace without victory'; one side or the other must win."[149] When Machen's side lost, the Protestant establishment did not disappear. Instead, its public face and the orientation of its cultural authority changed. The victors were the mainline denominations and the networks of their leaders embodied in Protestant umbrella organizations (the Federal Council of Churches, 1908–1950, and its successor, the National Council of Churches).[150] Representing roughly 60 percent of American Protestants in the decades leading up to the Sixties, the Protestant establishment's political profile at mid-century went well beyond what such a statistic might suggest. Leaders of the denominations and Councils were the generally accepted spokesmen for American Christianity on public affairs. They claimed to speak not only *for*

Protestants but also *to* Protestants and the larger American public on major public policy issues. At the beginning of the twentieth century, an essentially unified Protestantism had confidently assumed its authority to guide the moral commentary on American public life. By contrast, the post-1920s Protestant mainline leaders were far more self-conscious in institutionally programming their reform messages—itself a sign of eroding cultural authority.

The leaders of the mid-twentieth-century Protestant establishment preferred to think of themselves as moderates rather than liberals, and in fact a broad range of views were represented, from modernist to neo-Orthodox.[151] However, it is also true to say that "moderation" in the Protestant establishment typically meant being generally open to the secular influences of modern culture, and weighted on the liberal side theologically and politically. The denominational leaders and Council officials aimed for an ecumenicalism that emphasized Protestant inclusiveness and unity over concerns with biblical authority and doctrinal clarity, both of which could easily threaten unity. Thus inclusiveness did not include fundamentalists.

Following strongly in the tradition of the social gospel, the leaders of mainline Protestantism sought to apply their inclusive Protestant-Christian vision to the solution of social problems. This typically entailed advocating domestic initiatives to protect labor and promote industrial democracy, to end racial discrimination, and to alleviate poverty through social welfare programs and income redistribution. Many of these proposals and endorsements tracked closely with Roosevelt's New Deal.[152] In foreign policy the Protestant establishment views were humanitarian, internationalist, and at times pacifist. During the Second World War, Protestantism's leaders went so far as to urge creating a postwar "new world order" in which national sovereignties would be relinquished to a world government that could outlaw war, check unbridled capitalism, and protect human rights. After 1945, however, the growing recognition of a Cold War against the expansionist ambitions of atheistic communism quickly brought the Protestant establishment into close alignment with foreign policy leaders in Washington and the Western bloc nations of the new United Nations. Guided by such figures as the Presbyterian lay leader John Foster Dulles and the neo-Orthodox intellectual Reinhold Niebuhr, the social witness of postwar Protestantism became generally congruent with the American status quo and what became known as Cold War liberalism.[153]

The 1960s blew apart any idea of a mainline Protestant establishment.[154] On a variety of fronts, conflicts within the mainline churches found progressive-minded pastors and laity demanding a more authentic social gospel that confronted Americans' complacency and the great issues of the day. Heading the list were racism and civil rights, followed by poverty, hunger, colonialism, and other conditions of social injustice at home and in the Third World. Divisions soon became especially sharp and impassioned when establishment leaders who were aligned with Washington's anti-communist containment policies confronted younger pastors and congregants protesting the immorality of the Vietnam War. Thus mainline Protestantism found itself besieged from both sides. In foreign policy, its identification with hawkish Cold War liberalism antagonized progressives in and outside the churches. In domestic policy, its liberal social activism antagonized the more conservative elements within its denominational coalition.

Upheaval in the Protestant establishment was about much more than topical political causes. Along with the demand for "authenticity" in social action came the requirement for a Christianity that would have "relevance" for the modern generation. Here too the older certainties and coherence of mainline Protestantism crumbled on a range of fronts. Radical Protestant theologians advocated a "non-supernaturalistic" view of God and religion, essentially doubting the meaningfulness of anything like traditional Christianity to contemporary minds. In a book that was immensely influential among many leaders in mainline denominations, Harvey Cox of the Harvard Divinity School applauded the rise of secular urban civilization and its capacity to undercut, relativize, and privatize traditional Christianity. Secularization was now presented as the logical outcome of, and the successor to, biblical religion. In this view the Christian church should focus on social change toward a new, inclusive human community, the church being simply "a sign of the emergent city of man, an outrider for the secular city."[155] The very idea of a professional ministry, specially trained for a salaried career in church administrative structures, fell into widespread disrepute in leading Protestant circles. Meanwhile, on a more personal level, many young Americans reared in mainline church services and Sunday Schools were drawn to what they saw as a more relevant encounter with Christ outside the organized church. After the years of initial fervor in various "Jesus People" movements, many of these people appear to have moved on to conservative congregations.[156]

The Sixties marked a clear turning point. A Protestant establishment that had once taken for granted its privileged place in the wider culture was finally disestablished.[157] While the leaders of mainline Protestantism may have carried the moral high ground in terms of engagement with the humanitarian causes of the time, they lost to the evangelicals in terms of attracting people into their ranks. In the decades leading up to the 1960s, the mainline Protestant denominations had at least maintained their membership in relation to population growth. But even then, the mid-century evangelical/fundamentalist movement was growing faster to become what *Life* magazine in 1958 called a "third force" coming alongside Protestant and Catholic Christianity. By 1960, conservative Christian groups controlled more than 80 percent of the personnel and financial resources of Protestant missions abroad.[158] Worse was to come. From the mid-1960s onwards, the liberal Protestant denominations experienced actual net losses in membership while conservative evangelical churches continued to make mirror-image gains in overall membership and energy. In explaining this shift, social scientists and even analysts friendly to the cause of mainline Protestantism generally reached similar conclusions. The mainline denominations lacked certainty in their core theological beliefs, offered a confused message based on accommodations to secular society, and failed to hold people to a strict, life-changing view of what it meant to be a Christian. With the benefit of hindsight, we can now see that much of the change in conservative and mainline church memberships has been a function, not of people switching churches, but of generations of lower birth rates among women in the more liberal churches compared with those in conservative churches. More babies would seem a natural result of the greater happiness and better sex reported in the marriages of conservative Christians as compared to other couples, but we need not pursue that line of inquiry here.[159]

Whatever the explanation, the fallout from the Sixties was a shift in grassroots numbers and organizational power that would soon have major implications for American democracy and Christianity.

Thus while the mainline Protestant establishment endured its travail, the previously vanquished fundamentalist critics were waiting in the wings and growing in strength. Well before the 1960s, the doctrinally easygoing and politically liberal policy agenda frequently put leaders of the Protestant mainline denominations at odds with more conservative elements of their "united" Protestantism. Indeed, these denominational and Council reformers often doubted that their progressive policy agenda represented more than a minority view in the local congregations.[160] Amid mainline Protestantism's theological uncertainties and political engagements, the fundamentalist cause had passed to a new generation. Its leaders were convinced that traditional Christianity, far from being the relic of a primitive subculture, was the relevant, authentic answer to modern man's anxious condition. Under leaders such as the Chicago theologian Carl Henry and the Boston pastor Harold Ockenga, the National Association of Evangelicals for United Action (NAE) was formed in 1943 to unite conservative, traditionalist Protestants against what they liked to portray as the united forces of Protestant liberalism. The fundamentalist moniker was now self-consciously replaced with the term "evangelical." It was a way for the new generation to reassert the timeless relevance of the Christian "good news" of sinful human beings' redemption through Jesus Christ's atoning death and resurrection—what friends and foes called the old time religion.[161] Evangelical churches called for strict biblical preaching of the gospel of salvation, the sinner's spiritual rebirth, and an emotionally charged new life in Christ. This commitment to a common core of traditional Christianity inadvertently carried with it a potential grassroots advantage of political organization. Unlike its opponents in the Protestant establishment, the NAE grew through a relatively flat, grassroots membership structure that welcomed not only whole denominations but also individuals, congregations, schools, and missions—anyone who might feel they were being misrepresented by the Protestant establishment.

The postwar evangelical movement had been nurtured in the seminaries, Bible schools, missions, and congregations outside the Protestant establishment. At mid-century it was greatly energized by the reappearance of urban mass revivalism. The relevance of the old time Christian gospel was asserted through the immensely popular and professionally orchestrated "crusades" of the young Billy Graham, beginning with his surprising Los Angeles success in 1949. However, it is also true to say that the new fundamentalist/evangelical movement had little interest in heeding any call to become publicly engaged with the rapidly changing culture.[162] To be sure, for evangelicals, as well as for Catholics and other Protestants at mid-century, American power and American Christianity tended to merge into one righteous cause and intensified expression of the American public religion. The point is that for evangelicals, the threats of atheistic communism abroad and godlessness at home served mainly as prompts to call for personal conversion and spiritual revival in the nation, not for direct engagement in politics and public policy. In the growing evangelical churches, mainline Protestantism's gospel of social reform was generally viewed as an un-Christian distraction from the ultimate value of personal salvation in the midst of a degenerating world. An emphasis on social and political activism sidetracked the Gospel.

This position left evangelicals open to a general public perception as social reactionaries, and leaders of the Protestant establishment were not slow to take advantage of this political vulnerability. They charged that making personal conversion the sole answer to life's problems turned Christianity into a socially irresponsible private religion. Evangelism should not be an excuse for the un-Christian acceptance of the corrupt status quo—a backhanded endorsement of racial discrimination, economic injustice, and anti-catholic bigotry. On any fair reading of the events of this time, such criticisms were not far off the mark. At best, the growing fundamentalist/evangelical movement of the postwar years demonstrated an indifference, and often hostility, to the civil rights movement.[163] Evangelicals had little to say about the poverty that coexisted with America's prosperity, and they took the lead in opposing the election of John F. Kennedy on the ground of his Catholicism. For the great causes of the Sixties, white evangelical churches were not missing in action; they never showed up.

No one intended the paradox, but the rapidly growing ranks of white conservative evangelicals were one of the groups most liberated by the Sixties. In several converging ways, they were empowered to eventually become a force in national politics, quite apart from their growing membership rolls.

In the first place, America's first Catholic President became a settled and harmless reality, helping to make evangelicals' anti-Catholicism a moot point.[164] Second, and more important, the passage of civil rights legislation in the 1960s formally neutralized an issue on which evangelicals were immensely vulnerable. Traditionalist Christians were now free to assert their conservative defense of the social order without automatically opening up themselves to charges of racist and anti-Catholic bigotry. Third, it followed that with the end of legal segregation, white conservatives in the South could no longer be counted on to support the

Democratic Party. After a hundred years, openness to Republican politicians' appeals now became a realistic option. Fourth, the Sixties' fulfillment of the heretofore gradually emerging "public doctrine" threw into dramatic, bold relief a clear picture of conservative Christians' foe. The Sixties ethos of cultural openness and nonjudgmentalism, together with the related and expanding policy expectations for the national government, pushed to the fore a new social agenda that directly challenged evangelicals' traditional understandings of family, gender, sexual behavior, and godliness in general. More clearly than ever before, Christian believers in the old time religion thought they could see the true nature of their enemy in this world—soon to be labeled secular humanism.

Finally, and perhaps most remarkable of all, these reverberations from the Sixties created the potential for something that had never before been conceivable among evangelicals—the discovery of common ground with Catholics.[165] In light of the new cultural issues raised by the liberations of the 1960s, it became plausible to think that America needed not a Protestant or Catholic response, but a Christian response to the times. Before the Sixties, the strategic possibilities of a Protestant/Catholic alliance had looked quite different. Catholics' social teaching, along with their longstanding position as outsiders, had often led to sympathetic relations with the liberal and ecumenical reformers in the Protestant establishment on issues of economic justice and racial discrimination. Likewise, with their united Church hierarchy and figures such as Wilmoore Kendall and William F. Buckley Jr., Catholics formed a large and intellectually formidable anticommunist force well-disposed toward Cold War liberalism. However, the Sixties' cultural agenda on issues of family and sexuality struck at what many leaders of the Catholic hierarchy regarded as core moral teachings of the Church. The modernizing reforms regarding Church positions on religious liberty, democracy, the liturgy, and other issues had scarcely been announced by the Second Vatican Council (1962–1965) before a split roughly similar to that among Protestants broke out between more free-wheeling modernists and conservative Catholics. By the end of the 1960s, Catholics at all levels found themselves embroiled in heated internal disputes over issues of "artificial" birth control (that is, contraception), abortion, marriage, and gender roles.[166] The pathway toward previously inconceivable cooperation between American evangelicals and "papists" began to appear.

The turn to political activism among traditionalist Protestants as well as Catholics was not a spontaneous eruption. It was provoked. And it took time for any shared awareness of the provocation to grow. But even though it did not happen suddenly, after the Sixties there was an inexorable quality to the emergence of conservative Christians as a national political presence. With the unfair advantages of hindsight, we can now see that the tipping point for conservative Christians away from civic withdrawal and toward political engagement occurred during the 1970s.

Early in that decade, one of the first Catholic activists to effectively reach out to evangelicals was Phyllis Schlafly. The successful state-level campaigns against ratification of the Equal Rights Amendment to the Constitution began revealing both the new challenge to traditional family/gender values and the power of cooperation among Christian traditionalists. When the Supreme Court's 1973 *Roe v. Wade* decision upheld a woman's right to abortion, Catholic spokesmen at first stood virtually alone in opposition. Disappointed by mainline Protestant leaders who failed to follow through on their avowed support for restrictions on abortion, Catholic activists began cultivating help from evangelical Protestants, many of whom saw the decision as simply another reason to separate themselves from the larger culture. The catalyst for change was what evangelicals came to perceive as Washington's frontal attack on their subculture of Christian schools. The immediate issue involved Internal Revenue Service efforts, again following a federal court ruling, to deny tax-exempt status to Christian schools for practicing de facto racial segregation, even if they were purely privately funded.[167] Contrary to their hopes, this

IRS effort continued after the 1976 election of their fellow evangelical Jimmy Carter to the presidency. Worse, as the Carter administration proceeded, the realization grew that President Carter was quite willing to accommodate core Democratic constituencies and that these were determined to use government policy to advance their broad secular agenda against traditional views of family, sexuality, and religion in public life.

The midwives for delivering this realization were Richard Viguerie and Paul Weyrich, two Catholics and "movement conservatives" in the Republican Party who pioneered the new political technologies of direct mail, computerized information management, and grassroots political mobilization. Billy Graham had already served as the unwitting intermediary when conservative Christians were used and abused by the Nixon administration's electoral strategy for "Middle America." Then, after 1976, conservative Christian leaders felt themselves betrayed by President Carter's series of capitulations to secular and cultural liberals in the Democratic Party. Convinced of the need to stand up politically for their core cultural concerns, a more forceful mobilization of conservative Christians grew behind the presidential candidacy of Ronald Reagan and gained strength in the generally supportive atmosphere of his presidency.[168]

So was the post-Sixties mobilization of conservative Christians mainly a matter of Catholic brains and evangelical foot soldiers? That would be much too crude a view. Far from simply responding to Catholic leadership, Protestant evangelicals produced their own champions to fight against the cultural onslaught of the times. Jerry Falwell's founding of the Moral Majority in 1979 and Pat Robinson's TV ministry are obvious examples. However, there was a grander evangelical call to arms. Even an unsympathetic observer like Gary Wills had to conclude that more than anyone else, Francis Schaeffer galvanized evangelicals to take up the task of cultural criticism and political action.[169] During the 1960s and early 1970s, Schaeffer, a student and admirer of Machen, had electrified young evangelicals by showing that traditional Christianity, especially as inspired by the Reformation, need not be intellectually intimidated. It was fully equipped to critically engage all the art, music, philosophy, and other forms of cultural expression that society had to offer. Academics scoffed at his popularized scholarship, but Schaeffer, in a cascade of lectures and books after 1965, inspired hosts of American evangelicals to engage the ideas and history of western culture with a critically Christian mind.[170] Young Christians in particular felt liberated from the evangelical subculture's narrow-minded dismissal of the larger society's art, philosophy, music, and so on as "worldly." A good Christian should know about Existentialism. He or she could also fight against the plastic, dehumanized society that the Sixties hippies were rejecting. And it was OK to use movie screens instead of hymnals in church.

It would also be crude and obtuse to say that evangelical conservatives were mobilized in the 1970s simply in order to continue practicing racial discrimination in their Christian schools. The IRS tax-exemption issue was merely the dramatic example of a larger narrative being constructed: the courts and federal government were seen as now engaged in a concerted attempt to alter basic Christian patterns of American life. Beginning in 1976, Schaeffer's influential voice turned toward a call for political activism. Driven by the abortion issue as a virtually apocalyptic sign of the decadence and destruction of western culture, Schaeffer's new books, films, and speaking appearances became a pervasive presence in evangelical churches to make the Christian case for political engagement.[171] He pointed out that every previous religious awakening had produced cleansing reforms in our political institutions. The insinuation of secular humanism in our public schools that some had protested locally was now the national agenda in Washington. A "tyranny" hostile to the values of the people—as before the American Revolution—was at work. Continued political quiescence was not an option for Bible-believing Christians.

Thus in the reverberations following the Sixties, the division within both Protestant and Catholic communities has not really been between dogmatic and non-dogmatic Christians. The difference has been which dogma to support—the newer doctrine of individual choice and self-expression, or the traditional doctrines of the Christian past.[172] As Tocqueville rightly observed, "dogma . . . is the essence of religions" (412). At one dogmatic pole of religious activism, modernizers have emphasized personal choice, women's rights, and other aspects of human liberation. At the end of the other dogmatic pole, traditionalists have insisted on submitting any liberation to the authority of established biblical principles and traditional church teachings. In recent years Catholic intellectuals have been especially important in giving this latter conservative movement a coherent, non-denominational, and highly articulate voice.[173] The larger point, however, is that in the aftermath of the Sixties, conservative Protestants and Catholics have both come to see themselves as embattled co-belligerents on public issues of vital significance to their common religious faith, an ecumenical orthodoxy. Their politics has been mostly grievance-based, with a sense that the Christian way of life—their religion's version of "traditional values"—has now come under relentless attack and seems to be losing in modern America.

The Political Parties. These changes on the Christian scene have had their counterpart in the Democratic and Republican parties. The tumultuous Democratic convention of 1972 was an early confirmation of the leftward trend in the Democratic Party set in motion by the events and political causes of the Sixties. With anti–Vietnam War protestors and culturally liberal activists gathered behind the nomination of George McGovern, a distinctly secular segment of the Democratic Party came into unprecedented prominence. Since the 1960s, this vocal segment and its issues have continued to grow in importance within the Democratic Party. Abortion choice, women's rights, alternative life-styles, and criticism of American military power became prominent on the Party's agenda and have remained so. The common underlying theme has been a distrust of traditional authority in the cause of personal freedom. This, more than any spontaneous upsurge in political activities of Christian traditionalists, marked the coming of a new secular/religionist division between activists in the two parties.[174] In the years following 1972, this growth of secular activists' influence in the Democratic Party remained vastly underreported compared to subsequent media alarms about the countervailing and rather belated Republican mobilization among traditionalist Christians.

For the Republican Party, the fallout from the Sixties was a mirror image of this situation; it empowered an already strong conservative insurgency within the Party. This conservative movement was mostly separate from, and a generation earlier than, the appearance of conservative evangelicals on the political scene. The separation now seems counterintuitive, but it should not be surprising. For "movement conservatives," the tie to Christianity ran through Catholic sensibilities by way of intellectual leaders such as Russell Kirk and William F. Buckley Jr.[175] In his 1953 book that launched the movement, Kirk had grounded American conservatism in an outlook premised on western culture's traditional Christian theism. He declared the first "canon" of conservative thought to be

> belief that a divine intent rules society as well as conscience, forging an eternal chain of right and duty which links great and obscure, living and dead. Political problems, at bottom, are religious and moral problems. . . . We do wrong to deny it, when we are told that we do not trust human reason: we do not and we may not. Human reason set up a cross on Calvary. . . . Politics is the art of apprehending and applying the Justice which is above nature.[176]

By 1964, there were enough impassioned conservative activists in the Republican Party to capture the presidential nomination for Barry Goldwater, with his campaign against big government in Washington and military/political timidity in facing communism abroad. However, by the end of that year it was far from clear whether the new conservative forces could ever win a national election. For Republican Party moderates, such as the rising young politician George Bush (defeated as candidate for a Texas Senate seat), Goldwater's crushing loss signaled the need to return to a more moderate, mainstream Republicanism. For movement conservatives like Ronald Reagan, it was a call to spread their "dedication to a philosophy" to an ever-wider popular audience of ordinary working Americans.[177]

The growing turmoil of the Sixties then pushed the conservative cause in exactly that direction. Beginning in 1966 Reagan was rewarded with two terms (1967–1975) in the California governor's office. By the early 1970s, "neo-conservatives"—Democratic Cold War liberals dismayed by the feckless social engineering of Great Society domestic programs and leftist Democratic attacks on their anti-communist policies—began supplying weighty new intellectual talent to the Republican conservative wing. By the end of the decade, the fervent and growing body of conservative Republicans could share the feeling of Billy Graham's fellow religionists that they had been cynically taken advantage of by Richard Nixon and Republican centrists during the 1970s (by now conservative onslaughts had reduced "liberal" Republicans to an inconsequential remnant in the Party). For both of the heretofore separate camps, Ronald Reagan seemed to present a more authentic conservatism, an immensely personable and telegenic blend of Kirk-Schaeffer critiques of the Sixties' political and cultural blunders.[178]

With Jimmy Carter's surprising vault to the presidency, *Newsweek* labeled 1976 the Year of the Evangelical, but at the time it was quite unclear what that might mean politically. By the time of the 1980 presidential contest between Carter and Reagan, the political implications of resurgent evangelical Protestantism were not in doubt. Christians honoring traditional values should be for Reagan. Traditional Christians were, of course, being politically exploited by the Republican conservative movement. The deeper truth is that political professionals and evangelical leaders were now learning to exploit each other.

And what of Ronald Reagan himself in this rapidly boiling political/religious conservative stew? In 1953 Russell Kirk had written that in the "preservation of the ancient moral traditions," conservatism equals talent for re-expressing conviction on those principles to fit the time.[179] On that reckoning, Reagan's conservatism thermometer reading was off the charts. From the beginning of his political career in the 1950s, Reagan had seen and effectively presented himself as a spokesman for the rediscovery of America's traditional values.[180] However, it was primarily what I have called the sanctified vision of America that he reasserted and put on the political/cultural offensive. Rather than a warrior for conservative social causes, Reagan was essentially a sunny denier of any fundamental culture war at home, and a stern affirmer of America's destiny to defeat communism abroad. His enduring assumption was that when the nation's sanctified vision was re-invoked, Americans would respond out of a deeper cultural identity that remained fundamentally fixed and intact. Thus as a rising politician and governor of California, Reagan fought against campus unrest and condemned leftist intellectual influences. However, neither then nor as President did he vigorously use government to promote the culturally conservative policy agenda that the "religious right" was urging on him. In his own way, Reagan was oblivious to the Sixties. To embrace an aggressive cultural conservatism seemed too much like being disillusioned with America, too much like thinking ill of something he loved. Ironically, Reagan's final official warning to the nation was about Americans' loss of memory. He urged the younger generation to recover for themselves the idea of a consecrated nation, in a time when parents were no longer teaching their children about this idealized America.[181]

CULTURAL WARRIORS AND DISGUSTED BYSTANDERS

During and after the Reagan years, the post-1960s religious and political cleavages have manifested themselves in a gradual sorting process between the two parties. Ideologically-oriented liberal and conservative members of the electorate have been more clearly arranging themselves into the Democratic and Republican parties respectively. And the meaning of those ideological terms has increasingly come to emphasize liberal and conservative cultural values rather than simply economic issues. Secular and religious activists continued to be more deeply embedded in the Democratic and Republican parties respectively. But in scoring the capacities for grassroots political mobilization, the advantage has lain with conservative Republicans. The Democrats have had liberal interest group organizations gravitating to Washington policy-making headquarters, especially as the membership and power of labor unions continued to decline. The Republicans, by contrast, in their informal grassroots conservative alliance with tens of thousands of evangelical churches and their millions of congregants, have had people across Main Street America already potentially mobilized. The celebrated young strategist for Richard Nixon's "southern strategy" in the late 1960s would eventually acknowledge that he had thoroughly missed "the depth and importance of religion" in the post-Sixties building of the Republican Party. Forty years later in 2006, he was proclaiming that the Republicans had become "the first religious party in U.S. history."[182]

But can you have a culture war if the people don't come? What was true even in the 1960s and the years immediately following remains true today: distinctly ideological citizens—for or against Sixties thinking, pro- or anti-Christian and secular policy agendas—were and have remained a minority of the total American public. There is good evidence that most ordinary Americans, who tend to be rational and thus only sporadically attentive to politics, see no contradiction in being religious and patriotic on the one hand, and open-minded and liberally tolerant on the other. In terms of their attitudes and preferred policy positions (rather than the choices they are given), most Americans are not polarized, nor have they become more so.[183] In red and blue states alike, the general electorate is largely moderate or ambivalent in its orientation to a host of social issues. Compared to other developed nations, the overall orientation in America is toward "traditional values." But within America, the general public has the quite un-newsworthy quality of being centrist and moderate. An exhaustive study of American data from the World Values Surveys between 1980 and 2000 concludes: "Most Americans are religious centrists, located between the extremes of religious orthodoxy and moral progressivism. Cultural values are not polarized. Most Americans cluster toward the traditional pole of the traditional/secular-rational dimension. There is some evidence of the polarization of moral visions, but this is a tendency, not the basis of two morally opposed camps, because absolutists and relativists still have a lot in common."[184]

In fact, rather than being divided into two warring moral camps, attitudes among the vast majority of Americans on social and cultural issues have been converging rather than polarizing. Since the 1970s public opinion on issues having to do with minorities and the poor, the status of women, crime, homosexuality, personal morality, and so on have become less, not more, polarized. Americans have become more generally tolerant and supportive of equal rights, more committed to individual choice and a live-and-let-live attitude toward what goes on among consenting adults. Even on the politically explosive issue of abortion, Americans appear no more polarized than they were in 1980.[185] When people are asked the more searching question about the actual circumstances when abortion should be legal or not, there does not appear to be a very great difference between churched and un-churched Americans, evangelicals, mainline Protestants, or Catholics. In cases where the polls do show that Americans are closely divided, as on gay marriage, they are not deeply divided in the sense of perceiving the issue to be particularly important.[186] All such information is normally eclipsed, however, because the mass media and political commentators usually consider a good story about polarization more important than an accurate portrayal of good evidence. As one careful study of the subject puts it, "Reports of a culture war are mostly wishful thinking and useful fund-raising strategies on the part of culture war guerrillas, abetted by a media driven by the need to make the dull and everyday appear exciting and unprecedented."[187]

Religious polarization in the electorate is real, but it occurs mostly at the far ends of the spectrum where Americans are either extremely "religious" or extremely "non-religious." Politically speaking, it is the moderate middle that holds power, with stable patterns of religious cleavages in party voting that go back for decades. This is true even when one includes conservative Protestants in the picture. By one estimate, Americans attached to conservative Protestant churches make up 32 percent of the electorate. However, of that percentage, 6 percent are African-Americans in such churches, and they vote overwhelmingly Democratic. White conservative Protestants make up 26 percent of the electorate, but their propensity to vote Republican is only slightly greater (52 percent on average in the 1992–2000 elections) than Republican voting by mainline Protestants (45 percent) and Catholics (41 percent). Even within the smaller subgroup of white evangelical Christians, voting is monolithically Republican only for that sub-subgroup of traditionalists who account for slightly under half of such white evangelicals.[188]

It is important not to misinterpret the polarization in party support that has appeared between those who attend church weekly and those who almost never attend. Starting abruptly with the 1992 election, a major gap opened between regular churchgoers and non-churchgoers (a little under 40 percent and about 50 percent of the electorate respectively since the 1970s). Since that time this "churched/un-churched" gap in party voting has declined slightly, but it has persisted on both sides. In other words, the more religious the citizen (defined as faithful church/synagogue attendance), the more likely that person is to vote for and identify as a Republican; and the less religious the citizen, the more likely is his or her allegiance to the Democratic Party. However, the reason for this development does not appear to be that voters' attitudes have themselves become more polarized. Rather, the explanation seems to be that a fairly stable distribution of religious-political attitudes among voters has been forced to choose between more polarized parties and candidates—with a Republican leadership more aggressively asserting conservative moral issues and a religious identity, and a Democratic leadership more sharply secular and non-traditionalist in its moral positions and identity.[189] Presented with the more polarized choices offered by post-Sixties political activists, ordinary Americans naturally make more polarized choices.

It is among the minority of politically active Americans—individuals busying themselves in the work of parties, interest groups, issues, causes, and the public talk of politics generally—that the culture wars have seethed. And this seething polarization has seeped over into the politically attentive, articulate segments of Americans with college and postgraduate professional educations.[190] Among political activists (certainly less than one-fifth of adult Americans), the divisions on social-cultural issues run much deeper than for any ordinary citizens identifying with each party, and those elite divisions have deepened in the past thirty years. Such activists follow a rational strategy for mobilizing money, political attention, activity, and final delivery of the vote. They target the party's base of committed partisans, rather than the broad, moderate, and mostly ambivalent centrist segment of the population. This in turn polarizes the political appeals, nominations, and candidate choices into which the mass of non-polarized voters then have to sort themselves.

Most ordinary Americans would probably agree with the comfortable adage that you cannot legislate morality. By contrast, the activists on both sides of the cultural divide believe you cannot legislate anything else. The question is, whose morality? To put the issue in the negative—as the combatants prefer to do—America's choice is between the repressive, bigoted morality of Christian theocrats, or the debauched, godless morality of secular humanists. It does not make sense to assess the culture wars by surveying people who are uninterested in the subject. The result of developments since the 1960s has been not a polarized American public, but a substantial parting of the ways between the politically active Americans who set the terms of debate for the general public constituted by ordinary Americans. Both sides perceive themselves to be under attack from a determined foe. Both enjoy the self-righteousness that comes with being the aggrieved victims of such aggression. And both find it useful to play the politics of fear against each other.

The Coming Rupture

With the sort of sensible modesty that keeps historians from becoming political scientists, Sydney Ahlstrom once advised his readers that "interpreting the present calls for a seer, not a historian."[191] Here we face no such inhibitions in interpreting the present, as well as the future that it has been setting in motion.

It is a serious mistake to dismiss culture-war talk because it is mainly a combat among a minority of political activists fixated on the religious/secular divide. That it is an elite phenomenon is clear enough. But this is the opposite of saying it is unimportant. Alongside evidence of the "myth" of a culture war among ordinary Americans, there is also good evidence that conflicts among elites are of vastly disproportionate importance for shaping a nation's political future. When modern democracies run into serious trouble, when nations are built, torn down, or acquire a national identity, it has less to do with polarization in the opinion of ordi-

123

nary citizens and much more to do with the polarization among civic elites.[192]

Thus it is true, but not entirely relevant, that ordinary Americans have a very non-ideological approach to politics. They would like politicians to get on with the practical problems of improving the schools, health care, retirement supports, transportation, the environment, and national security. Nonetheless, there are few things more practical than a person's philosophical-theological outlook. Such "abstract" outlooks become an inescapably practical matter as a self-governing people must now make policy choices that have unprecedented scope and implications. However much the average American would like partisans to just get over culture-war talk, it is not something that is now in anyone's power to get over.

The articulate activists are not wrong in perceiving a fundamental division of outlooks. Their contrasting secular and religious views go beyond just one more opportunity for deliberative democracy to work out a tentative fix for some social problem. Through government policy decisions, Americans are increasingly being asked to consider the most fundamental meanings of human existence, and thanks to accelerating technology, this challenge will only grow with time. The first wave of such existential policy-making has mainly concerned sweeping issues of life and death—abortion, in vitro fertilization, brain death, organ harvesting, embryonic stem cell research, feeding tube removal, assisted suicide, and the like. This leaves aside such relatively "simple" issues as whether government policy should prohibit or, through inaction, passively endorse artificial reproductive technologies for unmarried couples, same-sex couples, or single individuals.

The next wave of policy choices that is already beginning to break concerns the turning of humanity itself into another man-made thing.[193] This takes secularists and religionists, both insisting on their different worldviews of human dignity, into choices regarding the genetic design of enhanced minds and bodies, not only cloning but the creation of embryos from three or more genetic parents, whole brain transplants, organic integration of non-biological and human intelligence, and the merging of man, machine, and animal components into something trans- or post-*Homo sapiens*—in other words, policies, presumably democratically determined, that add up to decisions on what it means to be human. Until our own time, the issue has always been one of using science and technology to repair nature when it fails. Now the issue is whether to do what nature has denied—in effect, to make nature a human artifact. Confrontations with traditional Christianity are inevitable because the choices will be made not as interesting intellectual exercises, but as the decisive, practical exercise of government power over policies. To insist that only secular "public reasons" are acceptable in debating policy choices about the meaning and creation of life, about the management of death, about what it is to be human, is not preserving a public forum of reasoned argument. It is telling religious people to shut up.

Years before academics were spinning theories as to why religious people should have to give public—that is, secular—reasons when debating in the democratic marketplace of ideas, practical political and commercial realities had already begun enforcing that rule.[194] In the early 1960s, it was Christian theologians who initiated a public movement questioning the moral significance of scientists' applications of new technologies regarding things like "test-tube babies." In less than two decades, their voices had been thoroughly marginalized by the demands that on such important issues, the means and ends of public policy had to be discussed in terms held in common by all Americans. Thus what emerged was first, the massive commercialization of a multi-billion dollar conception industry, and second, a new "bioethics" profession. This new profession claims to provide guidance that is neutral toward religion and exclusively secular in arguing moral issues of science and medicine. In this now generally accepted view, all Americans can agree that the goal is to advance a form of human dignity understood solely as autonomy, as well as human beneficence and justice. Being neutral toward religion in this context essentially means eliminating what religion in general and Christianity in particular might have to say about such things. Money, of course, has much to say. In 1978 the first test-tube baby was born; twenty-five years and roughly 3 million babies later, the U.S. fertility industry posted revenues of approximately $3 billion. Using technology that was not available even a decade ago, three-quarters of American in-vitro fertilization clinics now offer pre-implantation genetic diagnosis to weed out undesired embryos before they are transferred to the mother's womb. What began as screening solely for fatal childhood diseases has expanded rapidly to include, at the customer's choice, selection to eliminate embryos with milder childhood diseases, adult disease predispositions (such as colon cancer or arthritis), and poor tissue donation potential. Of the clinics surveyed in 2006, 42 percent were at times eliminating embryos simply for the purpose of selecting boy or girl babies.[195]

The point here is not to offer lamentations or cheers for what happened to the theologians; it is simply to observe that this is what has happened. And it is very likely to continue to happen. This is because there *is* a "Christian Problem" for secular America.

When social scientists survey the general field of religion and politics, they can find good reasons to conclude that the greatest contribution of religion to liberal democracy is in religion's decline, thereby allowing greater individual freedom.[196] Religion is about allegedly absolute truths, and these essential truths of faith are revealed from above, not discovered or invented by humans. It is quite possible to see religion's politics of moral certainty as a recipe for oppression, not democratic compromise. Ever since the French Enlightenment, those of a secular-rationalist faith have argued that there is an inherently irrational, emotional, and arbitrary quality to religious conviction, which leaves only secular reasoning as the appropriate means for intelligent decision-making in the democratic process.[197] The older versions of this argument, standard fare from any village atheist, need not detain us here. As discussed earlier, traditional Christianity is no rejecter of reason, and any secular-rationalist worldview has its own inevitably faith-based premises. In recent decades, however, a more powerful version of the argument has developed out of the democratic faith. For the average citizen, the problem of "public reason in deliberative democracy" sounds like some intellectuals' tempest looking for a teapot in which to happen. But it is a serious issue and deserves more careful attention.

This view of the Christian problem is grounded in understandings of democracy as a discursive process.[198] The philosophical lineaments of this argument go back to the earliest work of John Rawls, extend through legal orthodoxies developed during the 1960s and 1970s abortion debates, and can be heard in the most recent pronouncements of Democratic politicians. That party's rising star, Senator Barack Obama, has put the point succinctly: "Democracy demands that the religiously motivated translate their concerns into universal, rather than religion-specific values. It requires that their proposals be subject to argument and amenable to reason . . . I cannot simply point to the teachings of my church or evoke [*sic*] God's will. I have to explain why abortion violates some principle that is accessible to people of all faiths, including those with no faith at all."[199]

The general argument is as follows. The civil bond among equal citizens is said to be the exercise of reason in the form of arguments seeking to justify collective action through government. Such deliberative democracy (or government by discussion, as it was called earlier) can naturally see religion as a way of dictating the terms of argument or putting an end to discussion altogether. The justifications offered by religion arise from a comprehensive worldview not necessarily shared by other citizens. Its reasons, if solely religious reasons, are inaccessible to other citizens. Thus because they refuse to share the naturalistic, common base of discourse applicable to all citizens, and rely instead on private, revealed knowledge of God, religious voices in public life inhibit and distort the public reasoning essential to democracy.

However, this is more than a philosophical matter of conversational inhibition and distortion. In this view, the Catholic-evangelical-conservative political coalition threatens the secular institutions of our democracy. By rejecting ways of reasoning acceptable to all and seeking to legislate their own sectarian versions of morality, religionists overturn the "liberal bargain" so painfully achieved after Europe's religious wars. According to this bargain, in exchange for state-protected individual rights of religious liberty, religionists would abandon their political ambition to use the state to bring society into conformity with their rigid views of "what God commands." Religionists seeking to impose their moral views on the rest of society threaten to create a volatile politics of impassioned absolutes, where opponents are demonized and the compromises necessary for democracy are made impossible. At the extreme end of this worry, there are imaginings of a conservative Christian theocracy lurking around every corner.[200]

American Christians should not expect to escape this secular criticism and wariness. They *are* in fact called to have a certain kind of undemocratic rigidity. Christians *are* absolutists, in that they believe certain essential truths about human existence have been divinely revealed through the life and work of a unique historical person named Jesus. Christians *are* exclusivist, in that they consider (as do all believers in the law of non-contradiction) that the truths they hold exclude the truthfulness of contrary views denying those truths. Likewise, Christians have to acknowledge that, if true to the articles of faith given in their religion, they are less (or, as they might prefer to say, more) than fully civic. They are required to give ultimate obedience to a "foreign power"—another kingdom which they care for more than they care for America itself. It should be obvious that for someone who truly believes in it, Christianity will and should permeate every aspect of one's life. For such committed believers, Christianity is *the* frame of meaning within which they enact their lives. And it should also be acknowledged that, being human, these Christians will often find it easier to flock together in a holy huddle with fellow believers rather than interact with fellow citizens (though that is not necessarily what their Gospel of love teaches). For reasons such as these, secular Americans can understandably view "pious" Christians as strange and possibly dangerous. They are fellow-believers before they are fellow-citizens. Popular critics now call citizens voting on their cultural values rather than their economic interests "deranged." More than that, moderate Christians, by tolerating their co-religionists who believe in the literal truth of the Bible, are said to be encouraging an irrational and dangerous religious extremism to flourish in America. By the beginning of the twenty-first century a significant minority of the electorate—one-quarter of white voters by one estimate—resembled secular activists in the Democratic Party in their intense dislike of traditionalist Christians.[201]

So there *is* a "Christian problem" in deliberative democracy. But this problem as just described is one of modest dimensions. As I pointed out earlier in discussing the "culture war," this problem cannot reasonably be equated with some generic threat of religious fanaticism or impending American "theocracy." The truly odd (and democratically threatening) thing is to imagine that American democracy would be safer and healthier if religion, which essentially means Christianity in the American context, could somehow be kept out of our contested public life. There are multiple reasons why it makes no sense to think democracy "demands" that serious Christians and other religiously motivated people translate their concerns into universal values and reasoning accessible to citizens of any or no religious faith.[202]

First, the democratic conversation in university faculty clubs may be something that proceeds by exchanging universally accessible reasoning (something I very much doubt), but it is not and never has been true of the democratic real world. American democracy is and always has been full of people trying to get their way on the basis of publicly unreasoned convictions. Why should the religiously motivated be held to standards of universal public reasons that no one else has to meet?

Second, from what we human beings know of one another, it is obvious that reasoned argument is not something that is accessible to all adult citizens. In fact, given that Americans are increasingly besotted by the modern media and permanent political campaigning that seeks, under the best professional guidance, to wholly bypass the recipient's brain, reasoning may be the thing *least* accessible to many fellow citizens. It is ironic that attention to idealized deliberative democracy should coincide in time with the post–World War II triumph of a professionally PR-managed anti-deliberative democracy.[203]

Third, if it is procedurally improper in democratic debate to include unproven religious beliefs seeking to impose moral strictures on others, why is it procedurally proper to allow unproven non-religious beliefs seeking to impose moral views on others? All sides are in the game because they want to win—that is, to do some moral imposing. What sort of pluralism or democracy is it where secularists are entitled to enact policies based on their belief systems but religious people are not?

Fourth, where the most profound issues of justice and humanity are in dispute, it is itself an injustice to tell religious people that convictions of their religious consciences concerning transcendent truths should be considered irrelevant and/or dangerous in the talk of democracy. If religious freedom means "nothing more than that religion should be free so long as it is irrelevant to the state, it does not mean very much."[204]

Fifth, religious passions are politically dangerous, but so are secular passions. Modern history should teach us that we have at least as much to fear from wars of secular ideology as from wars of religious faith. Besides, insofar as they were "religious," the sixteenth- and seventeenth-century European wars were about which religion the state would adopt and enforce. Invoking religious belief and argument on important moral issues of modern public policy is something quite different. Conservative Christians are trying to make their convictions prevail on abortion, same-sex marriage, Intelligent Design, and other issues, just as their opponents are. It would be more dangerous to democracy if they were not trying.

Sixth, there is the inconvenient fact of American history. The evidence it provides shows that on balance, our democratic institutions have survived very well with religiously motivated people invoking their religious convictions to try to make America a more godly place. The liberal bargain was not upset by the loud religious voices of abolitionists, early feminists, Catholic workers' advocates, Populists, Social Gospellers, or the young civil rights movement. There never has been a clear line between "public reason" and the religious beliefs of people trying to change American society for what they regard as the better.

Seventh, just because religious people hold absolutist beliefs and accept religious authority, it does not follow that they must be political authoritarians. That charge is simply the reprise of an old anti-Catholic argument now applied to any committed, Bible-believing Christian. Any reader who has come this far should understand that we live in a country where, on the basis of religious authority, people opposed political authoritarianism and illiberal state power. It was indeed a Great Denouement.

Eighth, if they hope to win majority support, it is certainly politically prudent for religious believers to find secular reasons supporting their preferred positions. That requirement for enlarging, diluting, perhaps even corrupting the purity of one's position is part of the genius of democratic stability. But who are democratic theorists or political pundits to tell religious citizens what forms of political expression are demanded from them? The First Amendment stipulates otherwise.

Finally, to return to the original theme of this essay, the issue is not religion as such but the substantive content of a particular religion called Christianity. Simply to invoke God's will certainly does make further discussion rather pointless. But Christianity, at least the traditional sort extending back through Augustine and Origen, insists that there should be no divorce of faith from reason, that believers are called upon to have an understanding faith rather than a blind faith. Reasoning, including public reasoning, is required because the problem is not God's will but flawed human beings trying to understand God's will. Moreover, Christian believers in the revelation of God are supposed to act on the knowledge that God requires a love of others equal to the love of oneself. Whatever differs from that in thought or deed, to the extent of the difference, is not Christianity.

This is easy to say and impossible to fulfill, but nonetheless it presents an inescapable standard that is supposed to demand Christians' unstinting attention and obedience. A religious belief pointed in that direction would see a better protection against all forms of inhumanity to man than a great many alternatives, including an indifference to whether God even exists. It is true that a politics of moral certainty is a recipe for oppression, not compromise. But this is true for any secular moral certainty as well as for a religious moral certainty. On that score, Christianity does inherently contain an inner corrective. Christianity's "prophetic stance" toward political society is ambiguous, being "humane and engaged but also hesitant and critical."[205] This hesitant and critical view, according to orthodox Christian doctrine, applies first and foremost to the believer's own motives and to the correspondence of his or her own behavior to that of the one person who showed what it means to be really human. This is not the same thing as the democratic faith in deliberative justification, but it would appear compatible with it.

In our nation's last religious awakening, Martin Luther King Jr. tried to teach Americans that Christian power is the power of a suffering love. What secularists have to fear is not Christianity but the abuse of Christianity by people seeking another kind of power. The history of dissent and martyrdom shows that such abuse of the Christian religion has been real and recurrent. History also shows that believing Christians have been willing to throw themselves on the side of dissent and martyrdom to resist the corruption of their religion by the sinful love of earthly power. For those Americans interested in particular political agendas, traditional Christianity has liberal and conservative implications, but it is neither conservative or liberal. It is radically itself.

Much more serious than the Christian problem for democracy is the "democracy problem" for American Christians. The different facets of this problem come into view if we consider the four political options that twenty-first-century Christians face in America, understanding that these are really place-markers along a continuum of engagement and separation.

First, nursing a politics of grievance, some activists on the so-called Religious Right see themselves as besieged by hostile forces and call for a vigorous counterattack. In this view, the loss of Christian values in public life is the direct result of a campaign by ideological secularists. As we have seen, that is partly accurate but it certainly is not the whole truth. The growth of a secular moral discourse is also the result of the mounting pluralism that comes from a nation of seekers who choose their own meanings. With so many multiple perspectives, a pragmatically secular public conversation becomes the one reliable default setting for keeping the conversation going.

The most committed cultural warriors in today's Religious Right dismiss any such subtleties in American democratic development. The most extreme of these essentially seek to subvert the existing order. This view, fortunately rare, can be found among "Christian Identity" and Reconstructionist groups, whose aim is to seize power in churches and eventually legislate a biblically "Christian nation." In essence, the Kingdom of God is to be imposed on earth by worldly power. For reasons already discussed, this is not an option open to orthodox, traditionalist Christians who believe in the fundamentals of their religion.[206] America as a nation of this world can only be the city of man and never the city of God.

That said, there are more numerous proponents of a softer version of this first option. They seek to establish bases of political power in different levels of government and the Republican Party, and from there to "recover" America through legislation expressing Christian values. That is, of course, exactly the vision that worries today's more secular Americans about the whole idea of Christians in politics. They would be surprised to learn that moving the city of man in a more godly direction by amassing political power is something that also worries traditional Christians and evangelical thinkers.[207] This belies a realistic Christian understanding of the problem of worldly power and even the most sincere believer's vulnerability to pride and error. It emphasizes making illegal what Christians consider wrong, at the expense of acting affirmatively on the duties they have to other people.

This is the option represented among the approximately one-sixth of eligible voters who identify with the Religious Right. Since the late 1970s it has produced an ever closer engagement of conservative Christians not just in Republican voting, but in manning the organizational apparatus of the Republican Party, something that is often deliberately hidden from the public.[208] On behalf of their religion, this should worry Christians. Indeed, as Tocqueville teaches us, it should worry any friend of self-government who wants religion to play its vital role in sustaining the ordered liberty of democracy. To do that, religion/Christianity must be itself, not something tied to the apparatus of political power. As usual, Tocqueville put it very well: "When a religion chooses to rely on the interests of this world, it becomes almost as fragile as all earthly powers. Alone, it may hope for immortality; linked to ephemeral powers, it follows their fortunes and often falls together with the passion of a day sustaining them" (274).

The second option for Christians is to accommodate secular democratic discourse and treat one's religious identity just like anything else in the world. This option seems reasonable, but there are also limits, which committed believers will discern. Christians can be committed to the larger democratic goal of talking through things with citizens unlike themselves,[209] and they should be able to demonstrate that their religious opinions are not simply self-referential and beyond reasonable democratic compromises about common goods. This attitude has the advantage of keeping the public conversation going and assuring everyone that democracy is safe from religion. A sense of proportion should tell us that on most issues most of the time, this accommodation works well.

However, a sense of proportion should also tell us that this cannot be true for all issues. For believing Christians, subordinating religion as just another piece of one's worldly identity is exactly what their religion warns against. It is the same accommodation to the culture by modernists in the liberal churches that traditionalist Christians have been opposing for decades. If that is what the democratic conversation requires, then there clearly is a democracy problem. This is especially true as fundamental policy issues on the meaning of human life loom on the horizon. On the one hand, it should be possible to hold a shared understanding between religionists and non-religionists that any comprehensive foundational arguments will occur within basic constitutional rules of fair hearing and basic justice. On the other hand, it is unrealistic to think that full-throated religious talk and political action can be kept at bay on policy issues dealing with essential articles of faith. It is for this reason, 500 years after the disaster of the Reformation, that religiously serious Protestants and Catholics may now be increasingly willing to see themselves as two moments in one Christian movement in history.[210] And America is not necessarily the centerpiece of that history.

With subversion and thoroughgoing accommodation ruled out, the third option—political engagement to find a reasoned public ethic—has been the main course pursued by many thoughtful Christians. By now, sufficient experience has accumulated to define in very stark terms the democracy problem for politically engaged Christian traditionalists.

In the first place, it appears that even thoughtful secular activists and religious activists really do not agree on enough to have a serious argument. Forty years ago, John Courtney Murray could express the hopeful view that "we hold certain truths; therefore we can argue about them." From there he thought the contending sides could go on with the process of reaching tentative conclusions at the "growing end" of the basic consensus.[211] Murray was writing about mid-twentieth-century America. Roughly twenty years later, similar Christian traditionalists—critical of how the fundamentalist Moral Majority was discrediting the public responsibility of religion—launched an effort at political engagement to restore religion's place of public reason to the "naked public square" that had been left by the collapse of the Protestant establishment.[212] The aim of Richard John Neuhaus and others who were ecumenically like-minded was not simply to promote more religious voices in politics. It was to produce a public moral discourse, whose reasoning would draw on transcendent meanings of natural law accessible to all. After another twenty years, by the beginning of the twenty-first century, more experience had accumulated. It seemed to show that given the divergent premises of secularist and Christian worldviews, such a public discussion faced an insuperable barrier.[213]

In the second place, even if there were more shared premises at an intellectual level, it is now clear that engagement in the "public square" must invariably take place on the terms set by America's modern political arena for a so-called democratic discourse. This arena and its rules are not designed to search for truth or to compare rational "deliberative justifications." It is a sophisticated, cynical game designed to manipulate imagery and opinion. In other words, it is a public arena fully invested in the consumption arts. This reality is something far different and more cynical than academics' ideal image of a civic forum or a free marketplace of ideas where, in the competition with error, truth has nothing to fear. It is an arena for the professional marketing of feelings rather than the exercising of reason, and truth has everything to fear. So too do religious activists who decide to engage in the game for public opinion. Those who can be flattered as "God's people" are always easily exploited by politicians inside and outside church walls. Worse than that, Christian political activists are under a constant temptation to invert the true priorities of their faith. According to that faith, flexing political muscle to change America counts as nothing in comparison to the Gospel power to change hearts with the methods of a spiritual kingdom that is not of this world. Christians caught up in politics can easily develop a devotion to power and riches that the first Christian explicitly commanded His followers to reject. Moreover, conservative Christians can be just as willing as liberal ones "to paste Christian labels on essentially secular causes."[214] When conservative Christians present policy opinions as religious doctrine, they risk teaching everyone that doctrine is nothing more than opinion. For reasons such as these, it is not surprising that Carl Henry, who in the 1940s had led the call for evangelical Christians' public engagement, died fifty years later regretting evangelicals' captivity to the market dynamics of American religiosity.[215]

In the third place, the political engagement of traditional Christians has encouraged a majoritarianism—a sort of halfway covenant with mass democracy—which is inconsistent with their faith. Outraged at court decisions over such things as abortion, school prayer, gay marriage, and other issues, Christian activists have mounted vigorous campaigns against a judicial activism that replaces decisions by legislatures of democratically elected representatives. It is a deceptively popular argument to make. With natural-law jurisprudence a relic of the past, politically engaged Christians easily succumb to viewing the essence of law as the will of the political sovereign, namely the people. The problem is that if Christians really do believe what they say, it has to follow that immoral policies on abortion, eugenics, euthanasia, gay marriage, genetic engineering, and so on are just as wrong if passed by fifty state legislatures as they are if decided by handful of Supreme Court justices. Here we are re-encountering an ancient tension between the democratic and Christian faiths. As long ago as the eighth century A.D., *vox populi, vox Dei* was a traditional proverb, and Alcuin, as abbot of Tours and adviser to the great Charlemagne, was compelled as a Christian to warn against it.[216] For an authentic Christian believer, when a government—democratic or otherwise—abrogates the law of God, it loses its legitimacy.

Unfortunately for Christian activists—or as secularists would say, fortunately for American democracy—there is little evidence that more democratic policy-making will produce the majorities for which they hope. In the midst of Christian activists' call for more political engagement by the faithful, this issue is generally overlooked. To date, at least, talk about "reclaiming America for Christ" appears to be mainly good fund-raising talk. It ignores Americans' predominant preference for a "lite Christianity" that marginalizes transcendent claims of faith in favor of cultural claims of self-fulfillment.

While approximately 85 percent of American adults identify themselves as Christians, only 42 percent of Americans say they are absolutely committed to the Christian faith, and a majority of all Americans (60 percent) say they think there is no single religion that has all the answers to life's questions. Between one-fourth and one-third of Americans say that they base their moral decision-making primarily on principles and teachings of religion. For self-professed Catholics this drops to 16 percent, and even among "born-again" Christians, only 40 percent say they rely on biblical or church teachings as their primary source of moral guidance.[217]

In terms of the core doctrinal content that supposedly unites Catholic, Protestant, and Orthodox churches into Christianity as such, recent research makes it clear that the mass of American Christians have very little idea of, or interest in, what it is. As we have seen, the roots of a non-creedal Christianity go far back in American history, and by the twenty-first century it has become fully in tune with a secular culture that endorses individual choice, tolerance of different truths, and distrust of anyone's party line about what morality ought to be. In a transformation of American religion toward tolerance of divergent views, the evidence indicates that Americans are more interested in having religious faith than in the doctrines that define the meaning of their faith.[218] Compared with secular Europe, Americans remain hyperactively religious. But their activity appears less oriented toward seeking a God of theological truth, and very much more toward seeking out a religious community that serves one's personal needs (both utilitarian and aesthetic). This is not surprising, since about half of American Christians say they believe that all religious faiths teach the same basic principles. Reciting the traditional Christian creed at worship, and meaning it, is a countercultural gesture.[219]

It is true that church-going is an outstanding behavioral characteristic of Americans compared with other developed nations. In terms of attending organized religious services, 40 percent of Americans report having attended a worship service in the previous week (that is, excluding weeks containing the major religious holidays). Less often discussed in this measure of religiosity is evidence that such self-reported church-going is apparently—over half the time—a lie. According to independent validation by actual counts, time diaries, and the like, the percentage of Americans actually attending any place of worship in the previous week is probably closer to 20 percent than the widely publicized and self-reported figure of 40 percent.[220] It seems that in America the frequency of going to church is roughly matched by the frequency of lying about going to church.

Beyond bearing false witness to one's pollster, the evidence on behavior outside church is more difficult to gather, but it all points in essentially the same direction. Not only American Christians in general but also born-again evangelicals "are as likely to embrace lifestyles that are every bit as hedonistic, materialistic, self-centered, and secularly immoral as the world in general."[221] As the distinguished preacher and Bible expositor James Montgomery Boice put it in 1996 shortly before his death, "The sad truth is that they [evangelicals] perhaps even more than others have sold out to individualism, relativism, materialism and emotionalism, all of which are the norm for the majority of evangelical church services today. Evangelicals may be the most worldly people in

America." Likewise, the overwhelming majority of Catholics fail to abide by the Church's authoritative teaching on artificial birth control, and apparently very few priests insist on conformity with the Church's natural-law doctrine of contraception.[222] The old hostilities between Protestants and Catholics have indeed diminished in modern America, inasmuch as most people in both Christian congregations now seem to regard individual choice as their *de facto* religious creed and commitment.

In twenty-first-century America, the principle of individual choice appears to be the rock on which must break all hopes of traditionalist Christians appealing to either natural law or democratic majorities. Majorities of Americans consider various things morally wrong, but they are deeply reluctant to make them illegal. This applies to many issues, from abortion and homosexuality to euthanasia and assisted suicide.[223] It will certainly apply to the emerging wave of genetic and other policies for remaking nature. For example, in the largest opinion survey to date, roughly three-quarters of Americans are worried about the future of genetic engineering in designing and treating children like products. However, only 38 percent support any government regulation based on "morality or ethics," while 61 percent support government regulation to ensure the safety and quality of reproductive genetic testing.[224]

Personal choice can easily appear as the sensible middle ground for religious and non-religious Americans alike. It says that where people have such varying opinions, government and law must leave the issue to the choices of individual consciences. Because they are based on one's personal sense of conscience, such choices are self-validating. In this distorted way, Protestantism in a democratic regime of consumer sovereignty has ultimately reaped what it sowed in the Great Denouement. It is a distortion because from the beginning, religious liberty had been grounded not simply on "freedom of conscience," but on the essential God-bestowed dignity of the human person with duties to the God of the Bible. Nonetheless, in modern America the exercise of individual autonomy of conscience is *ipso facto* sanctified, whatever it chooses. Anyone who says otherwise is a judgmental bigot and a potential danger to democracy.

With all moral views reduced to differences of personal opinion, everyone can coexist peacefully so long as no one insists too strongly on any standards for other people. Some Christians will find it possible to accommodate themselves to this public outlook. Other, more orthodox Christians (as well as traditionalist Muslims, Jews, and other religionists) will hear this as a polite way of being told to leave the room. In either case, retailing social morality as the aggregation of individual choices can produce collective results that probably never would have been acceptable as wholesale public policy decisions (policies such as eliminating population groups with certain "defects," or privileging adults' reproductive freedom over the right of children not to be designed by some other human being). It is the same dynamic of choice that has produced the larger popular culture which traditional Christians find salacious, degenerate, and alienating.

Finally, then, for traditional Christians there is the increasingly attractive fourth option of separatism, or what Albert Hirschman called "exit." I expect that many, perhaps most, readers will consider it silly even to be discussing such an option. After all, we live in a time—not unknown in our history—when being super-patriotic and super-Christian is often regarded as the same thing. The overwhelming majority of seemingly traditional Christians (77 percent of conservative white Protestants and 87 percent of self-identified evangelicals) see America as founded on Christian principles, and a clear majority of these people think that Christian morality should be the law of the land. Pollsters find that conservative Protestants have more pride in America than any other religious or non-religious social group. Who would want to exit?[225]

All that, however, is on the surface of things and concerns only current events. In a Tocquevillian spirit, we should try to be attentive to deeper currents. It is here and looking toward the future that we will find devout believers recognizing that Christian political activists who identify their country with their faith are cheapening their religion. In fact, something of an odd-couple agreement is emerging on this option between secular activists (Christians should keep out of public affairs for the good of the country) and those who have been called the new pietists (Christians should keep out for the good of their religious way of life).

The chief worry of such pietists, as with their Pilgrim forefathers who left Leiden, Holland, is likely to be for their children. This view has been fueling the fast-growing home-school and Christian academies movement, although this certainly does not represent full withdrawal into a neo-Amish world.[226] Rather than a sudden exodus, what we may find is a gradual, on-again, off-again disengagement of committed believers in orthodox Christianity from the larger political culture. This may be especially attractive to the coming generation of younger evangelicals, who seem to have a certain empathy for the pre-Constantinian home-church communities of early Christians.[227] The self-critical impulse of their religion may well convince such traditional Christians that the real issue is not to blame or fix the larger culture, of which they have been an active part, but to thoroughly turn their own lives in the right direction. Separatism may well be the course followed by chastened patriots who sense that they have abandoned their first love. The attraction will not lie in separatism but in the yearning to be single-hearted. This is the early Christian vision of an unfeigned singleness of heart, a living-in-truth that makes the whole person available to God and to the united community of fellow believers. The historian John Lukacs once wrote that a person cannot be deeply middle-class and deeply Christian at the same time, and those taking this fourth option will be testifying that one cannot be enculturated by America and deeply Christian at the same time.[228]

In following the path of the Leiden Pilgrims and the early Christian church, believers will be occupying ground where two thoughts have to be held together in a strange union—a vision of reason and revelation, of works in the real world and faith in an unseen world that is even more real. Occasional interventions in the public debate may occur. However, separatists will believe that sustained involvement in America's political culture serves mainly to corrupt. Those taking this fourth option will indeed be trying to return to the vision of a tender, loving Christian community of sanctification, a people commanded to be in the world but not of the world. And from the world's point of view, we can expect that their aspirations for a godly community will be regularly defeated both from without and within the community. But somehow they will see that this does not ultimately matter. In the strangeness of their vision, the most real things in the world are the shadows of an unseen world that knows us by name.

For traditional Christians reluctant to separate, there is simply a sad sense of estrangement. Writing as a new grandmother in the mid-1990s, the distinguished professor of ethics Jean Bethke Elshtain questioned whether there would be a "culture worthy of endorsement and engagement" by the time her granddaughter became an adult.[229] From one day to the next, the elegiac withdrawal can be very quiet and unnoticeable. Such Christians (and no one really knows how many) will be primarily committed to participating in their religion's tradition of Bible study, the Daily Office, and charitable service, taking heart in simply keeping their faith alive amid what they see as the ruins of American culture and Christianity.[230] In any event, it is important to recognize that these intimations of exit are coming not from "backwoods fundamentalists," but from among some of the leading Christian minds in the nation. The democracy problem is becoming a rupture when conscientious Christians doubt if they can any longer give moral assent to the existing regime. Christian discipleship and American citizenship then start forcing very fundamental choices.

And so we come full circle. Although the correspondence is certainly not exact, there is an emerging similarity between twenty-first-century America and the situation that Tocqueville found so tragic and dangerous in his French homeland. It is a condition of devout, serious Christians alienated from the quest for democracy, and of devout, serious democrats hostile to Christianity. I am not saying we are there yet, or that we necessarily must reach that sorry state. But I am saying that this seems to be the general tendency in the movement of things. And in saying this I have tried to bear in mind that "aging scholars, like aging parents and retired athletes, tend to see the present as the past devitalized—all loss, faithlessness, and falling away."[231]

Thus chastised, I remain convinced that it is not this essay but American political development itself that has reopened the hoary issue of the compatibility of democracy and Christianity. In the coming years, the stresses created by this question will vary among the four-fifths or so of Americans who identify themselves to pollsters as Christians.[232] This tension between religious commitment and political allegiance will grow and vary depending on whether the person defines his or her life as a Christian American or an American Christian. Which is the "fundamental" term, and which the mere modifier? Each person's answer will make all the difference in the world and, some believe, beyond it.

2

DEMOCRACY AND CATHOLIC CHRISTIANITY IN AMERICA

Mary Jo Bane

HUGH HECLO IN HIS ESSAY ON DEMOCRACY AND Christianity in America makes the provocative statement that "it is reasonable to conclude that Christianity has probably been better for American democracy than American democracy has been for Christianity."[1] He then goes on to discuss what he sees as a "coming rupture" between the two as American democracy faces a new "Christianity problem" and Christianity faces a new "democracy problem."

In these comments I reflect on the Catholic experience with American democracy, with which Heclo does not deal. I contend that American democracy faced a "Christianity problem" in the nineteenth and twentieth centuries with the arrival of large numbers of relatively intolerant Catholic immigrants, a problem that was solved mainly through politics and through the contributions of Catholics as individuals and communities to American democracy. I then argue that Catholicism faced a "democracy problem," which it solved mainly through doctrinal development, with largely positive practical and theological effects. This history suggests to me that the problems which Heclo argues are facing contemporary democracy and Christianity may be addressed in the same ways, making engagement more possible and separatism less likely.

In making these arguments I use a conception of religion that is not defined solely by doctrine, and one in which doctrinal development is not heresy but an integral aspect of a living religion. I make these arguments from and about the Catholic tradition, although I suspect that they may be applicable to some threads of the Protestant tradition as well. I speak from Catholicism for three reasons: First, it is my own faith tradition and the one about which I am most knowledgeable. Second, because Catholicism takes theology and doctrine seriously, and articulates doctrine in authoritative documents, it is easier to document doctrine and its development in this tradition. Finally, ever since the great waves of immigration of the nineteenth century, Catholicism has been the single largest Christian denomination in America, currently claiming the allegiance of about a quarter of the population.[2]

The Great Denouement

In what ways has Catholic Christianity interacted with American democracy? Let me begin with Heclo's "great denouement," which came about, he argues, because the Christian churches at the time of the Revolution and the drafting of the Constitution developed the doctrine of religious liberty through theological, not simply practical, reasoning. Heclo says: "At bottom, government involvement with religion was not a political or philosophical mistake. It was a religious error. Authentic Christianity was the response of one's whole being to God's inner call; and that required that man's mind be left free from coercion."[3] Heclo suggests that Catholics in the English colonies of North America participated in the project of enshrining this line of reasoning into the structures and practices of the new American republic. Indeed they did. But this was not because religious liberty was a theological principle for Catholics, at least before the great Vatican II

Council of the mid-1960s. At best it was a practical necessity; at worst a great evil.

But luckily for American democracy, its Revolution was fought and its Constitution drafted during a brief period when Catholicism departed in many ways from its history and its future.[4] At the time of the Revolution, Catholics were an extremely small proportion of the population in the English colonies of North America, no more than one percent.[5] Among them were a small group of well-educated, middle- and upper-class Irish immigrants including Charles and John Carroll (a signer of the Declaration of Independence and the bishop of Baltimore, respectively), who are best described as Enlightenment Catholics and their church as republican Catholicism. This small group practiced a humanistic Catholicism that indeed celebrated religious liberty and saw no conflict between Catholicism, the ideas of the Enlightenment, and democracy. As Catholic parishes were being organized in this early period, often without resident priests, boards of lay trustees were formed that owned the properties, and parish governance had democratic features including hiring of pastors by the congregation.

This enlightened, republican Catholicism was tolerated by the Vatican mostly because the Vatican was at a low point in its historical power and influence and had other things on its mind than the tiny church in North America—for example, the destruction of churches and execution of priests in France after their revolution, and the kidnapping of two Popes by Napoleon. Preserving the existence of the Papacy seemed more important than whether a few Catholics in North America were developing their own forms of thinking, worship, and governance.

If the Vatican had forcefully expressed at that time its doctrines denouncing religious liberty as a serious error (as it did both before and after this period), or if the Vatican had been in a position to enforce its doctrines in the American church, or if Catholics had been a larger proportion of the American population at the time of the Revolution and Constitution writing, religious issues in the new republic might have been much more contentious. As it happened, the small Catholic minority within the population joined with Baptists, Methodists, and others in a practical compromise that at least would prevent the establishment of Anglicanism or Congregationalism at the national level. If Catholics had been a larger proportion of the population, and if the views of the Vatican had been better known, it might have been much more difficult to establish tolerance as the norm of the new republic—why should a religion which is not itself tolerant be tolerated by others? But the Vatican was weak and far away, and the Catholic population was small and tolerant. Thus the new republic was able to achieve a "great denouement" in regard to religious liberty. It was very lucky.

The Catholic Immigrants

The relationship of Catholicism to democracy during the period of immigration was very complex.[6] It could easily have gone badly wrong. The waves of immigration that contributed to dramatic population growth and societal change during the nineteenth century began, more or less, with the Irish potato famine of 1845. Between then and around 1865, a million and a half Irish immigrants came to America. As a result of this immigration, by 1860 perhaps 8 percent of the U.S. population was Catholic. The Irish clustered in a few cities and states and were, in those places, a much more real and visible presence than they had been in the colonies. The immigrant presence generated a nativist backlash; the Irish-dominated American church responded in a way that both created a strong American Catholic church and contributed to the cultural and civic underpinnings of American democracy. It was a complicated story.

In addition to sending great waves of immigrants to America, the potato famine in Ireland also contributed to a particular style of Catholicism, described vividly by Charles Morris.[7] Since, according to a prominent cardinal of the time, God had visited the famine on the Irish people as punishment for their sins, they needed to repent, submit to the authority of the church, abstain from (or at least not enjoy) sex, and participate in devotions to the Sacred Heart, the Blessed Virgin, and assorted saints. This style of Catholicism was consistent with theological developments in the larger church at the time, which became known as ultramontanism. (The movement was centered in France but looked "beyond the [Alps] mountains" to the Vatican for direction.)[8] The Vatican aggressively reasserted its authority after the debacles of the French revolution—authority within a strictly hierarchical church, and authority in a sense over the world, which could only be saved by becoming Catholic. This theological development found expression in a number of papal declarations on the primacy of the church, and most starkly in the declaration of papal infallibility in 1870.

The nineteenth-century "infallible" Popes were no defenders of religious freedom. In 1824, Pope Leo XII issued an encyclical condemning a variety of evils of the time, among them religious toleration. An 1832 encyclical repeated the condemnation of "that absurd and erroneous teaching, or rather that folly, that it is necessary to assure and guarantee to whomever it may be the liberty of conscience." Because people "will perish eternally if they do not hold the Catholic faith," if freedom of conscience is allowed, "the pit of the abyss is open."[9] As Noonan summed it up, "What is incontestable is that in absolute terms, without qualification as to context, the pope pronounced freedom of conscience and freedom of religion to be pernicious errors."[10]

The Irish immigrants who poured into America in the mid-nineteenth century were not the elite, educated immigrants of earlier times, but displaced farmers and workers. They brought with them a rigid and devotional style of Catholicism, and were accompanied by a clergy, most (though not all) of whom had been educated in Rome, had absorbed ultramonantist theology, and were fiercely loyal to the Pope. These clergy had been educated to

151

believe, as did the Pope, that error had no rights, that the Catholic church was the only path to salvation, and that both modernism and religious liberty were inventions of the devil.

One can imagine that these attitudes might have posed a problem for American democracy. And indeed there are some fairly horrific stories of anti-Catholic and nativist backlash against Catholics and foreigners. The most famous of these events is probably the burning in 1834 of an Ursuline convent in Charlestown, Massachusetts, after charges circulated (later shown to be baseless) that the convent had kidnapped young girls, kept them prisoners, and forced them to provide sexual services to priests.[11] Two decades of violence against Catholics followed. In the 1880s and 1890s the violence subsided somewhat, but nativism remained strong in the political arena. By 1890 the Know-Nothing Party, the platform of which was anti-foreign and anti-Catholic, had a million members and had captured electoral office in a number of states and cities.

The immigrants responded to (and to some extent fed) nativist anti-Catholicism by coming to perceive themselves and to act as a persecuted, beleaguered minority. The cities in which they settled were developing segregated housing patterns. Within these segregated neighborhoods, Catholic national parishes became the primary form of church organization. The first ones were Irish and therefore English-speaking. But later waves of Catholic immigrants, first from Germany and then from eastern Europe, worshipped in German or Polish or other parishes, according to the customs and in the language of their native countries. These parishes also built schools and developed a network of social activities and benevolent societies, all reflecting the culture and language of their countries of origin.

The sense of being a beleaguered minority was reinforced by a theology which held that there was no salvation outside the Catholic church and that interaction and intermarriage with Protestants were sure routes to hell. This fed the impetus to build Catholic schools, a tendency which was reinforced by the fact that public schools at the time were in fact Protestant schools, often requiring prayer and Bible reading from translations of the Bible that were considered by Catholics to be heretical.

Meanwhile, back at the Vatican, the papacy was asserting its authority over the papal lands as well as over the church. Theological controversies pitted neo-scholastics against historicists. Most important for our story is the theological controversy within the church over the relationship of church and state. Some American bishops and some European theologians were starting to make the argument that the American model of religious freedom and separation of church and state was theologically sound, and that Catholicism was most faithful to its origins when it was freely chosen and separate from the state. This group lost the argument. In 1895, in a letter addressed to the Archbishops and Bishops of the United States, Pope Leo XIII, after first expressing his "esteem and love" for the "young and vigorous American nation," went on to say:

> It would be very erroneous to draw the conclusion that in America is to be sought the type of the most desirable status of the Church, or that it would be universally lawful or expedient for State and Church to be, as in America, dissevered and divorced. . . . [The Church in America] would bring forth more abundant fruits if, in addition to liberty, she enjoyed the favor of the laws and the patronage of the public authority.[12]

Ten years earlier, in an encyclical on "the Christian Constitution of States," the same Pope denounced "that harmful and deplorable passion for innovation which was aroused in the sixteenth century," from which came "all those later tenants of unbridled license" that included the principle "that each is free to think on every subject just as he may choose."[13] Instead, he says, the state

> is clearly bound to act up to the manifold and weighty duties linking it to God, by the public profession of religion. . . .

153

Since, then, no one is allowed to be remiss in the service due to God, and since the chief duty of all men is to cling to religion in both its teaching and practice—not such religion as they may have a preference for, but the religion which God enjoins—. . . . it is a public crime to act as though there were no God. So, too, it is a sin for the State not to have care for religion. . . . All who rule, therefore, would hold in honor the holy name of God, and one of their chief duties must be to favor religion, to protect it, to shield it under the credit and sanction of the laws.[14]

Leo makes it clear in the course of developing his argument that "the religion which God enjoins" is the religion of the Catholic church.

So we might conclude that the American Catholic church around the end of the nineteenth century was surely a threat to democracy: a large (now about 16 percent of the population), growing (with higher fertility rates than the rest of the population), inwardly focused subgroup whose doctrine asserted the desirability of an established Catholic religion. The threat, however, did not precipitate a rupture. Instead, three developments occurred.

The first was rivalry between the Irish and the Germans. The Irish were the first large wave of Catholic immigrants to America. They established parishes, attracted priests from both America and Ireland, and came to dominate the Catholic hierarchy of bishops. German Catholic immigrants, who came later, established German parishes, and as time went on they asked for authorization for German-language schools and exclusively German-speaking priests for their parishes. The latter request especially was a threat to the Irish hierarchy. They lobbied vociferously and effectively in Rome against the "special privileges" requested by German American Catholics, and retained their control over the clergy and the hierarchy. Although national parishes remained the norm in Catholic America, the victory of the Irish-American bishops meant that Catholicism was not quite as isolated from American society as it might have been.

The second development was the desire of the Irish American Catholic hierarchy to exercise political power in cities with large Catholic populations. These powerful bishops wanted protections, and indeed privileges, for their Catholic flock; they wanted, for example, fair treatment in public schools and, if they could get it, public financing for Catholic schools. Although they lost most of the specific fights, they did develop into a strong political force. (In the early 1840s Cardinal Hughes in New York endorsed a slate of Catholic candidates for the legislature that agreed with him on the school issues. They won in the city, then won an important victory in the state legislature. Hughes withdrew the Catholic slate he had recruited for the next election, having made his point about Catholic electoral muscle.) And in doing so, they figured out that a platform calling for an established Catholic church might not be the optimum strategy for getting what they wanted. So this message, which was in fact the official Vatican position, was muted, indeed not heard, in America. Catholics, led by their bishops, built in their parishes a strong and rich Catholic religion that was developing, on this important issue, its own implicit doctrine.

The third and most important development was that the strategy of building strong and separate Catholic institutions not only reinforced the power of the hierarchy but also served both the immigrants and American democracy very well. The bishops and their clergy built an authoritarian Catholic church, which asserted and modeled a hierarchical structure and emphasized the importance of obedience. They insisted that Catholics pray only with each other, marry only other Catholics, belong to Catholic fraternal societies, and educate their children as Catholics. They then used their authority and the institutional structure of the church in support of education, strong families, hard work, temperance (not all their efforts were successful), responsibility, and loyalty to the country. Catholics, on average, went to school, worked hard, served in the armed forces, and saved money to buy homes. Their children became professionals and moved to the suburbs.

There were many ironies in this strategy. One was in the pattern of developing and staffing Catholic schools. According to Catholic teaching at the time, there were only two appropriate places for women: the home, where they were to defer to their husbands and raise lots of pious children, and the convent. Given those alternatives, many young Catholic women chose the convent, in which they could be relatively independent, get an education, and practice a profession. They staffed the growing numbers of Catholic schools and managed to provide young Catholics with a pretty good education, at very low cost, in a disciplined and orderly environment. (Another irony was that unmarried Catholic women who were not nuns staffed the public schools of the nation's large cities.) From these schools emerged the Catholic middle class, mostly Irish to be sure, who were in many ways model Americans in their habits, values, and families. And from these strategies grew the American model of mostly peaceful religious pluralism.

Later, at the time of Vatican II, the "success" of the American Catholic church was an important element in bringing about a dramatic shift in Catholic doctrine on religious freedom. That story will come later. Here, I want to make two points. First, Catholicism during the immigrant period posed a potentially serious "Christianity problem" for American democracy. The problem was managed in spite of, rather than because of, important Catholic doctrinal positions. It was managed partly by the chance rivalry of Irish and Germans. It was managed by politics, because the new immigrants settled in concentrated neighborhoods in a few large cities where their leaders, including bishops, were able to build political power and turned out to be pretty good at deploying it. It was managed by Catholic immigrants who developed a successful subculture that was powerfully shaped by religion, even as it muted and later explicitly rejected important doctrinal positions. A significant point here is that religion is more than its doctrine; it is also practice, institutions, habits, and ways of thinking. American democracy allowed the Catholic immigrants to develop a way of life as a subculture within a pluralist society. That subculture was rich in sacraments, symbols, rituals, social structures, and opportunities for community. It provided structure, education, and support; it opened up opportunities in politics and, through politics, in public sector careers; it was very Catholic, very American, and very successful.

My second point is that this period posed a serious "democracy problem" for Catholic Christianity. That problem was eventually solved by a dramatic change in doctrine, first implicitly in the immigrant church and then, at the Second Vatican Council, explicitly. In the case of Catholic Christianity, however, I believe this has proved to be a positive development for the religion, not a negative one. That is because doctrine develops and changes, even in the Catholic church, the most explicitly tradition-bound of all Christian religions.

Religious Liberty as Doctrine

In December 1964 the fourth session of Vatican Council II adopted, by a vote of 1,997 to 224, a draft of a Declaration on Religious Liberty. The key paragraph of that declaration reads as follows:

> The Vatican Council declares that the human person has a right to religious freedom. Freedom of this kind means that everyone should be immune from coercion by individuals, social groups and every human power so that, within due limits, no men or women are forced to act against their convictions nor are any persons to be restrained from acting in accordance with their convictions in religious matters in private or in public, alone or in association with others.[15]

The Council described what it was doing in this declaration as "search[ing] the sacred tradition and teaching of the church from which it draws forth new insights in harmony with the old."[16] The implication of the language in the declaration was that the church was simply restating an old doctrine in a new context.

The declaration on religious freedom may have been so long overdue, so intuitively correct, coming after so many countries in the world had incorporated the right of religious freedom into their constitutions, that most Catholics at the time may have assumed this was indeed the historical teaching of the church. But it was not. Less than a hundred years earlier, as noted above, religious freedom had been denounced by two Popes as a pernicious error. Only a year before, in the third session of the Council, the draft declaration on religious freedom had come close to being rejected on the ground that those in error had no rights; the most the church could condone was tolerance, not rights. Religious liberty, the opponents claimed, could not be justified on theological grounds, though it could perhaps be condoned on practical grounds.[17]

The American theologian John Courtney Murray, who had been instrumental in drafting the declaration, characterized the opposition to it as being not so much against religious liberty as against "the affirmation of progress in doctrine that an affirmation of religious liberty necessarily entails."[18] The bishops hedged their language, but they knew that doctrine was being changed in the Declaration, and they voted overwhelmingly in favor of it. Religious liberty became an official teaching of the Catholic Church.

Religious liberty is not the only example of the development of doctrine in the Catholic Church. The Vatican Council II Constitution on the Church in the Modern World contained a condemnation of slavery,[19] which had been defended by the church for many centuries, and was only officially denounced by this 1965 Constitution. No one at the Council appears to have opposed this change in doctrine, although the record of acceptance of slavery goes back to Saint Paul. The condemnation of usury was gradually abandoned by the Church. In his masterful study of these developments, *A Church That Can and Cannot Change*, John

Noonan suggests that church doctrine on divorce is now in the midst of notable development.[20]

How can this happen? Noonan describes the process as one of the deepening of our understanding of revelation.[21] In the case of the doctrine of religious liberty (or lack thereof), biblical and theological study clearly contributed. The arguments in the Declaration on Religious Liberty are based on newly articulated understandings of the human person, and on a reading of the Gospels that emphasized the freely given and freely accepted invitations to discipleship that Jesus offered.

Two aspects of the historical context were also crucial. First was the fact that the Vatican Council took place in the aftermath of the rise and defeat of Nazism, and in the midst of the Cold War. The power of religious bigotry had become apparent in the rise of Nazi Germany and fascist Italy, and its consequences had been made brutally clear. In the communist Soviet Union and the countries of eastern Europe, the church was struggling to assert the rights of Christians to practice their religion. Some of the strongest statements in the Council debates supporting the Declaration on Religious Liberty came from bishops behind the Iron Curtain.

A second clear influence on the thinking of the Council, and important for our discussion here, was the perceived strength and vibrancy of the American Catholic church. Cardinals Spellman and Cushing (of New York and Boston) came to the Council from an America where Catholics were almost a quarter of the population; where church attendance was high, religious vocations plentiful, and intermarriage low; and where Catholics over the previous decades had financed and built an incredible array of churches, schools, hospitals, and social service institutions. The cardinals argued that the strength of the American church was nurtured, not hindered, by the constitutional framework of religious freedom and non-establishment, and they had the reality of a financially and institutionally strong church to bolster their argument.[22]

In this case, it seems clear that doctrine did develop, that the doctrinal development was positive for the living Catholic faith, and that American democracy contributed to this happy outcome. An indication of the extent of the change in attitude is the positive discussion of American Catholicism and its contribution to Vatican II in a new book by Joseph Ratzinger, now Pope Benedict XVI:

> American Catholics also recognize the positive character of the separation between church and state for both religious reasons and for the religious freedom that it guaranteed them. . . . On the basis of the structure of Christianity in the United States, the American Catholic bishops made a unique contribution to the Second Vatican Council. . . . They brought to the issue and to Catholic tradition the experience of the non-state church (which had proven to be a condition for protecting the public value of fundamental Christian principles) as a Christian form that emerged from the very nature of the Church.[23]

The Aftermath

Ten years after Vatican II, the state of American Catholicism was not so rosy.[24] According to polls conducted and reported by Andrew Greeley, between 1963 and 1974 Sunday Mass attendance by Catholics fell by 20 percentage points, and the proportion of income that Catholics contributed to the church fell by half. In 1974, only 32 percent of surveyed American Catholics believed the Pope was infallible, and only 16 percent believed that contraception was always wrong, down from 52 percent who had expressed belief in this firm teaching of the church in 1963.[25] Greeley suggests that such a dramatic change in Catholic attitudes over this relatively brief period was historically unprecedented.

What happened between 1963 and 1974? The Second Vatican Council, to be sure. Some have argued that the changes made by the Council in Catholic worship and rules for Catholic living (the

English-language Mass and the lifting of the prohibition of eating meat on Fridays, for example), as well as the implication of the Council that the church could change, weakened the church and led to the subsequent declines in belief and practice. But something else happened in the Catholic Church between 1963 and 1974 that may have been more important. In 1968, Pope Paul VI rejected the recommendations of a commission he had appointed to examine the church's teachings on birth control and reaffirmed the church's prohibition on all forms of artificial contraception. The Pope was apparently persuaded that since the church had taught in the past that birth control was wrong, it must be wrong, since the church could not make a mistake on something that affected the lives of the faithful so directly. If he allowed the teaching on birth control to develop and change, he thought, the authority of church and pope would be seriously undermined.

As it turns out—and this is well documented by Greeley's surveys, among others—what weakened the authority of church and pope was their rigidity on this issue. Married Catholics had already rejected the birth control teachings in practice; they knew from the Council-instigated changes in the Sunday liturgy and norms on fasting that church rules could change; and they expected the commission to recommend and the Pope to accept what they saw as eminently sensible changes in the church's teaching on birth control.[26] Large majorities of Catholics simply rejected church teaching on this issue. It seems pretty clear that the problem for Catholicism in the early 1970s was not democracy but its absence—a failure on the part of the hierarchy to learn from the experience of the laity, to respect their conscientious and conscience-driven insights, or even to explain persuasively why the decision was made as it was.

What is perhaps most surprising, however, about American Catholic reaction to the birth control debacle is how many American Catholics stuck with the church through it all. They didn't go to Sunday Mass quite so often, and they dismissed some of the allegedly authoritative teachings of the Vatican, but they mostly stayed. They increased their participation in the Eucharist, and they gave a number of indications that, as Greeley puts it, they liked being Catholic. Their allegiance was dealt another mighty blow in early 2002, with the revelations about clergy abuse of children and the subsequent cover-ups by the church hierarchy. Here too I would argue that the problem was not too much democracy in the church, but not enough transparency, honesty, or remorse. And in this instance as well I would point to the robustness of the church's hold on the loyalty of its members, disillusioned but mostly still Catholic.

Catholics and "the Coming Rupture"

My brief survey of the relationship of Catholic Christianity and American democracy over the centuries suggests that the relationship has been more complicated and also more robust than might be suggested by Heclo's account. American democracy has weathered the potential threats of a powerful religion with official doctrines inconsistent with democracy, and Catholic Christianity has not only weathered but profited from the challenges posed by democracy. The "coming rupture," if one is coming, may also be weathered, by the American and Christian genius for working things out through politics when possible, ignoring unpleasant differences when necessary, and continuing to develop doctrine as theology wrestles with reality.

I look first at the possibilities for political accommodations, again from the perspective of Catholicism. In November 2004, white Catholics constituted 19 percent of the voters, and they gave 53 percent of their votes to George Bush and 47 percent to John Forbes Kerry—a long way from the 68 percent of Catholic votes that went to an earlier Catholic JFK running for President. Catholics who identified themselves as traditionalist voted 72 percent for Bush; as centrist, 55 percent for Bush; and as modernist, 69 percent for Kerry. Sixty-nine percent of Latino Catholic votes went to Kerry.[27]

Before the election, a conservative group called Catholic Answers had distributed millions of copies of a voting guide that advised Catholic voters to attend to five "non-negotiable" issues: abortion, euthanasia, gay marriage, stem cell research, and cloning. The clear implication, which was actually articulated by a few bishops, was that faithful Catholics were morally obligated to vote against their fellow religionist.

Centrist Catholics were clearly an important swing group in the 2004 election: 7 percent of the electorate that gave 55 percent of its vote to George Bush. Judging from the surveys of the attitudes of these voters, it seems unlikely that that they voted on the basis of "non-negotiable issues," since their attitudes on the five issues are conflicted when they are not outright rejecting the hardline Vatican positions. It seems more likely that these Catholics voted as they did for the same reasons as other Bush voters—that is, they were worried about national security and they didn't much like John Kerry.[28] But at least some of them may have been put off by what they and others perceive as extreme secularism in the Democratic Party. Recent Democratic efforts to talk more about values, to find a position on abortion that is both pro-life and opposed to criminalization, and to express compassion for the poor without advocating big government may or may not succeed with these voters; much will depend, I suspect, on whether these positions are, and are perceived as, sincere. But it is clear that centrist Catholics are an important group of convertible voters, who are likely to be attracted by moderate stands on divisive issues and by policies that effectively address poverty. Perhaps politics, once again, will figure this out, and in doing so, will help to avoid a rupture.

The potential for doctrinal development within the Catholic church as a moderating force on the "coming rupture" is risky to try to assess. This is important, however, because Catholicism is theologically sophisticated at the same time that it is conservative about doctrine. Catholic theologians have done much of the intellectual work for orthodox Christianity over the centuries, and are likely to continue to do so. Certainly contemporary Catholic theologians are exploring issues of moral theology, religious pluralism, and the interaction of church and state, working out a diversity of perspectives grounded in revelation and Catholic tradition. But the most interesting theologian, and the most important, may be the theologian who is now the Pope.

Many liberal and moderate Catholics, myself included, were horrified when Joseph Ratzinger, the enforcer of orthodoxy in his role as head of the Congregation for the Doctrine of the Faith, became Pope Benedict XVI. But might he accomplish the Catholic equivalent of Nixon's going to China? Benedict XVI wrote his first encyclical, *Deus Caritas Est*, on love.[29] The first part of the encyclical is a beautiful and generous portrayal of God as love, and of love, including erotic love, as both a wonderful gift of God and the way in which humans find God. The second part is a meditation on charity as a duty of the church, accompanied by a careful discussion of the state's duty to do justice. The encyclical contains no anathemas, no instructions for voting, no partisan positions. *Deus Caritas Est* will be hard to use as a weapon in the culture wars.

There are some other hints of how Benedict's theology may develop. There is no indication in any of his writings, recent or past, that Benedict is a religious relativist; he clearly does not believe that all religions are equal in either their reflection of truth or their ability to lead humanity to goodness. He forcefully articulates his belief that monotheism, specifically in its Catholic Christian form, is true, that it has universal relevance, and that Christians have an obligation to bear witness to its truth and to invite others to embrace its practice. Benedict clearly accepts, however, the Vatican II formulation of religious liberty and the primacy of conscience, emphasizing that Christianity must persuade by the reasonableness of its doctrine and the attractiveness of Christian lives, not by any form of coercion.[30]

Likewise, there are no indications that Benedict sees room for development in Catholic teachings on abortion, euthanasia, homosexuality, or the importance of the family. His first encyclical did not speak directly to any of these issues (nor did his 2005 Christmas message or his 2006 Lenten message, which discussed poverty, development, and charity); this suggests that they may not be his highest priority as Pope. Nonetheless, in a recently published dialogue with Marcello Pena, Benedict reiterated an uncompromising position on the sanctity of life, the primary importance of the traditional family, and the dangers of moral relativism.[31]

Where there may be room for constructive theological development by Benedict, however, is in the arena of religion and politics. *Deus Caritas Est,* in the context of a discussion of charity and justice, emphasizes the autonomy of both the church as community and the temporal sphere of politics. The church cannot and must not, he says, impose its beliefs and modes of conduct on those who do not share the faith; instead, the role of the church is to "help form consciences" on the basis of reason and natural law and to "reawaken the spiritual energy without which justice . . . cannot prevail and prosper."[32]

In an earlier Doctrinal Note from the Congregation for the Doctrine of the Faith on "The Participation of Catholics in Political Life," Cardinal Ratzinger made the same points about the autonomy of the church and politics. He stressed the obligation of Christians to participate in democratic politics in "the promotion and defense of goods such as public order and peace, freedom and equality, respect for human life and for the environment, justice and solidarity."[33] He also stated that there can be a variety of political and policy approaches that express a correct working out of these principles. He seems to be saying, in short, that Christians have an obligation to take their firmly held beliefs and their challenges to the culture into the political arena, and to work at devising political and policy solutions in the context of democratic politics, through persuasion and the use of reason.

Thus the Pope appears to be developing a theology of what Heclo calls engagement and defining it as an integral aspect of

Christian discipleship. This would seem to leave open the possibility that some of the more contentious issues that politics will face could be addressed with creativity and compromise, rather than, for example, bishops simply announcing that criminal law is the appropriate instrument for delegitimating abortion. If the Pope moves in this direction, it could help to frame a constructive role in politics not just for Catholics but for other orthodox believers.

The Catholic sacramental imagination, as Greeley has described it, sees the world as full of grace, the gift of a good God. It tends to be hopeful, often so when there is not a shred of evidence suggesting reason for hope. I admit to the bias of the Catholic imagination. But I also think there is reason for hope, both in the history and in the present.

3

PLURALISM IS HARD WORK
—AND THE WORK IS
NEVER DONE

Michael Kazin

A S I THOUGHT ABOUT HOW TO RESPOND TO HUGH
Heclo's ambitious and insightful essay, a statement by
Richard Hofstadter kept coming to mind. In 1968, at the
end of his unappreciated masterpiece, *The Progressive Historians,*
Hofstadter sought to transcend the dispute between consensus
scholars like Daniel Boorstin and Louis Hartz, and the New Left
historians, who were insisting on the central role of conflict, especially over class and race, in American history. Neither group, at
the time, was particularly interested in religion.

In 1948 Hofstadter had published *The American Political Tradition,* a classic statement of the consensus position. But twenty
years later, he thought that each side was missing the point. Hofstadter predicted: "As more and more historians become aware
that conflict and consensus require each other and are bound up
in a kind of dialectic of their own, the question whether we should
stress one or the other may recede to a marginal place, and give
way to other issues." He added, "As practiced by mature minds,
history forces us to be aware not only of complexity but of defeat
and failure: it tends to deny that high sense of expectation, that
hope of ultimate and glorious triumph, that sustains good combat."[1]

In recent years, there has been a renaissance of scholarship about Protestant Christianity in America and its connections both to governance and to social movements. Such historians as William McLoughlin, Nathan Hatch, Mark Noll, Richard Fox, and D. G. Hart have produced compelling analyses of how evangelicalism triumphed not only as a theological position but also as a political style—and how the latter influenced the former.[2]

These works imply a growing consensus: during the nineteenth century, a majority of Americans came to embrace a messianic, anti-hierarchical, Jesus-centered faith. Ironically, at the zenith of the Protestant Century (which only ended sometime after World War I), Americans also began to grow more tolerant of other faiths. As Alan Wolfe writes, "Although premised on one religion's outlook on the world, Protestantism's affinity for individualism, its relatively nonhierarchical organizational style . . ., and—especially in its evangelical form—its commitment to reaching out and spreading the Word helped transform American culture in directions that made it all but impossible for one religion to insist on a privileged status in relationship to others." By the middle of the twentieth century, only atheists and agnostics were denied the pluralist embrace.[3]

Hugh Heclo has written a wonderful synthesis of this scholarship—and has added acute, often witty reflections of his own. In sum, he describes how the long dominion of Protestantism in America established and kept refreshing the individualist cast of American democracy. Better than any previous scholar, he explains how this relationship was shaken during the 1960s but not, I think, destroyed. I also applaud him for emphasizing that the Protestant concern with defining and promoting moral conduct in the public sphere has decisively and continuously influenced American politics and politicians. If we truly have a civil religion, an unwritten pact that both assumes and encourages tolerance toward different faiths within a nationalist framework, then what Heclo calls "the expectation in the first place that one ought to be good" is essential to it.

But what's the point of writing a response if one only dispenses praise? So I want to dissent from one of Heclo's grander assumptions: I believe the consensus he describes was always more fragile and less satisfactory to most Americans than he supposes. He errs in seeing Christianity in the United States as a more or less unified entity that changed little over time, at least until the 1960s. Heclo does not simply rejoice in the marriage of Christianity and democracy in America—he is too good a historian and has too ironic a sensibility for that. But he downplays or ignores some of the most important and long-running cultural and political conflicts within that relationship. If, throughout our history, to be a theist is part of what it has meant to be an American, to battle over the content, meaning, and application of one's beliefs has been just as central to the national narrative.

The result has been an ongoing tension *between* religious Americans—most, but not all of them, Christians—about whether their faith is being practiced in a way that promotes democracy or restricts it to only certain groups in the population. Of course, this tension is sometimes relaxed, and the groups in question both adapt and change their composition and identity over time. But as long as most Americans ground their public moralism in their faith, the tension will probably never be resolved. To take one's religion seriously almost requires a certain amount of conflict with those who seriously disagree.[4]

Heclo neglects the *development* of this charged dialectic, in part, I think, because his focus is more on Christianity than on Christians. If one is analyzing the successful construction of a set of institutions rather than the actions of the people who struggled to define what those institutions should stand for, a sense of popular ambivalence toward those structures can get neglected. Heclo has also chosen to write an episodic style of narrative, which inevitably draws suspicion from a historian. He spends a good deal of time, as one would expect, on the beginnings of the Republic and its early decades, ending during the Second Great Awakening when Tocqueville came for a visit, accompanied by his friend

Gustave de Beaumont. Then, after a few asides about John Dewey, the Scopes Trial, and the Cold War, Heclo leaps into the 1960s for an extended stay.

What occurred during the intervening decades? Among other things, a long series of debates, some of them bloody, about what the relationship should be between democrats and Christians—and sometimes between American democracy and religion itself. It's hardly coincidental that those years included the greatest period of immigration in U.S. history—when, from the 1840s through the 1920s, 37 million people migrated legally across the Atlantic, north from Mexico, and east across the Pacific. Heclo gives barely a nod to how this mass immigration affected the marriage of Christianity and democracy. It is as if all those Catholics, Orthodox Christians, Jews, and Buddhists just leaped happily into a "melting pot" of faiths and races, as Israel Zangwill urged them to do in his 1908 play of that name, which announced that America was "God's Crucible."

But such an assumption neglects the always uneasy, sometimes hostile nature of the interaction between native-born Protestants and the religious newcomers. When Zangwill's drama opened on Broadway, it received the fulsome praise of President Theodore Roosevelt. In his muscular Christianity, TR showed no animus toward Catholics, Jews, or the Eastern Orthodox—as long as they adhered to what he considered to be moral and "true American" standards. Roosevelt also made clear that some coercion would be necessary to speed along the "melting" process and ensure that it would not go into reverse. "We must Americanize them in every way, in speech, in political ideas and principles, and in their way of looking at the relations between Church and State," he wrote in 1894. The immigrant "must not bring in his Old-World religious, race, and national antipathies, but must merge them into love for our common country, and must take pride in the things which we can all take pride in."[5]

That stance is remarkably similar to that which many contemporary native-born Europeans—from the unchurched majority as well as the shrunken precincts of the devout—take toward Muslim immigrants in such nations as the Netherlands, Denmark, and France. Like Theodore Roosevelt, they demand that the Islamic newcomers learn, with state guidance, to conform to national norms of speech, dress, and political behavior. The urgency of such requirements makes clear the natives' dread of the damage an unassimilable horde of foreigners could do to the political and cultural fabric of their nations and of Europe as a whole.

In the United States, the original great fear was that of tyrannical, medieval Catholic hierarchs and the allegedly servile brutes who filled their pews. Puritan settlers brought this dread with them from England, and the American colonists' participation in the Seven Years' War with France strengthened its hold over the dissenting Protestant imagination. On the eve of the Revolution, American evangelicals led protests against the Crown's recognition of the Catholic Church in Canada and accused Anglican bishops of plotting with English politicians to force a popish tyranny on free-worshipping Americans. Paul Revere illustrated the conspiracy theory with one of his most effective engravings, "The Mitred Minuet."[6]

Abolitionists and temperance reformers continued to rail against the Catholic "menace" in the decades just before the Civil War, and the great fear blazed on through the cultural and political skirmishes of Gilded Age America. A powerful 1871 cartoon by Thomas Nast shows frightened and praying schoolchildren on a beach, about to be attacked by a pack of bishops, their mitres shaped like the jaws of alligators—while in the distance sits a public school in ruins and the Capitol building with a cross on top, and the flags of the papacy and of Ireland flapping in the breeze. Nast dramatized conflicts that were taking place over required readings of the King James Version of the Bible in public schools, about how to teach the history of the Reformation and the subsequent wars of religion, and whether tax money could be spent on parochial education.

At the same time, there was often room for compromise. In

New York state, many local school officials kept the sectarian pot from boiling over by allowing Catholics to hold devotional services before the start of classes and inviting Protestants to hold evening prayer services inside the same buildings. But not until the era of World War II did many Catholics shed their suspicions of what their children were learning about their own faith in public school. And Protestant children in small inland towns learned to run quickly past churches where mass was being chanted, lest the whore of Rome seduce them into entering and snatch their souls.[7]

Meanwhile, in state after state, fierce battles over prohibition and immigration restriction, while demographically complex, tended to pit evangelical Protestants against other Christians, particularly immigrants and their children. The struggle over prohibition was particularly long-lived and impervious to compromise. At the head of the "dry army" were two evangelical Protestant organizations—the Women's Christian Temperance Union and the Anti-Saloon League, the latter run by Methodist, Presbyterian, and Congregationalist clergymen. Neither group was shy about pointing out that most brewers and saloon-keepers in industrial cities and factory towns were either Lutherans or Catholics. Not all prohibitionists were evangelicals, but it certainly seemed that all evangelical Protestants were in favor, publicly at least, of what Herbert Hoover would call "the noble experiment." The dry movement succeeded in amending the Constitution, and, throughout the 1920s, the Anti-Saloon League's lobbyists blocked any attempts in Congress to weaken the strict provisions of the Volstead Act. The "experiment" got wrecked by widespread grassroots law-breaking and a well-financed libertarian counter-movement. However, the gradual decline in Protestant nativism that followed the lopsided passage of immigration restriction laws during the same decade also had something to do with it. By the onset of the Great Depression, when more people were leaving the nation than entering it, dry crusaders had a difficult time convincing their fellow evangelicals to keep the old moral standard flying stiffly in the wind.

By then, however, religious animus had left an indelible stamp on American politics. Long before what the historian John Higham called "the tribal twenties," the influx of non-Protestant immigrants had had a large and formative influence on the party system. Hugh Heclo observes, "Tocqueville acknowledges and considers it irrelevant that most of education in America is entrusted to Christian clergy." He affirms Tocqueville's observation that clergy in the early 1830s were not affiliated with political parties. But Tocqueville was writing just before millions of Irish-Catholic migrants and smaller numbers of their co-religionists from Bavaria and the Rhineland began swelling the population of cities across America.

With the presence of all these Catholics, Tocqueville would have had to qualify his remark quite severely. In the North, many evangelical ministers endorsed the Whig Party. The great preacher Lyman Beecher campaigned for William Henry Harrison in 1840, and the messianic humanitarianism of the Whigs owed a great deal to such figures, who included Beecher's enormously influential abolitionist children, Harriet and Henry. Meanwhile, near election time, anyone reading a Catholic newspaper could not have missed the clear preference of its editors and of most local priests for the Democratic Party. This clerical division continued into the Gilded Age, as indicated by a Presbyterian minister's inopportune slur in 1884 that the Democrats were the party of "Rum, Romanism, and Rebellion." In fact, it was big news when anyone in the Catholic hierarchy broke with the Democrats, the party of religious toleration, as did Archbishop John Ireland in 1896 when he backed William McKinley over William Jennings Bryan.[8]

Such religio-cultural skirmishes lasted into the 1920s—when Al Smith and his allies battled the Ku Klux Klan, which recent historians have interpreted as a massive force of men and women dedicated to enforcing the Volstead Act and protecting the unofficial Protestant identity of most public schools. But it wasn't just reactionaries who reviled the Roman Church as a threat to the republic. During the 1908 presidential campaign, some Catholics spoke kindly of William Howard Taft because the Republican nominee, in an earlier stint as governor-general of the Philippines, had negotiated the lucrative sale of huge tracts of land there that were owned by various monastic orders. After Taft's election, his opponent, William Jennings Bryan, received a flood of letters charging that the Vatican had ordered Catholics to vote for the GOP. "How can it be said that our elections are free," asked one correspondent from Cambridge, "when one man in Rome can dictate the choice of . . . voters in this country?" Four years later, Eugene Debs called on his Socialist comrades to "expose" the American Catholic hierarchy "as the rottenest political machine that ever stole the livery of heaven."[9]

American Catholics only shed their image as foes of democracy after the Democrats, their ancestral party, surged into power with Franklin Roosevelt and then led the nation into the Second World War and through the dangerous beginnings of the Cold War. Through the 1950s, both secular liberals and conservative evangelicals accused Catholics of harboring a "dual loyalty" that was not so different from that of Communists who followed the dictates of the USSR. But most Protestants had grudgingly come to accept Catholics as "good Americans"; after all, such pillars of the Church as Bishop Fulton Sheen and Cardinal Francis Spellman played leading roles in the national purging of the Red Menace. In 1960, John F. Kennedy's candidacy and election certainly helped complete the process, although he had to disavow any role for religion in public life in order to assuage lingering fears of papal influence.[10]

Of course, as Hofstadter understood, all these conflicts took place within certain shared assumptions about the limits of political theology and the value of a common, if abstract, civil religion. There was no government-sponsored *kulturkampf* in America, nor did any influential citizens call for re-establishing state churches anywhere, not even in Utah. Meanwhile, Catholics were riven by their own "national question": first German and then

Italian, Polish, Hungarian, and Mexican parishioners demanded priests who spoke their language and were steeped in their traditional rituals of worship and celebration. Some new immigrant churches behaved almost like independent congregations—although the largely Irish hierarchy always managed to pull them back from the brink. But in early-twentieth-century metropolises like Chicago and New York, there was often more cultural pluralism *within* the Catholic Church than between Catholics and Americans of other faiths.

No discussion of pluralism can neglect the role played by American Jews. It was both unsurprising and highly significant that Jewish thinkers were at the forefront of the intellectual movement in the early twentieth century that articulated a cosmopolitan position toward ethnic and religious differences. Fearing both the growth of anti-Semitism and that of nativist bigotry more generally, such writers as Horace Kallen, Franz Boas, Bruno Lasker, and Lillian Wald thought it urgent to parry Christian supremacy—while, at the same, time ridiculing the pernicious nonsense about the supremacy of a "Nordic" race.[11]

Soon after Hitler took power in Germany, opposition to anti-Semitism became the litmus test for American liberals of any faith or none at all—although admitting Jewish refugees from Nazi rule never became a popular cause. But the habitual, if almost always nonviolent, anti-Semitism of most American Christians only came to an end after World War II when they learned about the Holocaust and realized that most Jews wanted to shed their cultural and political exoticism and join the home-owning middle class. Only then was it possible for Will Herberg's trinity of religious identities to gain legitimacy and for most Americans to consider as uncontroversial President Dwight Eisenhower's famous (or infamous) statement, "Our form of government has no sense unless it is founded in a deeply felt religious faith, and I don't care what it is."[12] At the time of Tocqueville's visit, the triumph of pluralism was hardly predictable; it had taken a century of dialectical development to produce the kind of relaxed diversity of faiths that, at least for now, most Americans take more or less for granted.

Despite the erosion of denominational lines in recent decades, there remain important conflicts between major religious groups in America over what ends democracy should serve. Hugh Heclo offers a fine sketch of what "traditionalist" Christians find alarming about contemporary American society. But equally lively alternative traditions on the left, of both ideology and behavior, continue to course through debates about the place of religion and the godly in public life. These minority traditions both derive from and shape the meanings of morality and prophecy for groups which, as Lincoln noted as the Civil War neared its end, "read the same Bible and pray to the same God, and . . . invoke His aid against the other."

The first alternative tradition is that of activist liberal Protestantism itself. Adherents of a Social Gospel are neither as influential nor as self-confident as they were a century ago—or during the 1960s. But many members of such shrunken denominations as the Episcopalians and the United Church of Christ (descendants, ironically, of what were once the established churches in colonial Virginia and New England) are, if anything, more united in their left-leaning interpretation of the Gospels than ever before. For large numbers of people in these denominations, to follow Christ means to welcome gay marriage and preserve abortion rights, to condemn military intervention overseas, and to welcome conflict with conservative authorities—secular or religious. In their view, "charity" has become a synonym for condescension and compromise. As William Sloane Coffin, the late firebrand of the UCC, put it, "Charity in no way affects the status quo, which accounts for its popularity in middle class churches, while justice inevitably leads to political confrontation."[13]

For their part, most Jews, despite their prosperity and high class status, have remained stubbornly liberal on both economic and cultural matters, practicing a species of what one might call "altruistic modernism." This outlook combines the hallmarks of cultural modernism: the freedom to choose one's religion and sexual partners, fluidity of class and ethnic lines, and an openness toward living in a society continually repopulated by immigrants and other cultural strangers. But Jewish modernism is paired with and defined by altruism: Jews tend to feel they have a duty to help the oppressed (or at least to feel guilty about not doing so), to bring about social equality, to practice *tikkun olam* (to repair the world) and the Golden Rule. Activist or not, American Jews are eternally suspicious toward evangelical crusades of any variety—from the right-to-life movement to the invasion of Iraq. The motto of *PM,* a radical daily paper with a largely Jewish staff published in New York City in the 1940s, put it well: "We are against people who push other people around."

The United States provided Jews with an environment in which this ideology could flourish. Even though an informal, folkloric kind of anti-Semitism was once widespread in America (President Harry Truman sneered, after speaking with a delegation of unhappy Zionists, that "even Jesus couldn't satisfy these people"), the hatred of Jews never animated a political party or a major social movement. And Truman, despite his prejudices, still supported the creation of the state of Israel.

For their part, many Catholic thinkers—whether or not they wear a clerical collar or habit—still refuse to share the individualist, anti-statist ethos that animates most Protestants. As two forceful advocates of the Catholic critique recently put it, "We don't think taxes are too high, government is too big, or that the Declaration and Bill of Rights are infallible. We are not against bureaucracy; it does big jobs that can't be done otherwise, and has a certain moral worth that we ought to think about more deeply. . . . We don't believe humans are perfectible, but that bit of wisdom calls for moral realism, not complacency or dropping out." Drawing not just on American texts but on a variety of encyclicals stretching back to *Rerum Novarum* in 1891, such Cath-

179

olics view solidarity and subsidiarity as guideposts for democratic practice.[14]

The current campaign for a living wage illustrates the strength of this tradition. In support of the policy, Catholic union leaders like John Sweeney of the AFL-CIO, local priests, and student activists at numerous Catholic colleges cite the work of Monsignor John Ryan and the social encyclicals. They either ignore or reject considerations of supply and demand in favor of what Ryan called "distributive justice." At Georgetown University, students who, in the spring of 2005, staged a nine-day hunger strike in support of a living wage cited Catholic social thought more frequently than any secular doctrine. This helped them put pressure on the university president, John DeGioia, who holds a Ph.D. in philosophy and regularly teaches courses about ethics and human rights.

If Hugh Heclo tends to minimize the rivalries and conflicts that have done much to form the history of European-Americans, he says hardly anything about the religious politics of black Americans. Citing the French sage, Heclo claims: "The future of democracy-as-equality is not in doubt for Tocqueville."

In the distant future, perhaps. But in the 1830s, Tocqueville famously warned about the possibility of race war in America. And whatever positive observations he made about blacks were overwhelmed by his affinity for blaming the victim. Recall such statements from *Democracy in America* as "The Negro has no family: woman is merely the temporary companion of his pleasures" and "If he becomes free, independence is often felt by him to be a heavier burden than slavery . . . he is sunk to such a depth of wretchedness that while servitude brutalizes, liberty destroys him."[15]

Gustave de Beaumont, Tocqueville's traveling and research companion, took a quite different and more empathetic view of the matter. In 1835, the same year when the first volume of *Democ-*

racy in America was published, Beaumont came out with *Marie,* a didactic novel written to expose what the author called the deepening "abyss which separates the two races and pursues them in every phase of social and political life." Beaumont was particularly hard on pious whites. The father of Marie, his hero's beloved and a beautiful and refined mulatto, is a rigid sabbatarian. He complains: "They no longer arrest people who travel on Sundays . . . If this disastrous trend is not stopped, all is over, not only with private morality, but with public morality too; there is no morality without religion! No liberty without Christianity!" But this same man refuses to allow his daughter to marry her well-born European suitor because in her veins run some drops of African blood.[16]

Such passages belong to a tradition already begun by black Americans themselves. In contrast to most whites, who believed their religion affirmed and promoted democratic ideals, black Christians tended to see their faith as a prophetic warning, even a scourge of those who quoted the Bible and mouthed the civic religion but betrayed both of them in practice. The writings of David Walker, Frederick Douglass, Henry Turner, Sojourner Truth, W. E. B. Du Bois, and many others are eloquent on this point. As the historian Albert Raboteau writes, "By criticizing white America, blacks assumed a position of moral authority that made them the true exemplars of Christianity in America." That assumption remains alive today. "God cannot be pleased" was the first sentence that Representative Elijah Cummings, chair of the Congressional Black Caucus, uttered at a press conference that Caucus members held to protest the Bush administration's response to hurricane Katrina.[17]

Since the 1960s, white liberal Protestants have echoed this style of jeremiad. They apply it not just to race relations but to military intervention and other examples of what they view as conservative backsliding. Jim Wallis is the best-known example of this tendency, although he grew up in the kind of evangelical, premillennialist church that has become a bastion of the Christian right. In his best-selling *God's Politics*—a series of energetic sermons on a variety of political issues—Wallis calls for a prophetic vision that would begin with the "God question—'How are our kids doing?'" He then moves on to brisk condemnations of terrorism, empire, war, poverty, racism, and corporate greed—all with apt quotes from Scripture.

His point, of course, is that conservative evangelicals are misreading the Bible; the Good Book contains far more references, Wallis points out, about helping the poor than about forbidding homosexuality. Wallis scolds "false Christians," such as General William Boykin, the protégé of Donald Rumsfeld who, in the fall of 2003, claimed that America's "Christian army" was at war with the "idol" of Islam's false god: "Brother Boykin, I believe you are a product of bad theology and church teaching. . . . Why were you never taught in Sunday school about the real meaning of the kingdom of God and the universality of the body of Christ? And why have you never heard that only peacemaking, not warmaking, can be done 'in the name of Jesus'?"[18]

Wallis has lived for a long time in an African-American neighborhood in Washington, D.C., and the "blackening" of such activist Protestants on the left has only increased in the decades since the political and spiritual revival of the 1960s. This is a largely unacknowledged cause of the division that rent the ideological wings of contemporary Protestantism during the heyday of black power and the movement against the Vietnam War, and it shows few signs of closing.

Yet here too, a certain status quo endures. One can view the passions of Wallis and his fellow left Christians as fulfilling the promise of their faith—to guarantee, in Heclo's words, that "there was now a new Israel for all men and women." Or one can point to the continuing, if informal, segregation of the overwhelming majority of churches in America, liberal as much as conservative, as evidence that the turmoil of the 1960s just ended up reproducing older patterns of worship and public piety—even though a certain radical Baptist minister who won the Nobel Peace Prize gets quoted in churches all over the nation.

In other ways as well, what occurred during the 1960s was less of a break in the history of Christianity and democracy in America than Heclo believes. The creation of what Wade Clark Roof has called a "generation of seekers" repeated a pattern seen during the Second Great Awakening and also in the disillusionment with both the Social Gospel and orthodox Protestantism that followed World War I. During each of these periods, large numbers of Christians broke away from their old churches and either joined new ones or followed a more individualist path to spiritual contentment. After World War I, there was as sharp and bitter a split between militant secularists and traditionalist Protestants as after the 1960s; the Scopes trial was merely the best-known skirmish in that particular battle. But by the 1930s, neither Menckenites nor fundamentalists had much influence over the national body politic, and both presidents and pastors were sanding the rough edges off the rhetorical hostilities of the previous decade.[19]

Early in a new century, we may be entering a similar period when strong religious differences matter less in the public sphere than the rhetoric of each side would suggest. Most Americans seem to be transcending the turmoil generated by both the Christian right and its secular and/or liberal enemies during the period from the late 1970s through the immediate aftermath of the attacks on September 11, 2001. The liberal Catholic Peter Steinfels recently labeled the emerging consensus one of "soft secularism"—a respect for religious believers, even the most orthodox ones, as long as they don't press a strong "claim to influence public life." Steinfels is troubled by this development; it rules out any serious dialogue between the devout and the atheist or agnostic, impoverishing talk about the moral basis of politics and leaving each group alone to reinforce the ideas and prejudices of its own adherents. Ironically, Steinfels comments, "soft secularism is the contemporary counterpart to the broad Protestant hegemony that reigned over respectable opinion in nineteenth-century America and still dominates parts of the country."[20] One can regret the cautious, constantly spinning nature of political talk about religion that increasingly marks the current environment. But it is a far cry from the "coming rupture" that Heclo fears.

So Hofstadter's dialectic between conflict and consensus continues to shape how Americans understand both our politics and our religion. It both liberates us and traps us within assumptions of thought and habits of behavior that have become hidebound traditions in our allegedly hypermodernist nation. We may never resolve the question of what role Christianity should play in democratic life because we cannot bear to give up either the ideal of a godly people or the ideal of a self-governing, self-reliant one—although, as Heclo explains, those ideals, if adhered to rigorously, are incompatible. Perhaps, to paraphrase F. Scott Fitzgerald, Americans collectively exemplify the characteristics of a first-class mind: they are able, on a fairly consistent basis, to keep two opposing ideas in their heads at the same time without going crazy.[21]

4

WHOSE CHRISTIANITY?
WHOSE DEMOCRACY?

Alan Wolfe

THERE IS NO SUCH THING AS RELIGION" — OR SO I begin my course on "Religion and Politics" each year. You can imagine, therefore, my pleasure at hearing a similar thought expressed by Hugh Heclo right at the start of his fascinating and provocative Tocqueville Lecture. "Religion as such has had little significance for American political development," he writes. Only social scientists, he continues, believe in something called "religion." For everyone else, there are religions, and for Americans, the most important of those religions is what Heclo calls that "richly variegated thing called Christianity."

And it is precisely with this description that my problems with Heclo's analysis begin. Heclo offers a learned and nuanced *tour d'horizon* of American Christianity, carefully describing how it has changed over time; once a faith which originated in Europe, it successfully met the challenge of flourishing in the United States. In its detail, Heclo's Tocqueville Lecture misses little and comprehends much.

Yet Heclo is also a social scientist interested in making generalizations, and for that purpose, his efforts to establish a link between Christianity on the one hand and democracy on the other do not succeed. The problem, in a nutshell, is this: if religion as such has had little significance for American political development, the same is true of Christianity. There has been no single body of doctrine, no common set of liturgical practices, no agreed-upon list of sins, no account of the specifics of salvation, no conception of grace, no translation of the Bible, no agreement on the relationship between church and state, and no consensus on the way to spread the word of God that is shared by all those Americans who call themselves Christian. Most Americans have not been Christian; they have been Catholic, Baptist, born-again, Lutheran, Pentecostal. Social scientists want to study something called Christianity because it is a unique religion when compared with Judaism or Islam. But within itself, Christianity is so many things that one generalizes about the whole only at one's peril.

The problem this poses for Heclo's analysis should be obvious: the fascinating and illuminating details he offers in the body of his essay about the many ways Christians disagree with each other appear to contradict the claims he wants to make at the beginning and at the end. Generalize to make sweeping conclusions, and one ignores the detail. Pay attention to the detail, and generalization becomes impossible. Heclo is quite aware of this problem: "Without over-generalizations," he writes, as if he had critics like me in mind, "there can be no lectures, not even bad lectures." His is anything but a bad lecture. But the over-generalizations, I believe, lose in precision what they gain in insight. I hope a few brief examples will make the point.

"Of all religions," Heclo writes, "Christianity is inherently and fervently doctrinal in nature." I find this description far too narrow because the exceptions to it are far too great. Some forms of Christianity are indeed doctrinal, but others, including a large number of its evangelical Protestant forms, view doctrine with suspicion, associating it with Catholicism and its presumed distrust of the believer's ability to glean all the doctrine he needs from reading the Bible; I would never describe the Southern Baptist Convention as a denomination that is "fervently doctrinal" in nature even though I would characterize it as one that is fervently

Christian. To be sure, Christians cannot avoid doctrine because, as Heclo notes, their faith in Jesus forces them to ask questions about how a human being could also be divine. And it is also true that Christians should hold fast to doctrine, given the central role that creeds play in so many of their histories. But it does not follow that all Christians lean more toward orthodoxy than orthopraxis; what most distinguishes contemporary fundamentalists is not their doctrine—so long as you accept Jesus into your heart, doctrine matters little—but their insistence on avoiding sinful behavior. Heclo here confuses a part with the whole. He assumes what needs to be known, which is where, along a spectrum of attitudes toward doctrine, a specific form of Christianity locates itself.

At other times, Heclo's use of the term "Christian" suggests the opposite problem; it confuses the whole with the parts. "The Christian claim is that God invaded historical time by taking on the form and substance of a living human being in a particular place and time," he writes. As description, this is true—that is, it effectively differentiates Christianity from other world religions in which God does not send his son to earth. But because identifying the differences between religions takes us to such a broad realm of generality, knowing that Christians believe that Jesus is the son of God tells us very little about the role of that belief in shaping human affairs. It certainly tells us little about what Heclo is trying to explain, which involves a distinctive attitude toward human history that he associates with the United States. "The hold of recurrent time on republics—a political life cycle of birth, maturity, and decay—has been decisively broken in America," he writes, citing both the devout Jonathan Edwards and the doubting Tom Paine. I agree with Heclo that Americans view historical time differently than Europeans do, but I see no relationship between this form of American exceptionalism and Christianity. How could there be? America is exceptional, but Jesus is close to universal. If all western democracies are Christian but only one of them views time millennially, then the explanation of the latter cannot possibly be the former. By attributing to Christianity a determining role in American political development, Heclo rules out ipso facto any form of American exceptionalism; for if America is special, it cannot be because it is Christian, and if America is not special, its Christianity explains everything and therefore explains nothing.

There are at least three major conflicts within the generic thing called "Christianity" that make generalization about it so difficult. The most obvious, and therefore the best place to begin, involves the differences between Catholicism and Protestantism.

Although Heclo is fully aware of these differences, he, as Mary Jo Bane points out in her comments in this volume, spends little time on Catholics; he gives them their due from time to time, but he also devotes most of his essay to Protestants. This makes a certain amount of sense; if most Americans were—and still are—Protestant, then the social scientist who wishes to address religion in America is obligated to deal primarily with the dominant one found here. Yet Catholicism is nonetheless our single largest religious denomination—comprising roughly one-fourth of Americans—and has been that for the past century or so. And so the question poses itself: when we talk about the relationship between Christianity and democracy, are we talking about the hierarchical, priestly, devotional, parish-rooted, Vatican-led, ethnically connected, primarily urban form of Christianity linked with Catholicism, or the congregationally organized, believer-trusting, liturgy-avoiding, plain-spoken, and Southern and Midwestern ones generally associated with Protestantism?

One way to answer this question is to claim, quite plausibly, that in the United States strong differences between religions, including differences between Protestants and Catholics, tend to evaporate. It has been argued, for example, that all American religions take on aspects of the dominant religion, leading Catholics, Jews, and even Muslims to form "congregational" faiths.[1] There may not have been a unified thing called Christianity in sixteenth-century Münster or Flanders, according to this line of reasoning, but there is such a thing in twenty-first-century Scottsdale.

Yet this way of defending Christianity in general does not work to support Heclo's efforts to specify the relationship between democracy and Christianity. For one thing, the "congregational" thesis, if I may call it that, extends beyond Christianity; if Jews and Muslims adopt Protestant styles of worship, then we are back to the even more general thing called religion. Heclo does not choose to go there and neither, at least for the sake of these comments, do I.

In addition, Heclo, as befits the Tocqueville Lecture, is concerned with the period in which American democracy was formed, and in that period, Protestants and Catholics were quite distinct. Both came here from Europe, and in Europe their differences were pronounced: lives were lost, churches were burned, and kings lost their thrones over such questions as whether the Bible should be translated into vernacular language, whether a priesthood was required to interpret its meaning, or whether those priests should or should not be allowed to marry. In importing its citizens, America imported at least some of their religious disputes. In Tocqueville's time, for example, American culture was being strongly shaped by settlers and the descendants of settlers who came from a Scotch-Irish background, and when they left there for Tennessee and back-country Virginia, they brought with them a furiously anti-Catholic form of evangelical Protestant revivalism.[2]

Having brought large numbers of Irish Protestants to our shores in the early nineteenth century, we then turned around and welcomed large numbers of Catholics from the other regions of Ireland later in the century. This looked like a formula for replicating the European wars of religion on this side of the ocean; and that, for a long time, was exactly what happened. There is a debate taking place these days over whether the United States is experiencing a culture war; I find myself on the side of those who believe that, as far as the general American public is concerned, rumors of the culture war are greatly exaggerated.[3] Yet I would never doubt, nor would most historians, that we did experience a real culture war in the nineteenth century, especially in the decades after Tocqueville left our country. This Americanized *kulturkampf* gave us the Know-Nothing Party, battles over the King James version of the Bible, suffrage restrictions (many designed to prevent Catholics from voting), urban political machines (many designed to allow Catholics to vote more than once), Populism, the Spanish American War, and Prohibition—to mention just some of the major developments in American history shaped by distrust between Protestants and Catholics. Heclo knows all these things; indeed, they constitute a substantial portion of his essay. But whenever he makes a generalization, these important differences tend to disappear. Christianity becomes to Heclo what liberalism was to Louis Hartz: both are undeniable realities in American public life, and both frequently imply a consensus that may not always have been there.

Now it is undoubtedly true that many of these once furious debates between Catholics and Protestants have subsided in contemporary America. For the first time in our history, a generic thing called Christianity is emerging, as large numbers of switchers move from one faith to another and as young spiritual seekers respond, not to doctrinal differences between faiths, but to the vibrancy of specific sermons or the charisma of particular clergy.[4] But if there exists a convergence among Christians today, it is difficult to imagine that the Christianity which historically divided them is precisely what is now unifying them. On the contrary, it makes more sense to argue that there is something in contemporary American *culture* that causes all American religions to become similar to each other (just as there is likely something in Nigerian culture that makes all of Nigeria's faiths—Anglican, Catholic, and Muslim—conservative in a worldwide context). Once something resembling a generic Christianity emerges, in other words, it confirms a relationship between democracy and Christianity, but it is not the one discovered by Tocqueville and extended by Heclo: today democracy shapes Christianity more than the other way around.

In addition to differences between Protestants and Catholics, the second major difference among Christians, as I hinted in my comments about the significance of doctrine, divides one kind of Protestant from another. By the time Tocqueville arrived here, American Protestants had already found themselves split into two very different wings, whether they are called "new light" versus "old light," Puritan versus Arminian, or high church versus evangelical. Again, Heclo knows all these things and discusses them with acute understanding of their significance. But he does not, I believe, fully consider the implications for his major thesis that stem from the existence of these differences.

Consider the importance of Lyman Beecher, one of the most important figures in American religious history and a man to whom Heclo rightly devotes attention. In 1832, the year after Tocqueville arrived in America, Beecher moved west, settling in Cincinnati. Beecher, whom the historian Daniel Walker Howe describes as "the Henry Clay of the ecclesiastical realm," was an expansionist among Protestants; with solid evangelical fervor, he wanted to unite as many Protestants as possible, if for no other reason than to head off any emerging threats from Catholicism.[5] A strong believer in progress, Beecher, like so many nineteenth-century evangelicals (and like the leading Whigs of his era), wanted to move beyond a strict form of Calvinism which taught that human beings were pawns in the hands of a capricious God. To do that, Beecher accepted the notion that human beings are blessed with free will, a position far removed from the orthodoxies of Old School Presbyterians (who, by the way, were as likely to be Democrats as New School reformers were to be Whigs). Because no society as dynamically entrepreneurial as this one could have within its religious universe a faith which tells people that they have no control over their destiny, Beecher's view was destined—one is almost tempted to say predestined—to prevail. Jonathan Edwards is our greatest theologian, but we should never forget that his Northampton parishioners kicked him out of his church. Between optimistic and pessimistic forms of Protestantism, the latter invariably lose.

Interestingly enough, Beecher's form of Protestantism, which placed great importance on human moral agency, resonated with the very features of American democratic life which impressed Tocqueville—and, I hasten to add, which impress Heclo as well. As Peter Dobkin Hall suggests, the voluntary association was to society as Beecher's form of evangelical revivalism was to faith: a place in which individuals, through their efforts, could shape the world around them. In Hall's words, "The historical record indicates that the proliferation of voluntary associations in nine-teenth-century America involved groups whose theological convictions and religious practices led them to see secular civil society as the most promising arena for exercising moral agency."[6] (One is always tempted to point out, in discussing Lyman Beecher's role in all this, that without such a conception of moral agency, his daughter Harriet would have had a far more difficult time contributing to the abolition of slavery.) If we confine ourselves to the first decade of the nineteenth century, there was, as Heclo rightly suggests, a strong relationship between democracy and Christianity, but—and this is where his tendency to generalize gets him in trouble—the relationship existed primarily between democracy and only one of Christianity's many forms. High church Christianity—the Episcopal Church of the New England Federalists—made little contribution to democracy. The revival churches sprouting up in the Midwest, as Nathan Hatch argues in his book on the Jacksonian period, made a significant one.[7]

It would be one thing if these differences among Protestants concerned what, from the viewpoint of the present, seem like relatively minor matters of doctrine. But they did not; as arguments over free will suggest, Protestants were divided over the most profound theological and philosophical questions in the western tradition. Heclo rightly notes how Pelagian American Protestantism had become by the time of Charles Grandison Finney, but he does not pause long enough to reflect on its meaning: if something is a sin in one era and an accepted truth in another, how unified can the religion be that embraces both points of view? The very Protestant-ness of Protestants makes generalization difficult. If Protestants disagreed with each other over the majestic question of free will, can we expect them to have agreed with each other on the more mundane matter of who should have the suffrage? If they argued furiously over the sacred question of whether Jesus will return to earth before or after the Apocalypse, can we expect them to have been united on the profane matter of a free press? If some of them believed the Bible to be the literal word of God and others did not, would they have had the same position on the tariff? When it comes to differentiating between Christians, in short, it is helpful to point out that some are called Catholics and others are called Protestants. But when it comes to tracing the relationship between democracy and religion, all those who are called Protestants should be broken down into the kinds of Protestants they are.

Once we do that and recognize the bewildering variety of Protestant sects in America, however, we immediately face a third source of division among Christians: each of the many Protestant sects can be as different within itself as all Protestants are among themselves or as all Christians are among themselves. Consider the evangelicals who did so much to influence the course of American democracy in the nineteenth century; as Nathan Hatch points out, many of belonged to the rapidly growing movement called Methodism. Yet if Methodists were evangelicals in the nineteenth century, they are frequently taken as the very definition of a mainline Protestant denomination in the twentieth. So even if we reduce Christian to Protestant and then Protestant to Methodist, we still face the task of specifying whether we mean last century's Methodists or this century's. Nineteenth-century religion is an interesting topic to study and so is twentieth-century religion, but they are different topics. Most religions in theory posit the existence of transcendental truths oblivious to secular trends; most religions in practice adopt themselves to secular trends in order to survive and flourish. There were, when Tocqueville came here, no megachurches, no Promise Keepers, no *Purpose-Driven Life*. Heclo more or less argues that Tocqueville anticipated those events, and on this point I would agree with him. But if he did, their emergence has little to do with anything inside Christianity and a great deal to do not only with democracy—Tocqueville's explanation of just about everything—but with the emergence of exurbs, interstate highways, television, and therapy.

Not only is a contemporary religion such as Methodism different from the Methodism of nineteenth-century revivalism, but the Methodism that produced Hillary Clinton is quite different from the one that produced Laura Bush and, through her, attracted our current President. No other finding of sociologists of religion is more accepted that the one which demonstrates the extent to which mainline churches have lost members, and evangelical ones have gained them, over the course of the past three or four decades. Thanks in part to Mr. Bush's born-again experience, we are now all aware of the fact that while most contemporary Methodists are mainline Protestants, not all of them are. For sociological purposes, we divide Protestantism up into its various denominations. But in American religion, what counts is not the denomination but the congregation. To cite Tip O'Neill, all religion is local. Americans distrust denominations for the same reason they distrust Congress: they identify with the near over the distant, and this, however democratic it may be, makes a mess of the division of Protestants into denominations.

Even when you get inside specific American congregations, however, you are likely to discover what the sociologist R. Stephen Warner found in his exhaustive ethnography of one church in California: congregations are frequently divided, and what divides them is not so much the fine points of theology, but music, gender roles, preaching styles, and dress codes.[8] American religion may be more congregational than it is denominational, but it is also more individualistic than it is congregational. Each American is a church unto himself. (Heclo anticipates this when he writes that "every Protestant believer is in a way his own moralist.") As Heclo is quick to acknowledge, we live now in an era of seekers and switchers, Americans who have a good idea of what they want from religion and, when they do not find it in one particular church, they simply move on to another. It may therefore be true that members of any town's First Methodist Church like their pastor and enjoy the music, but it is not true that they can identify John Wesley or explain why they do not attend a church with the word Baptist in its name. Americans typically do not stay in one church long enough to learn that much about its theology and its history. Intermarriage, job relocation, small groups, soccer leagues—these are among the factors that lead people to join one church or to leave another. This is all very frustrating for the social scientist craving generalizability, as much as it may be exciting to the believer seeking fellowship or authenticity.

To bring this part of my commentary to a close, I would not say of Christianity in particular what Heclo says of religion in general, that it "can mean anything—from love your enemy's heart to eat your enemy's liver." (I know of no single Christian sect that teaches the latter, though someone reading this book may.) But Christianity can mean almost anything, from accepting a Muslim believer as a religious person to insisting that his faith is false, or from believing that God separated the races to believing that he treats members of all of them equally. Something about American religion surely played a major role in shaping American democracy. But whatever that something is, it cannot be a generic form of Christianity whose existence on this earth is difficult, if not impossible, to establish.

Enough on the question of Christianity. Heclo is also concerned with democracy; the whole point of his lecture is to examine the relationship that one has with the other. If it is difficult to define what specifically makes a Christian a Christian, it is not that difficult to define what makes a democrat a democrat. There are, of course, many kinds of democrats, but certain key features of democracy—popular suffrage, representative government, checks on the executive—are relatively uncontested, at least as political concepts go. The United States may not have been democratic in its earlier configurations, but by the time Tocqueville came here, its democratic character had been established. And that character has changed relatively little over time. Indeed, one of the reasons we have the Tocqueville Lectures—or so I assume—is that Tocqueville left us with such a powerful and convincing treatment of this thing called democracy that any discussion of the phenomenon so many years after his death will still have to take him as the starting point. There may not be any Tocquevilles around, but there are Tocquevilles manqués, as we saw recently with the publication of Bernard Henri Lévy's *American Vertigo*.[9]

Heclo offers a profound challenge to anyone who thinks about the state of democracy in America. We usually ask whether religion is compatible with democracy. But shouldn't we ask whether democracy is compatible with religion? For the most devout believers, God comes first and human affairs after. We should not, Heclo warns, dismiss their way of looking at the world; the cost of doing so, he suggests, is "myopia." Democracy is responsive to the people. If the people consider God to be a major factor in their lives, democrats had better pay attention.

Heclo's point here makes considerable sense to me. There is a way of theorizing about democracy—more specifically, about liberal democracy—that all too often treats the views of religious people as incompatible with the requirements of democratic citizenship. John Rawls came close to making an argument along these lines in *A Theory of Justice*, although he went on to modify his views in his later writings. In my book *The Transformation of American Religion*, I cite two other scholars who, I am sure, would raise Heclo's ire.[10] One, the anthropologist Vincent Crapanzano, writes that "one perquisite for democracy is an openness to the position of the other," a capacity he did not find among conservative Protestants; they believe that they "have special access to the truth," an absolutist point of view that renders dialogue impossible.[11] Along similar lines, the political philosopher Stephen Macedo discussed the case of Vicky Frost, a conservative Protestant who did not want her child exposed to ideas she condemned as secular humanist. "Liberal education is bound to have the effect of favoring some ways of life or religious convictions over others," Macedo concluded. "So be it."[12]

Strong faith creates a difficult dilemma for liberal democrats. If they welcome into the public realm individuals who put God first, they will have to share the liberal democratic stage with people who do not assign the same priority to liberal democratic values as themselves. But if they keep them out, they are not acting like liberal democrats, for they find themselves in the business of treating people they believe to be intolerant with intolerance on their part. Certainly a religious believer would bristle about being told that the most fairly arrived at decisions are those arrived at deliberatively, when for that believer the best decisions are those that are revealed.

What Heclo calls the "great denouement" offers a way out of this impasse. If secular liberals in the tradition of Rawls knew more about religion, Heclo implies, they would not be so quick to set reason and revelation against each other. For one thing, religious liberty in America has historically meant not freedom *from* religion, as many secular liberals insist, but freedom *for* religion, as many believers hold. Primarily because of our Protestantism, we developed a religious life quite different from the form found in Europe. There, clericalism confronted anti-clericalism. Here, neither existed. Our believers were not clericalists because they did not bring the power of the state down on behalf of their sects. And our non-believers were not anti-clerical because there was no state church they could attack. Religion was free to play the role of softening the direct confrontation between the individual and the state because it was embodied in civil society rather than in government. Freedom was not license; as Heclo rightly insists, "Autonomy was not a lack of controls but rather self-control, a combination of personal independence and moral responsibility."

This ability of religion to serve as a great denouement, at first glance, is even truer now than it was in the time of Tocqueville. In contrast to Macedo and Crapanzano, I argue in *The Transformation of American Religion* that American culture, including secular culture, has so thoroughly shaped religion that, rather than constituting a danger to democracy, religion, in order to survive, has little choice but to adopt the trappings of modern democratic cultural life. Subject to the dictate of the market in souls, it tempers its message to avoid turning off potential customers. Like politicians, clergy praise the wisdom of their flock rather than emphasize their sins. No one wants to be politically incorrect, or at least not excessively so. Religion is a powerful force that shapes how people act and what they believe. So is culture. When the two conflict in America, religion yields more to culture than the other way around.

This message may not be comfortable for secular humanists who continue to distrust religion, but neither is it a comfort to those, such as the theologian Stanley Hauerwas, who wish to imagine religious believers as "resident aliens," a counter-cultural alternative to the moral thinness of American life.[13] Relying in part on my work, Heclo writes that "Americans have arrived at a self-understanding that is religious . . . but also non-absolutist, inclusive, modest, and, above all, nonjudgmental of others." This is not a description of a nation engaged in a furious battle between reason and revelation. We have our arguments, but we do not have anything like the Spanish Inquisition.

Yet having said all this, I wonder if strong religious believers may still pose a problem for democracy, not because their convictions are so strong and sectarian, but because they are so weak and without content. Our culture is a confessional culture: we admire leaders who are sincere even if we pay less attention to what they are sincere about; we praise those who hold strong convictions even if we fear holding strong convictions of our own; we prefer politicians who appeal to our emotions rather than those who call upon us to increase our knowledge; and we want our leaders to be people of faith so that we need not pay that much attention to the policies they pursue. Watch one of the many preachers on a religious television station and then watch a candidate, even a secular one, running for office. The message may—or, in the age of Bush, may not—differ. The style is the same.

If Christianity has shaped democracy, in other words, it is not in the way it did so in the nineteenth century. Then, as Heclo points out, Christian theologians were anxious to establish the importance of autonomy; like Augustine, they understood that the greater the capacity of human beings to lead lives under their own control, the greater the glory of the God who populated the earth with such special creatures. When Christianity was more intellectual, more demanding, more eloquent, more sin-focused, it produced a certain kind of democratic citizen. Abraham Lincoln may not have been much of a conventionally religious person, but the Christianity of his era was indispensable to the magnificence of his rhetoric. Democracy required virtuous citizens, and, as Heclo notes, Christianity satisfied what politics could not offer. There really was a time when "there was a general consensus that reason and revelation overlapped sufficiently—not just for philosophers but for ordinary citizens trying to live decent lives—to make self-government a hopeful, going concern."

That period exists no longer. Contemporary Christianity could not produce Lincolnesque rhetoric because contemporary Christianity—more specifically, the evangelical form that receives so much attention in politics—resembles Oprah Winfrey more than Jonathan Edwards. (To make the implicit point explicit, I am not generalizing about Christianity as a whole here—if I were, I would be making the same mistake I charge Heclo with making—but talking only about evangelical Protestantism in its more generic forms; as I have argued above, there is a generic form of evangelicalism, strongly influenced by American culture, which crosses denominational lines.)[14] To survive in America's highly emotional, exquisitely individualistic, and depressingly anti-intellectual culture, American evangelical Christianity all too often absorbs, rather than confronts, the culture of narcissism. It gives its followers an important sense of empowerment, a sense of place and meaning, and an avenue for recovery from their dilemmas, but the focus—in evangelical forms, the relentless focus—is on what God can do for you, not what you can do for God. It is the small groups, not the large sermons, that count most in today's megachurch. You come out feeling uplifted. You do not come out feeling intellectually challenged.

This matters because, as Heclo is right to insist, Christianity's location in civil society gives it the special task of teaching the morality that makes democracy work. Unfortunately, however, today's Christian morality, even in its conservative evangelical forms, frequently has little to do with—it is in fact the very opposite of—what the classical thinkers meant by virtue. It does not require us to put aside our self-interest in favor of what is good for the whole. It tells us instead that God hears our prayers and knows what is in our hearts. Citizens shaped by this ethic have difficulty adopting the viewpoint of an impartial spectator or engaging with the Kantian categorical imperative because they all too rarely lift up their eyes to consider the needs of people in worlds very different from their own.

The shape of contemporary American Christianity therefore suggests that there are two ways in which reason and revelation can be at odds with each other. One, the traditional version, suggests that religion's dogmatism and sectarianism stand in sharp contrast to reason's requirements of proof and respect for pluralism. This is the conflict between reason and revelation that Heclo's "great denouement" softens. The denouement between reason and revelation posed in this form posits on the one side liberalism as it exists in practice and conservative religion as it exists in theory. When he discusses the relationship between democracy and Christianity in the latter part of his essay, Heclo assumes the role of prophet more than he adopts the tools of the social scientist. He is concerned with the world as Christians imagine it, a world in which absolute truth is compromised by value relativism and in which time-tested traditions are overthrown for personal convenience. His argument is that genuine Christians, those who really take their faith's doctrines seriously and believe in its conception of authority, will be so uncomfortable with the direction American democracy has taken in the wake of the 1960s that they may well come to consider existing political arrangements illegitimate.

But how many such old-fashioned Christians are there in the United States at this time? True, there are influential Christian intellectuals whose disgust with American culture tempts them into withdrawal, if not, at times, to question democracy itself.[15] But it would be wrong, I believe, to generalize from their examples to the revival of conservative Christianity as a whole. Many ordinary Christians—most evangelical ones—are conservative politically and find themselves more comfortable among Republicans than Democrats. But they are not withdrawing in disgust from the larger culture; if anything, the evangelicals flocking into the megachurches are joining America's emotion-laden and personal testifying culture with enthusiasm. For people such as these—conservative Christians in practice rather than in theory—a second, postmodern conflict between reason and revelation emerges. In this one, religion's refusal to judge, its unwillingness to state firm truth claims, and its tendency to blur all theological and doctrinal disputes confront reason from the side of multiple perspectives and epistemological skepticism. Too narcissistic and inward-looking for comfort, evangelicals have more in common with postmodern literary theorists than they know. Both distrust the authority of science and distrust abstract moral philosophical judgment as well.

There are—there have to be—exceptions to the generalization I have just made, and the most important of these is the movement on behalf of intelligent design. Here is the classic confrontation of reason and revelation, the modern-day Scopes trial. Yet even here, one side—the Christian side—refuses to return to Dayton, Tennessee. We are not defending a theological position, they claim; creationism does that but we are not, or so we say, creationists. No, we believers in intelligent design are followers of Thomas Kuhn; we are challenging the dominant paradigm and merely suggesting that good science look for a more explanatory theory. These claims, as it happens, are not true; intelligent design, it was shown during the Dover, Pennsylvania brouhaha, grows directly out of the creationist movement. Still, it tells us much about the form that today's conflict between reason and revelation takes that defenders of the latter will not adopt the language of the former. They argue for revelation in the guise of liberal ideas of fairness and pluralism of viewpoints—a position that, if taken literally, makes them irreligious or, if not taken literally, makes them hypocrites.

There was a "great denouement" to resolve the older conflict between reason and revelation. There is no great denouement to resolve the new one. Whether the resurgence of contemporary American evangelicalism constitutes a new Great Awakening I leave to others to debate. But even it does, this one has borrowed the enthusiasm of earlier awakenings without the content. Like so much else in contemporary America, it is flashy and exciting, but it does not cut especially deep. Between Joel Osteen, the feel-good preacher at Houston's 25,000-member Lakewood Church, and Jonathan Edwards, I would take Jonathan Edwards any day. I think Heclo would as well. But the prophetic form of Christianity upon which Heclo bases his pessimistic conclusions does not exist in sufficient strength to shatter the softening impact that American culture has had on American religion. One can, if one wishes, long for the return of Jonathan Edwards, but he is not coming back anytime soon.

* * *

And so I come to Heclo's conclusions about what will happen to the United States in the wake of the great denouement's failure to bridge the gap between America's secular and religious components.

Although Heclo notes that this failure originated before the 1960s, that decade plays an enormously important role in his analysis. Traditionally, Americans recognized the existence of a democratic realm "where everything was contested and open for innovation," linked to a religious realm that "set firm boundaries" around democratic innovation. But the 1960s changed all that. On the one hand, policy choices expanded, ranging into such personal matters as sexuality and intimacy. On the other, the ability of religion to guide individual moral conduct atrophied. "Reason and revelation in the autonomous religious realm did not agree on basic moral standards for guiding political action," Heclo concludes. Although Heclo agrees with scholars such as Morris Fiorina and myself that Americans themselves are not that polarized, the emerging gap between reason and revelation is fueling a furious and important culture war among elites. They see the country as divided between "the repressive, bigoted morality of Christian theocrats," as one side holds, and "the debauched, godless morality of secular humanists," as the other insists. Without standards to guide us, secular Americans have a Christian problem and American Christians have a democracy problem.

Heclo is not very optimistic that these problems can be resolved. Christians are absolutists, he points out. They do believe in certain truths that exclude others. They do have an allegiance to a higher power than their nation-state. Secular Americans are correct to view Christians with some suspicion (just as Christians are right to view secular Americans as hostile to them). We face "a condition of devout, serious Christians alienated from the quest for democracy, and of devout, serious democrats hostile to Christianity." Our situation more resembles the France that Tocqueville left than the America that greeted him. We Americans may think we are exceptional, but here we are faced with the conflict between reason and revelation that plagued Europe for centuries.

These are indeed dark conclusions, too dark for my own taste. There are, no doubt, many Christians who are absolutist in their convictions and many secularists who genuinely view faithful people as dogmatic sectarians. But the 1960s united Americans far more than they divided them. We should never forget that the 1960s had a spiritual as well as a secular side; large numbers of Americans came to believe in transcendental truths and otherworldly experiences during that decade, and their attachment to spirituality frequently lived on. And by that I do not mean that they became Wiccans and Buddhists. Some of the most conservative evangelical churches in America—for example, Calvary Chapel in California and its many offshoots—directly appealed to the "Jesus people" who emerged out of the 1960s.[16]

At the same time, many conventionally religious people—the category Heclo and others call "traditionalists"—were in fact touched by the individualism of the 1960s. The experience of being born again owes as much to the 1960s as it does to nineteenth-century revivals. By welcoming Jesus into one's life, the believer makes authenticity of experience more important than adherence to creed. As many scholars have noted, there is a rebelliousness in the act of being born again, a willingness to break with custom and authority, an assertion of individual will, a feeling of personal empowerment.[17] Without the 1960s, American Christianity would not have its rock music, its small groups, its insistence on holism, its testimonials and confessions, its home schooling, even its home churching. Christians may hate the drug culture and left-wing politics which they identify with the 1960s. But they are products of that decade, and their expanding numbers have as much to do with how they absorbed some key aspects of the 1960s as they do with rejecting the messages and personalities brought to us by the political and cultural movements of those years.

America, I conclude in contrast to Heclo, does have a Christian problem and it does have a democracy problem. But they are at root the same. Christianity needs to find a way to retain its commitments to authority and truth as Christians toy with individualism and this-worldly preoccupations. Democracy needs to find a way to preserve its sense of accountability and leadership as Americans focus on their own needs and shy away from grand collective enterprises. Christianity and democracy have both been influenced by American culture, and as a result, they share more in common, even in today's more contentious times, than Heclo acknowledges. There are no large numbers of conservative Christians entering into internal exile in the United States because even though the culture may be repulsive to them in some ways, it is extremely attractive in other ways. We as a country can count on our materialism, our individualism, our populism, and our emotionalism to keep us together, however much any lingering differences of doctrine or faith may divide us.

In conclusion, I want to say a word of praise on behalf of Hugh Heclo. Writing about Christianity is a difficult undertaking because any focus on one religion easily runs the risk of ignoring all the others. Some scholars run this risk more than others. One who illustrates the dangers here is Rodney Stark. His book, *The Victory of Reason,* claims that Christianity, and Christianity alone, made possible the emergence of modern science, democracy, and tolerance.[18] Along the way he deals with the contributions of other faiths—Islam's protection of the classical tradition, the Jewish life of the mind—by simply ignoring them. His excuse is that he is concerned only with Christianity because nearly all modern people are Christian. In his hands, a sociological fact is transformed into religious triumphalism.

Heclo also concentrates on Christianity, and for the same reason that Stark does: most Americans are Christian, hence any study of "religion" in American history most focus on the religion that was actually here. Now I have already made my point that Heclo's idea of Christianity is frequently too broad. But let me quickly add how much I admire Heclo for discussing the Christian contribution to democracy without entering into the triumphalism of a Rodney Stark. In part this is because Heclo discusses Christianity's weaknesses as well as its strengths. It is also a result of the appreciation he shows for how Christianity has changed over time; unlike Stark, he does not believe that once Christians made their presence known in the world, democracy was inevitable. Heclo appreciates contingency and recognizes complexity. His Christianity is more real than Stark's because it is more human. And since democracy is human as well, one comes to understand through Heclo's analysis how the faith of real people contributed to the success of an actual political society.

For this reason, it is not inappropriate to conclude that Hugh Heclo's Tocqueville Lecture follows in the spirit of Tocqueville's book. Like Tocqueville, Heclo admires both American Christianity and American democracy without being an apologist for either. It is an impressive accomplishment, one that, for all the criticisms I have offered in this response, represents a huge step in the much-needed direction of reminding political scientists never again to ignore religion the way we had done for far too many decades.

5

RECONSIDERING CHRISTIANITY AND AMERICAN DEMOCRACY

Hugh Heclo

IT IS UNUSUAL TO HAVE A CHANCE TO WRITE SOME-
thing, read your critics' comments, and then offer a rejoinder—all in the same book. Of course, I welcome the unfair
advantage of having the last turn at bat.

However, it is always the reader who truly has the last word.
My overriding hope is that what is said in this book will en-
courage more serious attention to the vital relationship between
Christianity and our American democracy. Since it is a relationship between many Americans' Christianity but everybody's democracy the stakes are high. By the term "serious attention" I
mean thinking with care, like grown-ups, and not succumbing to
the emotional sloganeering that dominates our public shouting
matches on this subject. In the prevailing climate of opinionated
extremes—a cocksure mutual deafness being the one thing that
unites secular and Christian political activists—such thinking is
especially hard work. Nonetheless it is important work, because
every attempt to interpret our past is also an implicit effort to understand our present and what may lie ahead. That is a very
Tocquevillian thing for us to do, and we should try to do it.

It is no exaggeration to say that today's America exhibits something approaching a mirror image of what Tocqueville perceived

in the 1830s. In the democracy he saw, the political world was a place where "everything is in turmoil, contested, and uncertain," but it was strictly limited in scope and undergirded by a "moral world [where] everything is classified, coordinated, foreseen and decided in advance" (40). Today one could arguably reverse his descriptors for those two worlds. What Tocqueville said about the moral world ("obedience is passive, though voluntary") is actually truer of our professionally managed political system, where the political class does politics and the mass of ordinary citizens have politics done to them. What he said about the political world ("there is independence, contempt of experience, and jealousy of all authority") is truer of our moral world, where to judge with fixed standards or decide anything in advance is considered undemocratic bigotry. The result is that it seems harder than ever to get our bearings in such a political society, and more important than ever that we should try to do so.

To that end I have sought, perhaps recklessly, to take the large view of a very big subject. Landscape artists have told me that the choice is not always between using a large brush or a small one. With care, one can paint finely with a broad brush, and that is what I have tried to do.

There are many things that have made us who we are, but the phenomena embraced by the two concepts of democracy and Christianity would surely have to be on any reasonable person's shortlist of those things. My working assumption has been that the interaction between the two should be regarded as dynamic rather than static. In other words, there is development arising from both sides—a tensioned, reciprocating influence between this religion and our democracy. Such a developmental perspective is especially important if we hope to use this large view to gain a better understanding of our present condition and what may lie ahead.

In my lecture I began—and ended—with the outlandish idea that the relationship between democratic self-government and Christianity is problematic. It is not what Americans have been taught to see—some foreordained harmony written into the nature of things. Because of his experience in France, Alexis de Tocqueville had a deep appreciation for this ambiguity. And because of his keen insight, Tocqueville could discern how the American experience produced principles helping to resolve that *problématique*. Christianity, separated from the apparatus of political power, could preserve both its essential nature as a religion and its necessary and rightful influence in democracy. Christianity was teaching Americans not simply how to be democratic, but how to sustain ordered liberty in democratic politics as well as how to uphold the spiritual nobility of human beings against the threats of a materialistic, mass democracy.

Tocqueville's insight then led me to examine a deeper development in America, one that had already shaped what he was able to see in the 1830s. This development was a profound historical achievement. It was a general respect, affirmed in law, for each individual's right to religious liberty. Centuries in the making and never fully completed, this Great Denouement of religious-political claims arose more from the advantages of a particular time and place than from some innate American genius for tolerance. Amid deeply felt religious differences, a Protestant political society gradually convinced itself of the truly Christian reasons for, as well as the enlightened political advantages of, liberty of religious conscience. With this achievement, a new space in public life was opened up—a space for freedom of action in the two distinct, though never wholly separate, spheres of religious belief and civil authority. All we have of this religious freedom, so carelessly enjoyed today, was won for us long ago.

My lecture then tried to describe how, after the eighteenth century and well into the twentieth, this free play of Christian beliefs and democratic politics in America set in motion a tensioned, push-pull interaction between these two powerful impulses (eliciting my image of a double helix). To make this twisting story manageable, I focused on the democracy/Christianity interaction with regard to three subjects: ideas of history, the individual, and political society. By the middle of the twentieth century, something like a mutual embrace between American democracy and Christianity had emerged. I argued that this century and a half of reciprocal influence was largely on the plus side of the ledger for American democracy and on the negative side for Christianity, veering toward un-Christian commitments to worldly progress, autonomous self-realization, and idolatrous patriotism.

The complacency, not to say inauthenticity, of this mutual embrace made it vulnerable to fundamental critique and political challenge. This occurred first with the civil rights movement and then with the broader cultural upheaval that became the Sixties. Amid the turmoil of this time, the best historically-minded observers of religion in American public life sensed that a crucial discontinuity was occurring. How and why was this happening? People like Sydney Ahlstrom, William McLoughlin, and the Niebuhr brothers were not sure. And neither am I. The best I can do, noting the similarity and contrast with America's tradition of religious revivalism and awakenings, is to consider the Sixties as a secular awakening. My lecture sketched the development of public doctrine in our schools, courts, and popular culture that laid the groundwork for this upheaval. By the end of the period, Christianity had lost much and perhaps most of its cultural authority.

Within this larger perspective, I turned to our own times. Despite the rise of the so-called Religious Right in politics and glib talk of an "American theocracy" under Republican presidents,[1] the central tendency of our era is an estrangement. It is a growing, reciprocal alienation between Christianity and American democracy. There is a "Christian problem" for what has come to be understood as deliberative democracy. To an even greater extent, there is a "democracy problem" for American Christians who take their faith seriously. These sets of problems are real, and they are playing themselves out in what we can expect to be a growing struggle between secular and religious political elites. Looming ahead are inescapable public policy decisions on issues weighted with human and religious significance. This threatens to turn estrangement into a coming rupture between serious Christians and our secular democracy.

Such is the story I have tried to tell. In response to my presumptuousness in doing so, three scholars whom I admire have commented in a most kindly and tolerant manner. In what follows I will begin with the common theme that unites the criticisms by Mary Jo Bane, Michael Kazin, and Alan Wolfe, and then consider more particular points brought forward in each of their essays. I will conclude by discussing why any American, non-Christian or Christian, should care about this story I am trying to tell.

Is There Any Such Thing as Christianity?

Taken as a whole, the three comments on my lecture raise an extremely important issue: each of these scholars, in his or her own way, suggests that I have spoken too broadly of Christianity, as if it were one thing. Mary Jo Bane rightfully gives sustained attention to the Catholic presence in America. Michael Kazin just as rightly emphases the many divisions and conflicts among all sorts of Christian groups in our history, so much so that he sees it as an error to view "Christianity in the United States as a more or less unified entity that changed little over time." As a good sociologist, Alan Wolfe pushes the point to its limits by telling us that "Christianity is so many things that one generalizes about the whole only at one's peril. . . . Christianity can mean almost anything."

For two reasons, I am very glad that these scholars' essays are appearing together with my lecture in the same volume. First, the three essays describe important complications that need to be appreciated any time we try to talk about Christianity in America. Topics having to do with Catholicism, anti-Catholicism, denominational conflict within Protestantism, variations in liturgy, doctrine, evangelical mission, moral stances—all this and much more needs to be part of the picture. Working on this lecture was like having to drive too fast through a fascinating and beautiful countryside; it was painful but necessary to neglect one thing after another in order to hew to main themes about the Christian religion itself in the American democratic context. But if my so-called lecture was not going to start resembling Ahlstrom's 1100-page tome, *A Religious History of the American People,* there was simply no alternative to pulling down the shades and keeping the accelerator pressed to the floor. Thanks to these three essays, I can now feel less guilty about short-changing so much of the variegated reality that constitutes Americans' experience with Christianity. My drive-by offenses have, at least to some extent, been redeemed.

Second, the general theme of the Bane/Kazin/Wolfe essays unintentionally offers readers a valuable cautionary tale. The notion that Christianity should not be talked about as if it were one coherent thing reveals a widespread academic blind spot that has persistently trivialized discussions of religion. To be sure, as a matter of behavioral description, it makes perfect sense to point out that Christianity in practice has been far less than a single, unified entity. That observation has its critical force against any claim that Christianity is *only* a single, unified entity. I am saying something different, however—namely that along with all the variations amply demonstrated in the historical record, Christianity *is* something. If it were not some thing, we would not be able to identify variations in the thing that it is. While we rightly want to be attentive to the variations, I do not think we should fall into the opposite error of claiming that Christianity is only the sum of its variations.

This is an important point to consider more closely, especially in our American context where Christian denominations have blossomed in bewildering array and where social science has often pursued a secularist agenda contrived to evade the substantive content of religion.

The underlying theme of the three commentaries is not really that I have done too little, but that I have done too much. They are not saying that I should refrain from talking about the whole of a thing until I have talked about all its parts. They are really saying that there is no one whole thing to talk about as regards Christianity in America.

While the other two comments lend support, the underlying logic of such a view is very well presented by Alan Wolfe. Averting our gaze from "the generic thing called 'Christianity,'" as he puts it, we must begin with the differences between Catholicism and Protestantism. From there, we must attend to the differences among the many Protestant denominations. But our journey into sub-Christianities has only just begun: we must now recognize that the divisions *within* each of the many denominations can be as great as are any differences among all Christians. But wait, there is more. In American Christianity, "what counts is not the denomination but the congregation." And yet there is no resting place here, for congregations are themselves divided—or rather pulverized—into individualized commitments, most of them having little to do with theology. And thus we come to how to think about Christianity: "Each American is a church unto himself." In effect, Christianity has been "sociologized" into a descriptive morass of pointillistic differences.

Obviously this is no genuine invitation to think about Christianity, because we are left with nothing to think about. If this religion that came to America is a free-form exercise defined by whatever particular persons calling themselves Christians happen to believe and do at any particular time and place, then there really is nothing of substance in this (or any other) religion to talk about. This is behavioralism in the social sciences run amok. It is also positivism in philosophy and nihilism in theology run amok. Relentlessly subdividing the subject into its descriptive behavioral particularities, we eventually end up with no subject at all. Christianity as such has no coherent content or meaning—so says such religious minimalism.

That is not true. It is not true because we can look over the centuries and see that there actually is a coherent content, indeed a massively coherent content to this religion. A little over twenty years ago Jaroslav Pelikan finished his monumental five-volume work, *The Christian Tradition: A History of the Development of Doctrine.*[2] I suspect that Alan Wolfe and others of like mind might respond: aha—you see, there is no such thing as Christianity. Its doctrines are so varied and changeable that it takes five volumes even to catalogue them. The answer to this objection is to actually study Christianity and what Pelikan demonstrates about its twenty centuries of life. To be sure, he shows that Christianity is something that can be complex and thus susceptible to development and variation. But it is *something.* That is why you can talk about it in so many ways.

Because Christianity does mean a certain thing—above all a certain person—its doctrine can and has developed. Development of doctrine does not mean a substitution of new for old doctrine, or an evasion of past doctrine, or a successful surrender to some outside source. As G. K. Chesterton put it, "When we say a puppy develops into a dog, we do not mean that his growth is a gradual compromise with a cat. We mean that he become more doggy and not less. Development is the expansion of all the possibilities and implications of a doctrine, as there is time to distinguish them and draw them out."[3] In other words, what Pelikan is showing as development is an advance in understanding the application of what is fundamental; it is a fuller comprehension of what was already there. Professor Pelikan was never one to use words carelessly. His title is not "A Christian Tradition," or "Some Christian Traditions." Or "Bunches of Different Things Christians Have Thought." "The" is a definite article, and it means there is one thing in view. In *Credo,* his later book, Pelikan summed up a lifetime of scholarship devoted to articulations of the Christian faith over the last two thousand years.

> The overwhelming impression that any new reader will carry away from reviewing any of the collections of creedal and confessional texts from various historical periods . . . must surely be their sheer repetitiveness. Above all the creeds from

the period of the early church, and then once again, though this time at much greater length, the confessions from the age of the Protestant Reformation, do seem to be making the same points over and over and over again. . . . The differences between them, which came out of theological controversy and when sent on to spawn still further theological controversy . . . must at least sometimes seem to any modern reader to be so minute as well as so marginal that only a specialist in historical theology would be able to tell the various confessional positions apart. . . . From this declaration of the Book of Acts that "those who received his word were baptized" we may infer that there was a close connection between the early creeds and the preaching of this "word," the primitive Christian proclamation—or, as it has come to be called also in modern English, the "kerygma" . . . Nor is it a great leap to suppose that this stock outline of the kerygma bore a distinct enough resemblance to the creeds that we now have, in whole or in part, to justify our viewing them as reflecting that outline.[4]

Nor is there any lack today of clear, straightforward explications of what this thing called traditional Christianity is, however rich the forms of its is-ness may be.[5]

To all of this the objection can be raised that doctrine is fine, but there are many American Christians who are far from doctrinal. Quite so. One of the themes throughout my lecture is that American Christians, evangelicals and modern Christians in particular, have been less than doctrinal—especially under the pressures of popular democracy. But so what? That supports the view that "Christianity can mean almost anything" only if we fall into the trap of limiting Christianity to a purely descriptive definition derived from whatever people calling themselves Christians happen to be doing at the time. Such description is important, but it is a grievous error to then conclude that this is all Christianity amounts to. Nothing is more dangerous than an error that is almost true, a half-truth pretending to be the whole truth, and this descriptivist claim is such a half-truth. American Christians might not know a doctrine if it bit them, but that does not mean the religion is non-doctrinal. When the stereotypical backwoods fundamentalist puts up a hand-painted sign on his fencepost saying that "JESUS SAVES," behind that little sign is a world of doctrine. Saved from what? Why does anyone need saving? Why can't they save themselves? How does this Jesus save? And who is this guy to be saving anyone? Like the Molière character who did not know he was speaking prose, our non-doctrinaire believer does not know he is speaking soteriology from the fencepost. But he is.

We might turn the issue around and note that the three commentaries have no comparable objection to my generalized use of the term "democracy." This appears to be because the authors, like many other people, presume there is a greater coherent meaning to democracy than to Christianity as such. Again, Alan Wolfe articulates the general position quite clearly. He points out that there are many kinds of democrats, "but certain key features of democracy—popular suffrage, representative government, checks on the executive—are relatively uncontested, at least as political concepts go."

Really? The fact is that it would be quite easy to start subdividing the alleged common core that Alan Wolfe presents into ever finer variations, and so conclude that democracy "can mean almost anything." Checks on the executive—isn't there a fundamental difference between a parliamentary democracy that scarcely dares impose checks and a presidential, separation-of-powers type of democracy? Representative government—hasn't Robert Dahl taught us how recently this idea has attached itself to the concept of democracy, indeed that the origin of the idea of representation is not even democratic?[6] Popular suffrage—what about those who claim that democracy confined to the political sphere and denied in the economic, market-capitalist spheres of life is no democracy at all? If Christianity has no coherent content and meaning because of the descriptive diversity and conflicts among its adherents, then there surely is no meaning to "democracy" either. It is merely the sum of different ways of being "democratic." Some democracies crush people in the name of the "people's democracy," and others celebrate individualism as if there is no common good. I would contend, in fact, that given the intellectually flabby, sloganeering quality of the democratic faith, the Christian faith's strenuously worked out doctrinal content gives it a far stronger claim to being something real.

In the end, the religious minimalists in social science usually do not really seem to mean what they say. They are drawn to recognize that there really is something there. All three commentators indirectly invoke a general concept of Christianity in delineating differences among its adherents. Mary Jo Bane does so along the Catholic/Protestant axis. Michael Kazin does so in picturing pluralist conflict in American religion. And Alan Wolfe, again being the most explicit, takes the argument all the way over to the other side; in the last third of his comments, it appears there really is such a thing as Christianity. In this vein he wonders if "strong religious believers may still pose a problem for democracy, not because their convictions are so strong and sectarian, but because they are so weak and without content." Religious minimalism now laments that "contemporary Christianity resembles Oprah Winfrey more than Jonathan Edwards." It appears that this Alan Wolfe is attacking the Alan Wolfe who told us earlier that there is scarcely any such thing as Christianity, speaking doctrinally or otherwise. To be fair, he tells us that he is not generalizing about Christianity but speaking only about "evangelical Protestantism in its more generic forms." That is a nice sideways move, but it does not overcome the fact that in the background is a standard to which the author is holding "generic" evangelical Protestants (not evangelical Catholics?). He says something is wrong with a contemporary Christianity that absorbs rather than confronts the culture of narcissism, a Christianity that focuses on what God can do for you and not what you can do for God. Now we are told that there is something deeply flawed in a postmodern Christian evangelicalism that fails to state firm truth claims, that blurs all theological and doctrinal distinctions, and even that refuses to judge! If Christianity can mean almost anything, as the first Alan Wolfe maintains, how can the second Alan Wolfe claim there is anything wrong with a contemporary Christianity, evangelical or otherwise, that does these or any number of other mutually contradictory things outside the Christian tradition? He concludes that we do have a Christian problem in this country. It is that "Christianity needs to find a way to retain its commitments to authority and truth as Christians toy with individualism and this-worldly preoccupations." With the second half of that sentence sucking the meaning out of the first half, both Alan Wolfes apparently want to have it both ways. My conclusion is that the second Alan Wolfe has the better of the argument.

A Closer Look at the Comments

To restate what has sometimes only been implied up to this point, I have been honored by the gracious comments in the three preceding essays. It would be a serious mistake to read my lecture and not to read the three insightful responses of Mary Jo Bane, Michael Kazin, and Alan Wolfe. Each in its own way helps us gain a more rounded view of the subject.

Mary Jo Bane demonstrates how important it is to pay special attention to Catholicism in any consideration of Christianity in America. She points out that in the first place, the small number of Catholics in the early Republic had neither the strength nor the opportunity to pursue the Catholic Church's official opposition to religious liberty of conscience and separation of church and state. This adds support to the more general point presented in my lecture regarding America's historical advantage in dealing with the problem of religion and politics. The colonies' struggle over religious liberty occurred in marked isolation from European power struggles and in the late Reformation era, when a kind of mutual exhaustion, as well as some useful social learning about the advantages of religious toleration, had occurred.

Nonetheless, even in America's earliest years Catholics were making a more positive contribution to the learning of liberty than simply being weak and few in number. Since at least 1636, there has always been a Catholic minority in America. One estimate puts their number at 30,000 out of an American population of 3 million in 1790, a proportion that is roughly double that of Muslims in the United States today. Supplemented by French clerics escaping persecution, the nation's Catholic population before the Irish immigration was mainly English, well-educated, and socially prominent. The patriot and drafter of the seminal 1776 Virginia Declaration of Rights, George Mason, could marry a Catholic without occasioning negative comment. The point is that from the outset, Americans had the benefit of living with a Catholic minority that accepted all the essentials of English-American culture while remaining loyal to their Catholic faith, people who were "truly Catholic and truly American according to the times."[7]

In Bane's account, the contribution of Catholicism to American democracy appears again with the surge of Catholic immigration after the early 1840s. Again, it is a rather negatively formulated contribution. Given the Catholic Church's official hostility to liberal democracy, this large new contingent of religionists was a potential problem. However, as she says, the problem was defused by rivalry between German and Irish Catholics, by the moderation American Catholic leaders had to exercise in achieving political power in their urban strongholds, and by the creation of separate institutions for a Catholic subculture.

All of this makes sense. One can argue, however, that this "problem-solving" strategy of a Catholic subculture had a downside for American democracy. When Catholics boycotted public institutions because "public" meant Protestant, voices with important things to say about the American condition turned inward and were not heard; this was especially true with regard to the social teachings of the church and the moral challenges posed by unfettered capitalism. Likewise, Protestants could dress up their anti-Catholicism with a doctrine of separation of church and state in the public schools. All this opened the way for public schools to drift into a hard-edged secularism. As one scholar of American Catholicism has astutely observed, more constructive leadership from both Protestants and Catholics might have found a way to use federalism (as Germany did) to allow state support for both Catholic and Protestant schools.[8] Our current muddled "neutrality" doctrine of church/state relations might have been the better for it. It is at least worth considering.

Mary Jo Bane next invites us to appreciate how American democracy has been good for Catholic Christianity by encouraging changes in official Church doctrine to favor free exercise of religion and separation of church and state. With two qualifications, I agree this was a positive development.

First, it may be a little misleading to rely on the future Pope Benedict XVI when he commends the American experience of the non-state church "as a Christian form that emerged from the very nature of the Church." My lecture seeks to correct the future Pope (a certain shamelessness is required in my line of work) by taking a larger perspective than that provided by the Church. I try to show that the American contribution was affirming individual religious liberty and a non-state church as "a Christian form" that emerged, not from "the Church," but from the very nature of the religion itself.

Second, I think we would do well to recognize that, even in this positive development of doctrine, there were some downsides for Catholic Christianity. In the wake of Vatican II there was a popular sense that since the Church changed its official teaching on religious liberty and church/state relations, why not do this on other unpopular issues as well? There was continuing pressure to radicalize 1965's *Dignitatis Humanae*. Hence the shock at what Mary Jo Bane calls a failure of Church leaders to learn from and respect the insights of the laity in Vatican pronouncements on birth control. That is only one indicator that many American Catholics are wanting more of the Protestant-style autonomy and less of the traditional guided morality that is supposed to characterize the Catholic community. This is another democracy problem for Catholic Christianity that is not going to go away.

This brings us to the essay's concluding thoughts, which concern what I have called the "coming rupture" between American democracy and orthodox Christianity. Mary Jo Bane is hopeful in seeing two "moderating influences" from the Catholic side regarding this possible danger. But it seems to me that these influences can just as easily be read to support my worries.

As Bane's essay points out, centrist Catholics (7 percent of the electorate) were an important swing vote in the 2004 election, and despite conservative Catholic appeals on non-negotiable human life policy issues, 55 percent of these centrist Catholics voted for Bush on the basis of something other than the non-negotiable moral issues. However, it is also true that more "conservative," observant Catholics *were* apparently influenced by such moral issues and voted even more disproportionately for the Protestant Bush and against their fellow Catholic, JFK II. That larger story of the 2004 election supports the point in my lecture about a possible rupture fueled in part by a split between traditionalist and non-traditionalist wings of Protestant and Catholic denominations alike.

Finally, Bane finds portents of moderating influence in Benedict XVI's first encyclical on the subject of love. With respect, I think that we are misconstruing the message if we think that the commitment to love will mean avoiding what she might consider doctrinal rigidity and what others call the condemnation of error regarding the fundamental teachings of the Catholic Church. As head of the Congregation for the Doctrine of the Faith, Joseph Ratzinger—or as she calls him, "the enforcer of orthodoxy"—was Pope John Paul II's man and not a way of balancing the Vatican ticket with Karol Wojtyla's kinder, gentler papacy. Both men have been fully committed to enforcing Catholic doctrinal orthodoxy against all worldly pressures, whether from the dark side of fascist and communist oppression or from the shiny bright side of liberal, democratic majoritarianism. After the fall of communism, a number of people were shocked to learn that Pope John Paul II was not the evangelizer of democracy, but the evangelizer of Gospel truth to which the will of democracy should be subordinate.[9]

As the 2002 Doctrinal Note from Cardinal Ratzinger's office put it, "The Church recognizes that while democracy is the best expression of the direct participation of citizens in political choices, it succeeds only to the extent that it is based on a correct understanding of the human person. Catholic involvement in political life cannot compromise on this principle."[10] I suspect that John Paul II and Benedict XVI will be found to have a single great theme in their papacies—the inalienable dignity and value of the human person, created in the image of God. Hence such "nonnegotiables" in the 2004 election on abortion, euthanasia, cloning, stem cell research. And hence John F. Kerry's problem.

In 2003, even the U.S. Conference of Catholic Bishops (not always a pillar of orthodox rigidity) had this to say about "the faithful citizen":

> Politics should be about fundamental moral choices. . . . It calls Catholics to bring their moral convictions to public life. . . . The faithful citizen is called to test public life by the values of Scripture and the principles of Catholic social teaching. . . . He and she are called to participate in building the culture of life. . . . A consistent ethic of life should be the moral framework from which to address issues in the political arena. . . . Catholics in politics must reflect the moral values of our faith with clear and consistent priority for the life and dignity of the human person, defending human life from conception until natural death and in every condition.
> . . . we cannot accept an understanding of pluralism and tolerance that suggests every possible outlook on life is of equal

value. . . . the legitimate freedom of Catholic citizens [is] to choose among the various political opinions that are compatible with faith and the natural moral law.[11]

It appears to me that for the development of doctrine that Mary Jo Bane hopes to see, there is much disappointment awaiting her. Nonetheless, she is absolutely correct in saying that Catholic theologians have done much of the intellectual work for orthodox Christianity over the centuries. An alliance of co-belligerency between traditionalist Catholics and Protestants has been emerging in our time, and I very much share her hope that Catholic thinkers will develop a "theology of engagement" to help form the conscience of that alliance.

Given Michael Kazin's deep knowledge of populism and American culture, I can certainly understand why he thinks I have spent too much time on "the consensus side of the street." He offers much evidence to show that I have understated the religious conflicts in our history which, together with various points of consensus, have produced a dialectic of development that "both liberates and traps" us.

I would not presume to put myself in the company of the admirable Richard Hofstadter, whom Kazin cites as a model. I would contend, however, that the organizing theme of my whole lecture is exactly the kind of tensioned relationship of consensus and conflict that Hofstadter espoused. It is on these grounds that I picture a double-stranded helix, an image of reciprocal, equivocal contestations of Christianity and democratic politics twisting together through time. Moreover, I describe the development as becoming more conflictual, to the point of being a helix whose two strands are coming apart in the last half of the twentieth century. I think that this amounts to more than my just strolling down the consensus side of the street.

It is true, however, that I spend little time talking about the particular conflicts that Michael Kazin identifies:

- The nineteenth-century conflict between Protestants and immigrant Catholics (though I do highlight the deeper struggle between their contending views of church-state relations, as well as the contrast between Protestant individualism and Catholic social thought).
- The divergent political party alignments of religious groups (but I do point out how, and why, Tocqueville was oblivious to that development).
- The Jewish contribution to America's cultural pluralism (I do cite an exchange between a Jewish supporter and President Washington, because I think it says something important about the cultural pluralism fostered by what I call the Great Denouement concerning religious freedom).
- The racial divide in American religion and politics (although I do discuss the civil rights movement growing out of black churches as the last of our traditional religious revivals, and I use Martin Luther King's words to point out the racial hypocrisy of mid-twentieth-century white churches).

It might well be added that I also do not focus on conflict over gender issues among religious groups, the never-ending fights among Baptists, schisms caused by the charismatic movement, and the like. The reason I don't spend time on these and other conflicts is that they are subjects that have been well worked over. There is a farmer's saying that there's no use plowing a field that has already been harrowed. And academics seem prone to be forever pulverizing the same ground. To keep doing that is the kind of dialectic that really does entrap our thinking.

Especially in light of current religious conflicts in the world, the striking thing about America's religious-political conflicts of the last 200 years is how rarely they centered on religious issues as such. I would contend that by contrast, Americans were more religiously divided in the years prior to 1800 than at any time since. This is not because there were huge numbers of Catholics, or non-Christians, or even a large number of Protestant denominations. It was because the religious differences within colonial Christianity were deeply felt, doctrinally sharp, and politically explosive. Good Puritan congregations could beat and kill Quakers. The young James Madison had his passion for religious liberty stirred by events such as local beatings and the imprisonment of unlicensed Baptist preachers at the hands of Anglican authorities.

By the time of Tocqueville's visit, things had changed. Catholics had always been in America and had come to be generally accepted. The conflicts associated with Irish immigration were less about their Catholicism than about the political, economic, and ethnic challenges these new people presented. The same was true of the Mormons and their persecution from Missouri onwards. Likewise, the "scandal of division" that grew with Protestant denominationalism had less to do with the Christian religion than with forces of race, class, region, and ethnicity.[12] Thanks in large part to the consensus on religious liberty, our nation's "religious" conflicts were only faintly religious. The Great Denouement was a great blessing which we Americans today too often take lightly.

In the same way, one could spend a great deal of time talking about the allegedly "religious" conflicts inflaming today's so-called culture war. However, as I tried to show in my lecture, we should look below the surface of competing publicists' self-serving hyperbole on this subject. When we do, what we mainly find is politicians *using* religion, not religious conflicts driving our politics. Few Americans care about the venerable religious differences over Christology, the means of salvation, infant baptism, and the like. To be sure, religious cleavages in American society and the impact of those cleavages on elections remain important, but they have remained important and largely unchanged for at least the last quarter-century.[13] Christian Americans, and even conservative white Protestant Christian Americans, are a many-splintered thing, but they can be organized as "values voters." That work is done by professional political managers who are adept at such organizing and manipulation. They are not busying themselves in simply upholding the Christian tradition, which by biblical standards would have to give equal time to preaching against divorce, greed, fornication, and indifference to the poor. Both conservative and liberal sides in the culture war have a vested interest in misrepresentation. As Greeley and Hout put it, "If they can puff up the otherness of the opposition, they can rally their base. And by exaggerating how strange the religious right is, demagogues can assure themselves that they will run afoul of very few real people." Typically, what is at issue is not religion but which side is more skilled at the demagoguery.[14]

Instead of replowing all this old ground, I spent a great deal of time in my lecture talking about a conflict that has been under-appreciated and that is growing. This conflict strikes at the fundamentals of our culture and political development. It is portentous enough to suggest an emerging rupture between American democracy and Christianity. Given the significance of this conflict, I do not think it leaves me spending too much time dwelling on consensus.

As for being episodic in my treatment (although I would prefer to call them points of inflection rather than episodes), I should plead guilty, at least in part. The alternative to being episodic is to be continuous, and without exceeding my original guidelines by several hundred thousand words, and extending the lecture to several days in length, that was not possible. However, where I think it matters most—over the centuries that produced our crucial doctrine of religious liberty and over the decades in trying to understand the turmoil of the Sixties—I have tried to sketch the ligatures of a long-term, continuous development of forces. On the latter subject in particular, I have tried to show a continuity of forces that came to fruition in what amounted to a secular awakening when the 1960s became the Sixties. I call this continuous line (with apologies to John Henry Cardinal Newman) the development of doctrine regarding democratic and religious faiths. Its description spans more than half of the twelve decades which Michael Kazin suggests I essentially ignored.

For the subject at hand, there is much that deserves to be ignored. By focusing too heavily on conflicts between Catholic Christianity versus Protestant Christianity, or some Protestant Christianities versus others, we risk overlooking the role of mere Christianity itself in American democracy. Likewise, the challenge posed by modern popular sovereignty, especially through policies regarding the fundamental meaning of human life, is not posed to Protestantism or Catholicism but to orthodox Christianity. If we do not see that, we will indeed remain stuck in the tired categories of the past in analyzing American political development. Americans can be Americans without being Christians, but heretofore they have not been able to be Americans without being heavily influenced by their nation's essentially Christian background.

Alan Wolfe's research and books are always teaching me new things, and I very much appreciate his kind comments. But I am afraid I am going to have to begin by trying to escape his embrace. If, as he says, he begins his course by claiming there is no such thing as religion, this is certainly not the thought I was trying to express at the outset of my lecture. What I did say is that religion as such has not been important in American political development, but rather it has been a particular religion called Christianity that has mattered.

Contrary to Wolfe's point of departure, I happen to believe there really is such a thing as religion. The fact that human beings in all times and places have offered different and muddled expressions about this thing suggests to me that we are more likely to be talking about something that is real, even if beyond humankind's poor efforts to grasp it, rather than something that just happens to be made up. This is why I begin my course on "Religion and Politics" with Rudolf Otto's wonderful little book, *The Idea of the Holy.* It does seem that in beautifully diverse ways, human nature is inherently religious. Rather than viewed as a flaw in our rational mind, a reverential religious mentality can be seen as a way to ensure that our public life is authentically human.[15]

Alan Wolfe then goes on to object that I do not follow through on Christianity with what I never said about religion: namely, I fail to realize that there is also hardly any such thing as Christianity. This issue has been discussed above in light of all three essays and need not be repeated here. Wolfe is surely correct that a person generalizes about Christianity only at one's peril, but I am willing to risk that peril, whatever it might be. I feel less imperiled when he goes on to say that what my overgeneralizations "lose in precision they gain in insight." A little less precision for a little more insight? This seems to me to be a very good trade-off.

Wolfe then raises the particular objection that my view of Christianity is too general to explain Americans' exceptional view of history, since Europe was also Christian and did not develop this same millennial view. Here I think he misses the point, because we have to compare the general with the general and the particular with the particular.

In fact, America and Europe did develop the same *general* view of history as linear and progressive, and this is because they did come from the same Judeo-Christian heritage. But they both also developed their own *particular* secularized—I would say bastardized—version of this heritage. In Europe it took the particular form of ideologies of progress such as positivism, socialism, Marxism, and later fascism—all aping the religious idea of a millennial purification of the world. In America this secularized religion of Progress took on a different particularity—partly because it came out of a particular branch of Protestantism and partly because it did so in the very process of forming the nation. The vision became attached to the idea of the nation itself.

The larger point remains that Christianity—the thing itself—has no philosophy of history or historical progress. What it has, and all it can have, is a theology of history. Karl Lowith, a secular

Jew, understood this better than many American Christians ever have. As he put it, "What the Gospels proclaim is never future improvements in our earthly condition but the sudden coming of the Kingdom of God in contradistinction to the existing kingdom of man." Reinhold Niebuhr extended the point by observing that "the New Testament never guarantees the historical success of the 'strategy' of the Cross."[16] With the strategy of vicarious suffering out of love for others comes the promise only of "tribulation in this world." But far from a message of doom and gloom, this is immediately followed by the word of joy: "Be of good cheer. I have overcome the world" (John 16:33). It is difficult to think of anything that is more un-Christian than to expect earthly happiness in some progressive age as a reward for godly living.

History aside, Alan Wolfe and I agree that today our modern democratic culture is shaping Christianity more than the other way around, and that it has been doing so for a long time. As noted earlier, he would like Christians to be more like Christians, that is, committed to authority and truth, even as they continue to "toy with individualism and this-worldly preoccupations"—a comfortable-sounding pilgrim journey. And since the same cultural forces affecting Christianity also affect our democracy, he thinks this democracy "needs to find a way to preserve its sense of accountability and leadership." On the whole, his is a rather contented view. There is nothing to be said about the terrible policy choices Americans will have to make affecting the very meaning of humanity. As a democracy, we "can count on our materialism, our individualism, our populism, and our emotionalism to keep us together." I suppose the question would be, keep us together as what—a collection of materialistic individuals driven by popular appeals to our emotions? Is that a formula for the long-term survival of democratic self-government?

From his concluding remarks, it actually would seem that Wolfe is more worried about American Christianity than American democracy. I am worried about both. What I call the coming rupture concerns a growing possibility that democracy and anything like a genuine Christianity will wholly disengage from each other. Alan Wolfe finds my conclusions "too dark" for his taste. They are also too dark for my taste, but that is irrelevant since any analysis, one hopes, is something more than a matter of personal taste preferences. Despite his preferential taste for the virtues of aristocracy, Tocqueville would certainly have been troubled by the idea of such a rupture, and so should any American, whatever his and her religious affiliation or lack thereof. I will conclude by trying to explain why.

Why Should We Care?

I have argued that, as this new century continues, there is the realistic possibility of a growing disengagement between American democracy and traditional Christianity. Should Christians care? Should non-Christian citizens care? Let us consider each in turn.

At first glance, traditionalist Christians would seem to be the last ones we should think of worrying about. Such people take their faith very seriously and this, as they would have it, means being fully committed to "the faith as received" from the eyewitness apostles in the earliest days of their religion. In any ongoing rupture with America's democratic regime, these Christians will essentially find themselves in a position similar to that of their earliest compatriots in the days of the Roman Empire. They will be one faith among many in a large, sophisticated world empire that is secular but nominally religious, spiritually-seeking in general but well-distanced from the truth claims of Christian revelation in particular. Believers may not turn their homes into virtual monasteries, but as dispersed groups they will form little enclaves trying to hold at bay the influences of public schools, the media, and general culture. Contrary to the hyped fear-mongering of today's televangelists, what they will face is more likely to be pervasive indifference and dismissal as anti-modernists rather than any outright persecution. Insofar as their congregations contain traditionally orthodox Christians, the once hostile forces of Protestantism and Catholicism—each of which a few centuries ago considered the other to be non-Christian—will recognize their kinship in the face of this secular, nominally religious society of seekers.[17] Although such old-fashioned Christians will sense they have little in common with other Americans, the alienation in question will produce a "persecution" that is mostly psychological. Still, I suspect some writer of popular biblical prophecy will discover that these traditionalist remnants within the Protestant and Catholic branches of Christianity are really the Bible's two last witnesses who are foretold to finish their testimony and then be killed by the beast that ascends out of the bottomless pit. Co-belligerency will mean, as prophesied, the two witnesses' dead bodies being left in the street of the great city, "which spiritually is called Sodom and Egypt" (Revelation 11:3–8). A highly profitable book and movie deal will no doubt follow.

The more sober truth is that orthodox Christianity would suffer from such a withdrawal into internal exile in this country. My original essay emphasizes that neither the legal doctrine of church/state separation nor the Christian doctrine of following a king whose reign is not of this world has made religion irrelevant to American politics. From the beginning of our nation, a conditional, non-idolatrous attachment to America has offered Christians committed to their first love an ongoing opportunity to turn their words into deeds. Free to follow the charge of being light and salt in their Master's cause, they have helped make America a source of hope for others. That hope is for justice, freedom, and above all love, things that do not seem to occur naturally in this world. In not pursuing that hope (even while duly noting all that discretion requires concerning attachments to worldly powers), American Christians would be diminished as resident pilgrims in the time and place to which they have been called. Without idolatry toward either, Christians can love their country as they love their neighbor. As one Christian writer has indelicately put it, "Calling ourselves 'a peculiar people' or 'resident aliens' should not become a religiously sanctioned way of giving the finger to our neighbors."[18] Disengagement from American democracy would produce just such a result, and it is something about which Christian believers should certainly worry. Properly discerned, giving an un-civic finger is an un-Christian thing to do.

Fair enough. But why should non-religious or nominally religious citizens care if orthodox Christians have such a serious problem with American democracy that they essentially withdraw? As good democrats engaged in deliberative discourse, aren't we all better off if religious fundamentalists do drop out of public life?

These are valid questions, but they are also too generic for our purposes. They draw us into an unhelpful loop of abstractions about "religion and politics." To return to the opening theme of my lecture, we need to attend to such questions in view of the particular religion that has been integrally related to American political development. Christianity is the religion which some fraction of Americans are likely to be "fundamentalist" about. The issue is whether non-Christians, or the immensely larger number of nominal American Christians, should want citizens who are trying to live their lives fully faithful to the Christian tradition to be an active part of the American democratic future.

Tocqueville's insights start us down the path to see compelling reasons why we should. Those reasons focus on the connection between individual character and the societal prospects for a healthy democracy. American Christians, like all other Christians before them, fail to live up to the ideals of their religion (as expressed in the person of Jesus). But we may all fail even more disastrously if we attempt to live without those ideals in our midst. In at least four crucial ways, traditional Christianity is one important force that can help teach "the art of being free."

First, as Tocqueville pointed out, traditional Christianity comes with an elemental moral code that helps stabilize and order an otherwise chaotic democratic society. It teaches people to be honest rather than lie, to be fair rather than cheat, to keep rather than break promises, to shun selfishness, and all the rest. Of course, there are many citizens who try to behave morally without the Christian God, or any god at all. And certainly there are many immoral Christians. The point is that traditional Christianity makes it its business to ferret out religious hypocrisy. Given the temptations to misuse freedom, it is likely one will be surrounded by a democratic society that simply works better if it has citizens in it who not only try to do the right thing but who know why, because of the teachings of their religion, they are under a personal and higher obligation to actually do it.

Second, the packet of moral imperatives that comes with traditional Christianity includes obligations that regularly lead such citizens to do good works for others. Of course non-religious people often do the same. Again, the point is that Christians are likely to bring a special commitment and energy to such work as a commandment of their creed. To love is a command, not an option. As the British atheist Roy Hattersley has pointed out in reviewing responses to recent natural disasters, if suffering human beings have to wait for atheists and agnostics rather than religious believers for help, they are likely to wait a very long time.[19] Christianity teaches that good works do not get you into heaven. But good works are likely to come from people who believe there is a heaven and that it is their real home. People who have been taught to believe that love is even greater than faith and hope are likely to be people who impart a benevolent, civilized tone to democratic society.

The third factor is the reforming impulse that traditional Christianity carries into society. The religion envisions itself not as a collection of isolated individuals, but as communities of personal attachment sharing a spiritual vision that is meant to be deployed in the world. Here people learn arts of association that, as Tocqueville would say, keep individuals from being atomized and lost in the democratic world of equality. But it goes beyond that. Of the many types of groups making up civil society, the church of Christ is one dedicated—again by the content of its creed—to pursuing a moral vision of the larger society. The inherent tendency is to bring an ethical awareness to every subject, not just abortion and homosexuality but also the environment, scientific research, taxation, and everything in between. The fact that in contemporary America one hears more from Christians on the political "right" rather than the "left" of such issues does not vitiate the general point. The perspective of the Christian mind is inherently reformist and ameliorating, and the positive contributions stemming from this perspective can be spelled out in detail and at great length.[20] Thus Christianity can serve as a democratically valuable force for both stability and ongoing reform.

Finally, once we disabuse ourselves of the heresy of fideism—that is, confining religion to the realm of irrational blind faith—it is clear that Christianity can help preserve the role of reason in democratic discourse about humankind's most fundamental issues. Traditional Christianity holds that faith and reason are not only compatible but essential to each other. In the heat of partisan argument, it is easy for the public to forget that secularist views also start from "unproven premises." Everyone engaged in the great conversation of democracy is arguing for courses of action that are elaborated conclusions built on faith in something or other. If that faith is purely in human reason itself, Christianity asks: is it reasonable to make such a "leap of faith"?

Traditional Christianity insists that we reason about who man is. Like every religion, it claims to have the crucial answers to the big questions of human existence. In the American context, Christianity's contentions help to limit the ultimate arbitrariness of democratic sovereignty by arguing that all is not permitted and man cannot do whatever he wills.[21] And so we return to the worry that lay behind Tocqueville's search for insight into the American experience. Democratic man is pointed in the direction of becoming wholly materialistic, shortsighted, and self-absorbed. Drunk with the sovereignty of his own will, he risks becoming disoriented and psychologically adrift to the point of being willing to give up his very liberty for security. Without transcendent moral reference points for ordering personal and public life, democratic societies will become debauched and alienated from what is most human. This was the worry of Alexis de Tocqueville, and it should worry twenty-first-century Americans as well. Non-believers may not believe the Christians' answers, but a democratic society is surely better off for having to confront the Big Questions rather than pretending they do not exist. Without a strong, publicly engaged Christian presence, America will become a different and not a better place.

But what about the danger for American democracy posed by Christians in the "public square" who claim to be fully convinced, through faith, of God's commandments to do this and to refrain from doing that? I have spoken about that worry in my lecture, but perhaps too abstractly, or maybe too politely. To automatically jam traditionalist, Bible-believing Christians into the category of arrogant, self-righteous, God-is-on-our-side religious prigs in politics is—what shall we say? Arrogant, self-righteous, willfully ignorant secular priggery? In the lecture I spoke of the "prophetic stance" in traditional Christianity, so well discussed by Glenn Tinder.[22] This is far from a call to act with self-righteous certainty in the world's affairs. In putting Babylon on notice, it is also a call that is supposed to put all Christians on a continuous and self-critical watch, demanding to know if they themselves are a prideful and prospering part of the city's wickedness. It lays a finger on the enlivening Christian pulse that has throbbed now for some two millennia, from the sincere worries of today's Christians active in politics, back through the Puritans and the Reformation controversies, through the medieval Catholic reform movements, into the Christian schisms of late antiquity, thence to the Church Councils of Roman Emperor Constantine, and finally back to the original questions of Jesus' Jewish disciples asking their mysterious, risen Jewish teacher when the earthly Jewish kingdom would be restored. His answer, suitably superior to human questioning, was that these truest of first believers were not to know such things. Rather they should get on, when empowered by God's Holy Spirit, with telling other people everywhere in the world what they had seen and experienced. And then, saying no more, this Jesus left them to carry on (Acts 1:6–9).

If it is truly growing out of such a Jewish/Christian tradition, the prophetic stance of today's Christians should have little to do with God-is-on-our-side politics. It should have everything to do with an are-we-on-God's-side politics of self-examination. For traditional Christians, every action that engages the allurements of the world, above all the grand temptation of political power and pride, should by the terms of this religion itself evoke humility, questioning, and doubt—not about God, but about one's own self-righteousness and capacity for self-deception. People with that sensibility, whether citizens or government officials, are a healthy presence in American democracy.

Believing Christians believe they know something—the essential, invaluable, big something—but they are assured by their own sacred texts that they do not know everything, and should act accordingly. While their belief in the truth of their religion may be annoying to others, traditionalist Christians who sincerely try to live out their faith are not people we should want to see retreat from active citizenship. In fact, they make for the kind of companions we should all like to have on board a wandering ship of state as it navigates dark seas. Insofar as they are sincere believers, Christians are likely to be the kind of shipmates who think, like the seventeenth-century Puritan Richard Baxter, "In necessary things, unity; in disputed things, liberty; in all things, charity." One could do much worse by way of fellow passengers.

NOTES

1. CHRISTIANITY AND DEMOCRACY IN AMERICA

1. James W. Ceaser, *Nature and History in American Political Development* (Cambridge, Mass.: Harvard University Press, 2006), 5, 97, 124–126.

2. Reasonable estimates are that, statistically, Protestants moved from near-complete dominance in the colonial and Revolutionary periods to roughly 80 percent of the American population in 1840 and then by 1860 to something around 60 percent, where Protestantism has since remained. William R. Hutchison, "Discovering America," in William R. Hutchison, ed., *Between the Times: The Travail of the Protestant Establishment in America, 1900–1960* (Cambridge, Mass.: Harvard University Press, 1989), 304 and 309, note 3.

3. A discussion of the secularist ideology's approved routes to democratic modernity can be found in David Martin, *On Secularization: Towards a Revised General Theory* (London: Ashgate, 2005).

4. Alexis de Tocqueville, *Democracy in America*, ed. J. P. Mayer and Max Lerner, trans. George Lawrence (New York: Harper and Row, 1966), 286. All subsequent page references and quotations from *Democracy in America* refer to this edition.

5. Peter Gay, *The Enlightenment: An Interpretation* (New York: W. W. Norton, 1995), chap. 7.

6. While Tocqueville frequently uses the generic term "religion," the contexts indicate he is usually thinking of Christianity when he does so. The important exceptions occur when he discusses religion existentially in terms of the universal human yearning for transcendent meaning; he sees all religion as a form of hope natural to the human heart, and its denial as an aberrational distortion of intellect, soul, and human nature itself (409–410). For the most part, however, Tocqueville is explaining his conviction "that at all costs Christianity

must be maintained among the new democracies." *Democracy in America,* 517.

7. André Jardin, *Tocqueville: A Biography* (New York: Farrar, Straus and Giroux, 1988).

8. Alexis de Tocqueville, *The Old Regime and the French Revolution,* trans. Stuart Gilbert (Garden City, N.Y.: Doubleday, 1955), 15.

9. *Democracy in America,* 37. Thus in urging the distinction between elements of Puritan versus English origin, Tocqueville sees the former as accounting for the large sweep of America's democratic landscape, while the elements of English origin consist of relics of aristocratic institutions that can be unexpectedly found in that landscape (41–42).

10. Ibid., 38. Later, Tocqueville becomes more sarcastic toward those "pedants" in Europe who declare the religious spirit Tocqueville admires to be a barrier to Americans' freedom and happiness. "To that I have really no answer to give, except that those who talk like that have never been in America and have never seen either religious peoples or free ones. So I shall wait till they come back from a visit to America" (270).

11. Joshua Mitchell, *The Fragility of Freedom* (Chicago: University of Chicago Press, 1995), 190.

12. "In the United States even the religion of most of the citizens is republican, since it submits the truths of the other world to private judgment, as in politics the care of their temporal interests is abandoned to the good sense of the people. Thus every man is allowed freely to take that road which he thinks will lead him to heaven, just as the law permits every citizen to have the right of choosing his own government" (364).

13. John G. West, Jr., *The Politics of Revelation and Reason* (Lawrence: University Press of Kansas, 1996), 1–3. In his account of "A Fortnight in the Wilds," Tocqueville does offer a brief report of a frontier revival meeting but seems unaware of political implications of such religious enthusiasm in even the most remote parts of America. Appendix V, *Democracy in America,* 745–746. The fictional letter of Tocqueville's younger sister criticizing his failure to report the mixture of religion in American government deserves repeating: "The phenomena I have just reviewed—the commitment in state constitutions to the public worship of God and the enforcement of this obligation by sabbatarian legislation; the use of public funds to endow churches, maintain ministries, commission missionaries, and benefit

religious education; the control of public education by the clergy; the enforcement of a decent respect for the deity and the principal tenets of Christianity by the criminal law; and the submission of the entire sexual life of the Americans to commandments derived from Christian Scripture—point in another, more worldly direction. My brother wrote, just before he ventured upon his analysis of the role of religion in America, 'The principal aim of this book has been to make known the laws of the United States.' It is evident that the bulk of the laws bearing upon religion were omitted from his account." John T. Noonan Jr., *The Lustre of Our Country* (Berkeley: University of California Press, 1998), 110.

14. Alfred Stepan, "Religion, Democracy, and the 'Twin Tolerations,'" *Journal of Democracy,* 11:4 (2000), 37–57.

15. Glenn Tinder, "Can We Be Good Without God?" *The Atlantic Monthly,* 264:6 (1989), 68–82, and *The Political Meaning of Christianity* (Baton Rouge: Louisiana State University Press, 1989), 8.

16. Peter Brown, *The Rise of Western Christendom,* 2nd ed. (Malden, Mass.: Blackwell, 2003), 174–176.

17. This is "the gospel" which Paul says he received and delivered to others. I Corinthians 15:3–8.

18. Jean-Jacques Rousseau, *On the Social Contract,* ed. Roger D. Masters (New York: St. Martin's Press, 1978), 130–131.

19. John T. Noonan, Jr., *Religious Freedom* (New York: Foundation Press, 2001), 117; and Noonan, *The Lustre of Our Country,* 48–49.

20. Speech to the Virginia ratifying convention on the Constitution, June 12, 1788. *The Papers of James Madison,* ed. William T. Hutchinson and William M. E. Rachal (Chicago: University of Chicago Press, 1973), vol. 8, 130.

21. By royal patent, the Catholic convert Lord Baltimore was allowed to found a colony in the Chesapeake area as a haven for English Catholics coming under pressure from the growing Puritan movement. The law of the new colony provided that no Christian should be molested "for or in respect of his or her religion nor in the free exercise thereof." In honor of King Charles's Catholic wife and the Virgin Mary, the colony was named Maryland. Noonan, *The Lustre of Our Country,* 54 and 365.

22. Comments of Jack Rakove in Ceaser, *Nature and History in American Political Development,* 105–108.

23. In addition to Noonan's work, see Thomas E. Buckley, *Church and*

State in Revolutionary Virginia, 1776–1787 (Charlottesville: University Press of Virginia, 1977); William Lee Miller, *The First Liberty: Religion and the American Republic* (New York: Knopf, 1986); Leonard W. Levy, *The Establishment Clause: Religion and the First Amendment* (New York: Macmillan, 1986); Michael McConnell, "The Origins and Historical Understanding of Free Exercise of Religion," *Harvard Law Review,* 103 (1990), 1486–1488.

24. Noonan, *Religious Freedom,* 125.

25. Quoted in Robert Louis Wilken's book review, "In Defense of Constantine," *First Things,* April 2001, 37.

26. This and the following quotations from Madison are taken from Noonan, *The Lustre of Our Country,* 72–75.

27. Gaillard Hunt, "James Madison and Religious Liberty," *Journal of the American Historical Association,* 4:1 (1900), 165–171. As President Washington wrote to a Jewish supporter, "The citizens of the United States of America have a right to applaud themselves for having given to Mankind examples of an enlarged and liberal policy, a policy worthy of imitation. All possess alike liberty of conscience and immunities of citizenship. It is now no more that toleration is spoken of, as if it was by the indulgence of one class of people that another enjoyed the exercise, of their inherent natural rights." President George Washington, "Reply to Moses Seixas, Sexton of Hebrew Congregation of Newport," in Edwin S. Gaustad, *A Documentary History of Religion in America to the Civil War,* 2nd ed. (Grand Rapids, Mich.: Eerdmans, 1993), 278–279.

28. As John Witherspoon, Madison's Calvinist teacher at Princeton, put it, "There is not a single instance in history in which civil liberty was lost, and religious liberty preserved entire." Thomas Miller, ed., *The Selected Writings of John Witherspoon* (Carbondale: Southern Illinois University Press, 1990), 140–141.

29. Noonan has a valuable discussion in *The Lustre of Our Country,* 61–75. Madison's text is worth serious attention: "We remonstrate against the said Bill, 1. Because we hold it for a fundamental and undeniable truth, that Religion or the duty which we owe to our Creator and the manner of discharging it, can be directed only by reason and conviction, not by force or violence. The Religion then of every man must be left to the conviction and conscience of every man; and it is the right of every man to exercise it as these may dictate. This right is in its nature an unalienable right. It is unalienable, because

the opinions of men depending only on the evidence contemplated by their own minds cannot follow the dictates of other men: It is unalienable also, because what is here a right towards men, is a duty toward the Creator. It is the duty of every man to render to the Creator such homage, and such only, as he believes to be acceptable to him. This duty is precedent both in order of time and degree of obligation, to the claims of Civil Society. Before any man can be considered as a member of Civil Society, he must be considered as a subject of the Governor of the Universe: And if a member of Civil Society, who enters into any subordinate Association, must always do it with a reservation of his duty to the general authority; much more must every man who becomes a member of any particular Civil Society, do it with a saving of his allegiance to the Universal Sovereign. We maintain therefore that in matters of Religion, no man's right is abridged by the institution of Civil Society, and that Religion is wholly exempt from its cognizance." James Madison, "A Memorial and Remonstrance," June 1785, in Noonan, *Religious Freedom,* 173–178. See also more generally Merrill D. Peterson and Robert C. Vaughan, eds., *The Virginia Statute for Religious Freedom: Its Evolution and Consequences in American History* (New York: Cambridge University Press, 1988).

30. Vatican Council II, Declaration on Religious Liberty (*Dignitatis Humanae*), 1965, paragraph 12, *www.vatican.va/archive/hist_councils/ii_vatican_council/documents,* accessed 2/13/06.

31. In fact, it was the opening of Jefferson and Madison's "Virginia Statue on Religious Freedom," introduced in 1779, finally passed in 1785, and generally regarded as the first law of its kind.

32. Thomas S. Engeman and Michael P. Zuckert, eds., *Protestantism and the American Founding* (Notre Dame: University of Notre Dame Press, 2004).

33. "Memorial and Remonstrance," in Noonan, *Religious Freedom,* 173.

34. Thus in terms of Henry May's four categories, one is dealing here with the "Moderate Enlightenment," which was "often inextricably mixed with Christian ideas." Henry May, *The Enlightenment in America* (New York: Oxford University Press, 1976), xviii.

35. See Isaac Kramnick and R. Lawrence Moore, *The Godless Constitution: The Case Against Religious Correctness* (New York: W. W. Norton, 1996); Daniel Dreisbach, *Religion and Politics in the Early*

Republic (Frankfort: University Press of Kentucky, 1996); and the debate between the authors of these two books in *Liberty,* May/June 1996, 13–14; November/December 1996, 11–13; March/April 1997, 2.

36. Jon Meacham, *American Gospel: God, the Founding Fathers, and the Making of a Nation* (New York: Random House, 2006), 22–27, 74–75.

37. Speech to Virginia ratifying convention, June 20, 1788, in Robert A. Rutland and Charles F. Hobson, eds., *The Papers of James Madison,* vol. 11 (Charlottesville: University Press of Virginia, 1977), 163.

38. This commonly held view was epitomized in George Washington's Farewell Address: "Of all the dispositions and habits, which lead to political prosperity, Religion and Morality are indispensable supports. In vain would that man claim the tribute of Patriotism, who should labor to subvert these great pillars of human happiness, these firmest props of the duties of Men and Citizens. The mere Politician, equally with the pious man, ought to respect and to cherish them. A volume could not trace all their connexions with private and public felicity. Let it simply be asked, Where is the security for property, for reputation, for life, if the sense of religious obligation desert the oaths, which are the instruments of investigation in Courts of Justice? And let us with caution indulge the supposition, that morality can be maintained without religion. Whatever may be conceded to the influence of refined education on minds of peculiar structure, reason and experience both forbid us to expect, that national morality can prevail in exclusion of religious principle." *www.earlyamerica.com* (accessed 5/10/06).

39. James T. Kloppenberg, "The Virtues of Liberalism: Christianity, Republicanism, and Ethics in Early American Political Discourse," *Journal of American History,* 74:2 (1987), 9–34.

40. West, *The Politics of Revelation and Reason,* 64.

41. James Turner, *Without God, Without Creed: The Origins of Unbelief in America* (Baltimore: Johns Hopkins University Press, 1985), chap. 2; Barbara A. McGraw, *Rediscovering America's Sacred Ground: Public Religion and Pursuit of the Good in a Pluralistic America* (Albany: State University of New York Press, 2003).

42. Ruth Elson, *Guardians of Tradition: Schoolbooks of the Nineteenth Century* (Lincoln: University of Nebraska Press, 1964); Sara Goodman Zimet, "Values and Attitudes in American Primers from Colo-

nial Days to the Present," in Sara Goodman Zimet, ed., *What Children Read in School* (New York: Grune and Stratton, 1972).

43. These and related points are presented in West, *The Politics of Revelation and Reason,* 73–78; Harry V. Jaffa, *The American Founding as the Best Regime* (Claremont, Calif.: Claremont Institute, 1990).

44. Robert H. Wiebe, *Self-Rule: A Cultural History of American Democracy* (Chicago: University of Chicago Press, 1995).

45. See the discussion and related sources cited in John W. De Gruchy, *Christianity and Democracy* (New York: Cambridge University Press, 1995), chapters 2 and 3.

46. William G. McLoughlin, *Revivals, Awakenings, and Reform* (Chicago: University of Chicago Press, paperback edition 1980), xiv.

47. Norman Cohn, *Cosmos, Chaos, and the World to Come* (New Haven: Yale University Press, 1993); Mircea Eliade, *The Myth of the Eternal Return* (Princeton: Princeton University Press, 1954); Christopher Dawson, *The Dynamics of World History* (New York: Sheed and Ward, 1956).

48. Karl Lowith, *Meaning in History* (Chicago: University of Chicago Press, 1949).

49. Ibid., 188.

50. Chapter 20 of St. John's revelation shows the angel of God binding Satan for a thousand years and the souls of martyrs for Christ's sake reigning with Jesus for those thousand years (all of these souls have part in the "first resurrection" with no power of the second death over them, while the rest of the dead remain dead until the thousand years are finished). After the thousand years Satan is loosed, producing a deception of all nations, the gathering of unholy forces against believers, a decisive, quick victory blow from heaven, God's final judgment of all human beings who have ever lived, and the end of historical time.

51. Governor John Winthrop's 1630 sermon aboard the *Arbella,* "Christian Charitee: Modell Hereof," is in Noonan, *Religious Freedom,* 122–123. For much richer accounts of Puritan millennialism than I can discuss here, see James West Davidson, *The Logic of Millennial Thought: Eighteenth-Century New England* (New Haven: Yale University Press, 1977); and Theodore Dwight Bozeman, *To Live Ancient Lives: The Primitivist Dimension in Puritanism* (Chapel Hill: University of North Carolina Press, 1988).

52. Patrick Wormald, Donald Bullough, and Roger Collins, eds., *Ideal*

and Reality in Frankish and Anglo-Saxon Society: Studies Presented to J. M. Wallace-Hadrill (Oxford: Blackwell, 1983).

53. President Ronald Reagan's farewell address to the nation eloquently played on these images: "I've spoken of the shining city all my political life, but I don't know if I ever quite communicated what I saw when I said it. But in my mind it was a tall, proud city built on rocks stronger than oceans, windswept, God-blessed, and teeming with people of all kinds living in harmony and peace; a city with free ports that hummed with commerce and creativity. And if there had to be city walls, the walls had doors and the doors were open to anyone with the will and the heart to get here. That's how I saw it, and see it still.

"And how stands the city on this winter night? More prosperous, more secure, and happier that it was 8 years ago. But more than that: After 200 years, two centuries, she still stands strong and true on the granite ridge, and her glow has held steady no matter what storm. And she's still a beacon, still a magnet for all who must have freedom, for all the pilgrims from all the lost places who are hurtling through the darkness, toward home." The speech appears in Davis W. Houck and Amos Kiewe, eds., *Actor, Ideologue, Politician: The Public Speeches of Ronald Reagan* (Westport, Conn.: Greenwood Press, 1993), 327.

54. Ernest Lee Tuveson, *Redeemer Nation: The Idea of America's Millennial Role* (Chicago: University of Chicago Press, 1968); Conrad Cherry, *God's New Israel: Religious Interpretations of American Destiny* (Englewood Cliffs, N.J.: Prentice-Hall, 1971); Steven H. Webb, *American Providence: A Nation with a Mission* (New York: Continuum International Publishing, 2004). In an earlier, too often neglected work, Richard Niebuhr presents the developments we are discussing as three overlapping phases in the "notes of faith" of a constructive Protestantism. The first, emphasizing the sovereignty of God, finds believers focusing on their eternal citizenship in heaven, with a relatively static view of society. The second "Kingdom of Christ" phase of revivals and awakenings focuses on the personal experience of Christ's love and reign in the believer, which, it should be noted, is not mere emotionalism but a rule of knowledge in men's minds. The third phase, "the Coming Kingdom," roughly corresponds to what I am discussing as millennialism. H. Richard

Niebuhr, *The Kingdom of God in America* (New York: Harper Torchbook, 1959), first published in 1937.

55. George McKenna, "An Holy and Blessed People: The Puritan Origins of American Patriotism," *Yale Review,* 90:3 (July 2002), 81–98.

56. Tuveson, *Redeemer Nation,* 102.

57. McLoughlin, *Revivals, Awakenings, and Reform,* 105.

58. Thus President Bush before 9/11: "Through much of the last century, America's faith in freedom and democracy was a rock in a raging sea. Now it is a seed upon the wind, taking root in many nations. Our democratic faith is more than the creed of our country, it is the inborn hope of our humanity; an ideal we carry but do not own, a trust we bear and pass along."

And President Bush after 9/11: "The advance of freedom is the calling of our time; it is the calling of our country. From the Fourteen Points to the Four Freedoms, to the Speech at Westminster, America has put our power at the service of principle. We believe that liberty is the design of nature; we believe that liberty is the direction of history. We believe that human fulfillment and excellence come in the responsible exercise of liberty. And we believe that freedom—the freedom we prize—is not for us alone, it is the right and the capacity of all mankind. . . . And as we meet the terror and violence of the world, we can be certain the Author of freedom is not indifferent to the fate of freedom." President George W. Bush, "Inaugural Address," New York Times, January 21, 2001, 14; and address to the National Endowment for Democracy, November 6, 2003. *www.whitehouse.gov/news/releases/2003* (accessed 1/15/06).

59. Jonathan Edwards, "Some Thoughts Concerning the Present Revival of Religion in New England," *The Works of Jonathan Edwards,* vol. 1, ed. Edward Hickman (Carlisle, Pa.: Banner of Truth Trust, 1974), 381. Thomas Paine, "Common Sense," in *The Writings of Thomas Paine,* ed. Moneurer Daniel Conway (New York: G. P. Putnam's Sons, 1894), 118–119. On Paine in relation to the religious atmosphere, see Stephen Newman and related references in "A Note on *Common Sense* and Christian Eschatology," *Political Theory,* 6:1 (1978), 101–108.

60. Walter A. McDougall, *Promised Land, Crusader State: The American Encounter with the World Since 1776* (New York: Houghton Mifflin, 1998).

61. See, for example, Claes G. Ryn, *America the Virtuous: The Crisis of Democracy and the Quest for Empire* (New Brunswick, N.J.: Transaction, 2004); Michael Northcott, *An Angel Directs the Storm: Apocalyptic Religion and American Empire* (New York: I. B. Tauris, 2004).

62. In saying this, there remains a very significant difference. Catholic teaching presents the Church as the visible society of the Kingdom of God on earth, a claim rejected by Protestant reformers. Reformers retained the idea of the church as the human society through which God's purpose in history is realized, but view this church as composed of all those born again in Christ and not the visible hierarchical Church known to history.

63. St. Augustine, *The City of God,* trans. Marcus Dods (Chicago: Encyclopaedia Britannica, 1952), chap. 20. For a helpful overview, see Arthur W. Wainwright, *Mysterious Apocalypse: Interpreting the Book of Revelation* (Nashville: Abingdon Press, 1993).

64. Niebuhr, *The Kingdom of God in America,* 193.

65. Charles E. Merriam, *The New Democracy and the New Despotism* (New York: Whittlesey House, 1939), 11.

66. Early Christian apologists, not least Paul, took special care in pointing out the glory to God that came from entrusting His good news about the Messiah to socially marginal people whom the world dismisses. Under Jewish law, shepherds, fishermen, tax collectors, and women were not the sort of proper people to give testimony about anything important.

67. Celsus, *On the True Doctrine* (Oxford: Oxford University Press, 1987).

68. See, respectively, Jacques Maritain, *Christianity and Democracy,* trans. Doris C. Anson (New York: Charles Scribner's Sons, 1944), 46; and Charles Taylor, *Sources of the Self* (Cambridge, Mass.: Harvard University Press, 1989). Recent examples of exaggerated claims identifying Christianity with success and progress on the world's terms are Rodney Stark, *The Victory of Reason: How Christianity Led to Freedom, Capitalism, and Western Success* (New York: Random House, 2005); and Thomas E. Woods, Jr., *How the Catholic Church Built Western Civilization* (Washington, D.C.: Regnery, 2005).

69. John Paul II, *Fides et Ratio: Encyclical Letter on the Relationship be-*

tween Faith and Reason (Boston: Pauline Books and Media, 1998), 46.

70. John T. McGreevy, *Catholicism and American Freedom: A History* (New York: W. W. Norton, 2003).

71. Carl J. Friedrich, *The New Belief in the Common Man* (Boston: Little, Brown, 1942), 3.

72. Thus in 1647 the Puritans' General Court of Massachusetts passed a law to create the first publicly supported schools with two declared aims: to foil the efforts of "ye old deluder Satan, to keep men from the knowledge of ye Scriptures," and to ensure that "learning not be buried with ye grave of our fathers." *www.extremeintellect.com* (accessed 5/27/06).

73. Peter Harrison, *The Bible, Protestantism, and the Rise of Natural Science* (Cambridge: Cambridge University Press, 1998), 93.

74. Cardinal Bellarmine, quoted in ibid., 100. In 1546 the Catholic Church's Council of Trent answered the Protestant reformers: ". . . no one, relying on his own skill, shall—in matters of faith, and of morals pertaining to the edification of Christian doctrine—wresting the sacred scripture to his own senses, presume to interpret the said sacred Scripture contrary to that sense which holy mother Church,—whose it is to judge of the true sense and interpretation of the holy Scriptures,—hath held and doth hold." *Decree Concerning the Canonical Scripture, Canons and Decrees of the Council of Trent*, Fourth Session, April 1546, *www.bible-research.com* (accessed 6/11/07).

75. A recent discussion of this more general issue is in Robert D. Woodberry and Timothy S. Shah, "The Pioneering Protestants," *Journal of Democracy*, 15:2 (2004), 47–61.

76. This compares with 89 percent in 1947 when this Gallup poll question was first asked. Gregg Esterbrook, "Religion in America: The New Ecumenicalism," *Brookings Review*, Winter 2002, 46.

77. A usefully brief summary of Puritan beliefs can be found in Nathaniel Philbrick's immensely informative and readable *Mayflower: A Story of Courage, Community, and War* (New York: Viking, 2006), 8–10.

78. See Sydney E. Ahlstsrom, *A Religious History of the American People* (New Haven: Yale University Press, 1972), 385 and Part IV generally.

79. The full story is of course quite complex, and for the period up to the

Civil War it is well laid out in two recent books: Mark A. Noll, *America's God: From Jonathan Edwards to Abraham Lincoln* (Oxford: Oxford University Press, 2002); and E. Brooks Holifield, *Theology in America: Christian Thought from the Age of the Puritans to the Civil War* (New Haven: Yale University Press, 2003). While Holifield lays greater stress on the trained clergy, a central theme in both books is the ultimate ineffectiveness of learned Protestant leaders' resistance to these popularizing trends.

80. Quoted in McLoughlin, *Revivals, Awakenings, and Reform,* 114; see also 121.

81. Debby Applegate, *The Most Famous Man in America: The Biography of Henry Ward Beecher* (New York: Doubleday, 2006).

82. Quotations are from Noll, *America's God,* 441 and 438.

83. Ibid., 442.

84. Niebuhr, *The Kingdom of God in America,* 193.

85. Sydney E. Ahlstrom, "Theology in America: A Historical Survey," in James Ward Smith and A. Leland Jamison, eds., *The Shaping of American Religion,* Volume I in the series *Religion in American Life* (Princeton: Princeton University Press, 1961), 319–320.

86. Alan Wolfe, *One Nation, After All* (New York: Viking, 1998), 56.

87. Robert Wuthnow, *After Heaven: Spirituality in America Since the 1950s* (Berkeley: University of California Press, 1998), chap. 1; Wayne Baker, *America's Crisis of Values* (Princeton: Princeton University Press, 2005), 57; Thomas Luckmann, "Shrinking Transcendence, Expanding Religion," *Sociological Analysis,* 50 (1990), 127.

88. For a survey of the many varieties see Wade Clark Roof, *Spiritual Marketplace: Baby Boomers and the Remaking of American Religion* (Princeton: Princeton University Press, 1999), and Brian D. McLaren, *A New Kind of Christian: A Tale of Two Friends on a Spiritual Journey* (San Francisco: Jossey-Bass, 2001). One author ably summarizes the contrast between the old (i.e., orthodox Christian) and the new spirituality: "The New Synthesis reverses each major tenet of the Revealed Word. The Word's insistence on history as faith's foundation gives way to myth as the universal mode of spiritual expression. Salvation through faith in God's grace yields to the mystical episode as the elemental religious experience. An evolving universe infused with divine consciousness supplants a wholly other God, while human beings evolving toward a divinity of their own are no longer created in the image of such a God." James A. Herrick, *The Making of*

the New Spirituality (Downers Grove, Ill.: InterVarsity Press, 2003), 251.

89. Pope John Paul II repeated the teaching against fideism traditionally upheld by both the Catholic Church and Protestant Reformers such as Luther, Calvin, Knox, and many others. "The truth conferred by revelation is a truth to be understood in the light of reason." John Paul II, *Fides et Ratio*, 48 and 64. Origen is quoted in Robert Louis Willken, *The Spirit of Early Christian Thought* (New Haven: Yale University Press, 2003), 14.

90. For a fuller discussion and related references, see Jean Bethke Elshtain, "In Common Together: Christianity and Democracy in America," in John Witte, Jr., ed., *Christianity and Democracy in Global Context* (Boulder: Westview Press, 2001).

91. H. Richard Niebuhr, "The Protestant Movement and Democracy in the United States," in Smith and Jamison, eds., *The Shaping of American Religion*, Volume I, 31–32.

92. Gordon Wood, *The Creation of the American Republic* (Chapel Hill: University of North Carolina Press, 1969).

93. A fuller discussion of this point would have to acknowledge important differences among not only Protestants but also conservative Protestants on the issue of "engaging the culture." See George M. Marsden, *Fundamentalism and American Culture* (Oxford: Oxford University Press, 1980), chap. 15; and more generally, H. Richard Niebuhr, *Christ and Culture* (New York: Harper and Row, 1950).

94. C. Howard Hopkins, *The Rise of the Social Gospel in American Protestantism, 1865–1915* (New Haven: Yale University Press, 1940).

95. Michael Kazin, *A Godly Hero: The Life of William Jennings Bryan* (New York: Knopf, 2006).

96. Nathan O. Hatch, *The Democratization of American Christianity* (New Haven: Yale University Press, 1989).

97. Charles Grandison Finney, quoted in McLoughlin, *Revivals, Awakenings, and Reform*, 123.

98. Gaines M. Foster, *Moral Reconstruction: Christian Lobbyists and the Federal Legislation of Morality* (Chapel Hill: University of North Carolina Press, 2002).

99. H. Richard Niebuhr, *The Social Sources of Denominationalism* (New York: Henry Holt, 1929), and William R. Hutchison, *Religious Plu-*

ralism in America: The Contentious History of a Founding Ideal (New Haven: Yale University Press, 2003).

100. Theda Skocpol, *Protecting Soldiers and Mothers: The Political Origins of Social Policy in the United States* (Cambridge, Mass.: Harvard University Press, 1992).

101. Clifford Putney, *Muscular Christianity: Manhood and Sports in Protestant America, 1880–1920* (Cambridge, Mass.: Harvard University Press, 2002); Thomas Winter, *Making Men, Making Class: The YMCA and Working Men, 1877–1920* (Chicago: University of Chicago Press, 2002).

102. Robert Bellah's article still repays attention: "Civil Religion in America," in William G. McLoughlin and Robert N. Bellah, eds., *Religion in America* (Boston: Beacon Press, 1968), 3–23.

103. Harry S. Stout, *Upon the Altar of the Nation: A Moral History of the Civil War* (New York: Viking, 2006).

104. McLoughlin, *Revivals, Awakenings, and Reform*, 144.

105. Marsden, *Fundamentalism and American Culture*, 146–147.

106. Maritain, *Christianity and Democracy*, 58–59.

107. Will Herberg, *Protestant-Catholic-Jew* (Garden City: Doubleday, 1956).

108. Martin Luther King, Jr., "Letter from Birmingham Jail," April 16, 1963, 8. *www.kingpapers.org* (accessed 7/7/07).

109. Andrew Greeley and Michael Hout, *The Truth about Conservative Christians: What They Think and What They Believe* (Chicago: University of Chicago Press, 2006), 83.

110. Variations within the conservative mainstream of the Protestant establishment are described in Marsden, *Fundamentalism and American Culture,* chapter 15, and within Protestantism more generally by William R. Hutchison, *The Modernist Impulse in American Protestantism* (Cambridge, Mass.: Harvard University Press, 1976). Not surprisingly, American Catholics were more self-confident in following Pope Pius X's 1907 condemnation of theological modernism as the "synthesis of all heresies," while accepting limited aspects of the modernist agenda (particularly economic reforms in pursuit of charity and social justice) as consistent with Catholic teaching. See Thomas E. Woods, Jr., *The Church Confronts Modernity: Catholic Intellectuals and the Progressive Era* (New York: Columbia University Press, 2004).

111. The series was reissued in 1917 as a four-volume set, which has been

reprinted by Baker Books, Grand Rapids, Michigan, in 1998. What became popularly known as "the five points of fundamentalism" are the inerrancy of Scripture, the deity and Virgin birth of Jesus Christ, his substitutionary atonement for human sin, his bodily resurrection from the dead, and his premillennial return (or, in Presbyterian circles, the authenticity of biblical miracles). The most cogent intellectual presentation of the fundamentalists' case against modernism is J. Gresham Machen, *Christianity and Liberalism* (Grand Rapids, Mich.: Eerdmans, 1923), reprinted 1981.

112. On the most portentous of these battles, see Bradley J. Longfield, *The Presbyterian Controversy: Fundamentalists, Modernists, and Moderates* (New York: Oxford University Press, 1991), as well as Marsden, *Fundamentalism and American Culture,* chap. 19.

113. Contemporaneous accounts presented the results as indecisive or possibly favorable to the anti-evolution cause, but this did not hinder the subsequent development of the Scopes legend as a decisive defeat for old-time religion. Edward J. Larson, *Summer of the Gods* (New York: Basic Books, 1997), chaps. 8 and 9.

114. Michael Kazin, *The Populist Persuasion: An American History* (New York: Basic Books, 1995), 80.

115. Daniel Bell, ed., *The New American Right* (New York: Criterion Books, 1955); Mark Noll, *The Scandal of the Evangelical Mind* (Grand Rapids, Mich.: Eerdmans, 1994).

116. Christian Smith, ed., *The Secular Revolution* (Berkeley: University of California Press, 2003), especially chaps. 1, 3, and 8.

117. See her debate with Judge Charles R. Grant, "Religious Teaching and the Moral Life," *The Arena,* June 1897, 17:91.

118. John Dewey, "Christianity and Democracy," in *The Early Works of John Dewey,* vol. 4 (Carbondale: Southern Illinois University Press, 1969), 8. The idea of teacher as prophet is discussed in Dewey's *My Pedagogic Creed* (1897) and analyzed in E. Rosenow, "The Teacher as Prophet of the True God: Dewey's Religious Faith and Its Problems," *Journal of Philosophy of Education,* 31:3 (1997), 427–437.

119. Walt Whitman, "Song of the Open Road."

120. Given the well-developed Church teachings on natural law, Catholic leaders were far more aware and articulate than Protestants in criticizing what was happening. As Georgetown University's Stephan McNamee pointed out, "The utter irony of the situation is that the American philosopher [Dewey] who most radically applied the ax to

the principles upon which this democratic government, as we know it in the United States, is erected, is openly hailed as *the* philosopher of democracy!" Quoted in McGreevy, *Catholicism and American Freedom*, 193.

121. Leigh Eric Schmidt, *Restless Souls: The Making of American Spirituality* (San Francisco: Harper, 2005).

122. R. Laurence Moore, "Secularization: Religion and the Social Sciences," in William R. Hutchison, ed., *Between the Times: The Travail of the Protestant Establishment, 1900–1960* (New York: Cambridge University Press, 1989); Christian Smith, "Secularizing American Higher Education," in Smith, ed., *The Secular Revolution*. More generally on this point, see George M. Marsden, *The Soul of the American University* (New York: Oxford University Press, 1994); and Julie Reuben, *The Making of the Modern University: Intellectual Transformation and Marginalization of Morality* (Chicago: University of Chicago Press, 1996).

123. Patrick J. Deneen, *Democratic Faith* (Princeton: Princeton University Press, 2005).

124. Noonan, *Religious Freedom*, xi.

125. Steven D. Smith, *Foreordained Failure: The Quest for a Constitutional Principle of Religious Freedom* (New York: Oxford University Press, 1995). A fuller account of the relevant cases, which supports Smith's point, is John Witte, Jr., *Religion and the American Constitutional Experiment; Essential Rights and Liberties* (Boulder: Westview Press, 2000). That the "separation of church and state" is a twentieth-century innovation in jurisprudence rather than a principle historically founded in the First Amendment is powerfully argued in Philip Hamburger, *Separation of Church and State* (Cambridge, Mass.: Harvard University Press, 2002). The history of our modern conflicts over "legal secularism" is surveyed in Noah Feldman, *Divided by God: America's Church-State Problem, and What We Should Do about It* (Gordonsville, Va.: Farrar Straus Giroux, 2005).

126. Richard John Neuhaus, *The Naked Public Square* (Grand Rapids, Mich.: Eerdmans, 1984). See also Stephen L. Carter, *The Culture of Disbelief* (New York: Basic Books, 1993).

127. *Lynch v. Donnelly,* 465 U.S. 668. Docket Number: 82-1256 (1984).

128. While no single study tells the whole story, one can see the pieces beginning to fit together in Stuart Ewen, *Captains of Consciousness: Advertising and the Social Roots of the Consumer Culture* (New

York: McGraw-Hill, 1976); Warren Susman, *Culture as History* (New York: Pantheon, 1984); Daniel Horowitz, *The Morality of Spending* (Baltimore: Johns Hopkins University Press, 1985); William Leach, *Land of Desire* (New York: Pantheon, 1993); Jackson Lears, *Fables of Abundance* (New York: Basic Books, 1994); Roland Marchand, *Creating the Corporate Soul: The Rise of Public Relations and Corporate Imagery in American Big Business* (Berkeley: University of California Press, 1998). On the cultural messages of marketing to youth, see Juliet B. Schor, *Born to Buy: The Commercialized Child and the New Consumer Culture* (New York: Scribner, 2004).

129. Gary Cross, *An All-Consuming Century: Why Commercialism Won in Modern America* (New York: Columbia University Press, 2000), 132, 127.

130. Alan Brinkley, *The End of Liberalism: New Deal Liberalism in Recession and War* (New York: Knopf, 1995); Robert M. Collins, *More: The Politics of Economic Growth in Postwar America* (Oxford: Oxford University Press, 2000); Elizabeth Fones-Wolf, *Selling Free Enterprise: The Business Assault on Labor and Liberalism, 1945–1960* (Urbana: University of Illinois Press, 1994); Lizabeth Cohen, *A Consumers' Republic: The Politics of Mass Consumption in Postwar America* (New York: Knopf, 2003).

131. Norman Ornstein and Thomas Mann, eds., *The Permanent Campaign and Its Future* (Washington, D.C.: American Enterprise Institute and Brookings Institution, 2000).

132. For a detailed account of this resistance, and its failure, see Cross, *An All-Consuming Century,* 112–143.

133. Nathan Miller, *New World Coming: The 1920s and the Making of Modern America* (New York: Scribner, 2003).

134. A survey of the critics is in Daniel Horowitz, *The Anxieties of Affluence: Critiques of American Consumer Culture, 1939–1979* (Amherst: University of Massachusetts Press, 2004).

135. Quoted in Kazin, *The Populist Persuasion,* 174.

136. Ronald Berman, ed., *Solzhenitsyn at Harvard* (Washington, D.C.: Ethics and Public Policy Center, 1980), 69–71. See also Joseph Pearce, *A Soul in Exile* (Grand Rapids, Mich.: Baker Books, 2001).

137. The Supreme Court famously described this idea in the 1992 case *Planned Parenthood v. Casey:* "At the heart of liberty is the right to define one's own concept of existence, of meaning, of the universe,

and of the mystery of human life." 505 U.S. 833 (1992). Docket Number: 91-744.

138. For a contrary view that such figures were debasing a previous secular purity in the American public arena, see Susan Jacoby, *Freethinkers: A History of American Secularism* (New York: Metropolitan Books, 2004).

139. David L. Chappell, *A Stone of Hope: Prophetic Religion and the Death of Jim Crow* (Chapel Hill: University of North Carolina Press, 2004).

140. In focusing on the movement as such, one is necessarily leaving aside the initiatives begun decades earlier with the Legal Defense Fund and other activities among NAACP elites.

141. An early account along these lines is in John Herber, *The Lost Priority: Whatever Happened to the Civil Rights Movement in America?* (New York: Funk and Wagnall, 1970). This history is carefully reviewed in Taylor Branch, *At Canaan's Edge: America in the King Years, 1965–68* (New York: Simon and Schuster, 2006).

142. Maurice Isserman and Michael Kazin, *America Divided: The Civil War in the 1960s* (New York: Oxford University Press, 2000), 300.

143. Anthony King, ed., *The New American Political System* (Washington, D.C.: American Enterprise Institute, 1978); Richard A. Harris and Sidney M. Milkis, eds., *Remaking American Politics* (Boulder: Westview Press, 1989); Morris P. Fiorina, *Culture War? The Myth of a Polarized America*, 2nd ed. (New York: Pearson Longman, 2006), 187–198.

144. Hugh Heclo, "Sixties Civics," in Sidney M. Milkis and Jerome M. Mileur, *The Great Society and the High Tide of Liberalism* (Boston: University of Massachusetts Press, 2005).

145. Sydney E. Ahlstrom, *A Religious History of the American People* (New Haven: Yale University Press, 1972), 1085. On this theme, see also pp. 2, 1078, 1094.

146. The full quotation is worth repeating: "At the close of the sixth decade of the twentieth century, commentators on the American scene seem to be of two minds in regard to the status and significance of religion in our culture. On the one side there are those of the intellectual avant-garde who insist that 'God is dead,' and that Western culture has entered into a 'post-Christian era.' On the other side are those who call attention to 'the surge of piety in America,' with its accompanying increase in religiosity (if not of authentic religious faith).

... In short, sophisticates seem to have given up on God altogether, while the naïve masses simply 'infinitize' their personal and social values and call the nebulous aggregate 'God.'" Smith and Jamison, *The Shaping of American Religion*, 5.

147. McLoughlin, *Revivals, Awakenings, and Reform*, xv and 179.

148. Isserman and Kazin, *America Divided*, 241.

149. Machen, *Christianity and Liberalism*, 6.

150. These "mainline" denominations (following the term for the upscale Philadelphia suburbs connected by the city's mainline commuter train) have customarily included the Presbyterian Church (USA), Episcopalians, Congregationalists (now the United Church of Christ), Methodists, Disciples of Christ, United Lutherans, Reformed Church in America, and American Baptist Churches (but not the Southern Baptist Convention). For a general account of the associated social structures, see E. Digby Baltzell, *The Protestant Establishment: Aristocracy and Caste in America* (New York: Random House, 1964). My discussion of the more political aspects of the Protestant establishment in the period leading up to the Sixties is indebted to the various excellent chapters in Hutchison, *Between the Times*.

151. While accepting historical and scientific critiques of the Bible (and thus rejecting its inerrancy), neo-Orthodox leaders in the Protestant establishment such as Reinhold Niebuhr reasserted traditional Christian doctrines concerning man's inherent sinfulness and God's saving revelation of Himself to man through the Christ of the Bible.

152. Charged with radicalism, President Roosevelt quipped that his program was "as radical as the Federal Council of Churches." Quoted in Robert A. Schneider, "Voice of Many Waters: Church Federation in the Twentieth Century," in Hutchison, *Between the Times*, 110.

153. This did not prevent some more liberal internationalists among Protestant leaders from being investigated as Communist "fellow-travelers" by the House Un-American Activities Committee in the early 1950s. On the whole, it seems fair to say that Cold War liberal elites were mainly impressed and influenced by Niebuhr's political acumen and realism but had little or no interest in his Christianity. Ronald H. Stone, *Reinhold Niebuhr: Prophet to Politicians* (Washington, D.C.: University Press of America, 1981). A useful recent survey of the rise and fall of Cold War liberalism is contained in Peter Beinart's *The Good Fight* (New York: HarperCollins, 2006).

154. Scholars from a wide variety of perspectives offer overlapping ac-

counts of the Sixties as a watershed in the disestablishment of mainline Protestantism. See Robert Wuthnow, *The Restructuring of American Religion: Society and Faith Since World War II* (Princeton: Princeton University Press, 1988); Jackson W. Carroll and Wade Clark Roof, *Beyond Establishment: Protestant Identity in a Post-Protestant Age* (Louisville: Westminster, 1993); Donald E. Miller, *Reinventing American Protestantism* (Berkeley: University of California Press, 1997); and Lyle E. Schaller, *Discontinuity and Hope: Radical Change and the Path to the Future* (Nashville: Abingdon, 1999).

155. Harvey Cox, *The Secular City* (New York: Macmillan, revised edition, 1966), 126. For a sense of this theological and pastoral fervor among self-styled "Christian atheists," see Thomas J. J. Altizer and William Hamilton, *Radical Theology and the Death of God* (New York: Bobbs-Merrill, 1966); and David L. Edwards, ed., *The Honest to God Debate* (Philadelphia: Westminster Press, 1963).

156. On the latter two points, see Marion S. Goldman, "Continuity in Collapse: Departures from Shiloh," *Journal for the Scientific Study of Religion,* 34:3 (1995), 342–353; and Matthew J. Price, "After the Revolution: A Review of Mainline Protestant Clergy Leadership Literature Since the 1960s," *Theology Today,* 59:3 (2002), 428–450.

157. Schematically, this could be seen as the third Protestant disestablishment in American history, the first being the displacement of the learned Protestant clergy by more populist evangelical churches after 1790 and the second being the modernist/fundamentalist fracture after 1920. See Wade Clark Roof, "The Third Disestablishment and Beyond," in Dorothy C. Bass et al., eds., *Mainstream Protestantism in the Twentieth Century: Its Problems and Prospects* (Philadelphia: Presbyterian Church, USA, 1986), 27–37; and more generally Robert T. Handy, *A Christian America: Protestant Hopes and Historical Realities* (New York: Oxford University Press, 1971).

158. Henry P. Van Dusen, "The Third Force's Lesson for Others," *Life,* June 9, 1958, 122–123. On missions, see Grant Wacker, "The Protestant Awakening to World Religions," in Hutchison, *Between the Times,* 267.

159. For an early account sympathetic to the mainline cause, see Dean M. Kelley, *Why Conservative Churches Are Growing: A Study in Sociology of Religion* (New York: Harper and Row, 1972). Largely supportive follow-up studies are by Steve Bruce, *A House Divided: Protestantism, Schism, and Secularization* (London: Routledge, 1990);

Roger Finke and Rodney Stark, *The Churching of America, 1776–1990: Winners and Losers in Our Religious Economy* (New Brunswick, N.J.: Rutgers University Press, 1992); and Donald E. Miller, *Reinventing American Protestantism: Christianity in the New Millennium* (Berkeley: University of California Press, 1997). Regarding birth rates, marital happiness, and family relations, see Greeley and Hout, *The Truth about Conservative Christians*, 105–111, 142, 159–161; and W. Bradford Wilcox, *Soft Patriarchs, New Men: How Christianity Shapes Fathers and Husbands* (Chicago: University of Chicago Press, 2004).

160. William A. King, "The Reform Establishment and the Ambiguities of Influence," in Hutchison, *Between the Times*, 137.

161. Joel A. Carpenter, "From Fundamentalism to the New Evangelical Coalition," in George Marsden, ed., *Evangelicalism and Modern America* (Grand Rapids, Mich.: Eerdmans, 1984). The rapidly growing major evangelical denominations have been Assemblies of God, Church of the Nazarene, Church of God in Christ, and the Southern Baptist Convention. A cogent discussion of doubts as to whether anything was gained after the 1940s in putting a fresh face on fundamentalism by adopting the term "evangelicalism" is in D. G. Hart, *Deconstructing Evangelicalism: Conservative Protestantism in the Age of Billy Graham* (Grand Rapids, Mich.: Baker Academic, 2004). In contrast to the NEA, the American Council of Christian Churches, created by the fire-breathing, super-fundamentalist, and occasionally paranoid anti-communist Carl McIntire, never approached mainstream Protestant status.

162. Carl F. H. Henry, *The Uneasy Conscience of Modern Fundamentalism* (Grand Rapids, Mich.: Eerdmans, 1947). For an early appreciation of Billy Graham in light of the cultural movements of the time, see William G. McLoughlin, *Billy Graham: Revivalist in a Secular Age* (New York: Ronald Press, 1960). A fuller retrospective assessment is William Martin's *A Prophet with Honor: The Billy Graham Story* (New York: William Morrow, 1991).

163. To his credit, Billy Graham insisted on racially integrated audiences. Many of the charges and counter-charges regarding social irresponsibility were conducted through mutual bombardments between the mainline journal *Christian Century* and the evangelicals' *Christianity Today*. For a general account see Mark Silk, *Spiritual Politics: Religion and America Since World War II* (New York: Simon and

Schuster, 1988). A thoughtful analysis of the polite dispute between Graham and Reinhold Niebuhr is offered in Andrew S. Finstuen, "The Prophet and the Evangelist," *Books & Culture,* 12:4 (2006).

164. While Kennedy's candidacy clearly aroused mutual distrust between evangelical Protestants and Roman Catholics, the hostility should not be exaggerated. In contrast to the ferocious anti-Catholicism of the nineteenth century, the conflict in mid-twentieth-century America was more like two butterflies fighting. Neither had the stinger or the venom to do the job.

165. Patrick Allitt, *Catholic Intellectuals and Conservative Politics in America, 1950–1985* (Ithaca: Cornell University Press, 1993).

166. See McGreevy, *Catholicism and American Freedom,* chaps. 8 and 9.

167. In 1971 the federal district court in the District of Columbia ruled in *Green v. Connally* (330 F.Supp. 1150) that, by definition, any organization practicing racial discrimination could not be considered a charitable institution and thus could not qualify for tax-exempt status. An account of the importance of this issue in 1970s political mobilization of evangelicals is contained in Randall Balmer, *Thy Kingdom Come: How the Religious Right Distorts the Faith and Threatens America* (New York: Basic Books, 2006). For a more general discussion of the evangelicals' turn to political action, see Michael Cromartie, ed., *A Public Faith: Evangelicals and Civic Engagement* (Lanham, Md.: Rowman and Littlefield, 2003).

168. Well-balanced historical accounts can be found in William Martin, *With God on Our Side: The Rise of the Religious Right in America* (New York: Broadway Books, 1996), and the second edition of George Marsden's *Fundamentalism and American Culture* (New York: Oxford University Press, 2005).

169. Garry Wills, *Under God: Religion and American Politics* (New York: Simon and Schuster, 1990), 320. Assessments of Schaeffer's career are in Dennis T. Lane, ed., *Francis A. Schaeffer: Portraits of the Man and His Work* (Westchester, Ill.: Crossway, 1986). A critique of his confused theological positions is in Gary North, *Political Polytheism: The Myth of Pluralism* (Tyler, Texas: Institution for Christian Economics, 1989), chap. 4.

170. Among the titles appearing between 1968 and 1975 were *Escape from Reason; The God Who Is There; Pollution and the Death of Man; Genesis in Space and Time; Art and the Bible; Two Contents, Two Realities.* These and other works mentioned in the text can be

found in the five volumes of Francis A. Schaeffer, *The Complete Works of Francis A. Schaeffer* (Westchester, Ill.: Good News/Crossway, 1985).

171. The most important works in this later period were *How Then Should We Live? The Rise and Decline of Western Thought and Culture* (1976); (with C. Everett Koop), *Whatever Happened to the Human Race?* (1979); and *A Christian Manifesto* (1981). In the last book before his death in 1985, Schaeffer returned to his 1930s separatist roots, warning about believers' accommodation to the world: *The Great Evangelical Disaster* (Westchester, Ill.: Crossway, 1984).

172. Robert Wuthnow, *The Struggle for America's Soul* (Grand Rapids, Mich.: Eerdmans, 1989), chap. 2.

173. See Damon Linker, *The Theocons: Secular America under Siege* (New York: Doubleday, 2006).

174. Geoffrey Layman, *The Great Divide* (New York: Columbia University Press, 2001); Louis Bolce and Gerald De Maio, "Our Secularist Democratic Party," *The Public Interest,* 149 (2002), 3–30.

175. George H. Nash, *The Conservative Intellectual Movement in America Since 1945* (New York: Basic Books, 1976). On Kirk in particular, see W. Wesley McDonald, *Russell Kirk and the Age of Ideology* (Columbia, Mo.: University of Missouri Press, 2004). Russell Kirk's Catholic leanings eventuated in his baptism and reception into the Church at the time of his 1964 marriage. His development as a Christian and a Catholic is traced in Eric Scheske, "The Conservative Convert: The Life and Faith of Russell Kirk," *Touchstone,* June 2003, 41–48. Whittaker Chambers's account of his painful religious journey, from Communism to Quakerism, also had a Catholic "sensibility" that was strikingly influential in the nascent conservative movement of the early 1950s. See Whittaker Chambers, *Witness* (New York: Random House, 1952), 481–485.

176. Russell Kirk, *The Conservative Mind: From Burke to Santayana* (Chicago: Henry Regnery, 1953), 7–8.

177. Pieces by Bush and Reagan reacting to Goldwater's landslide defeat appeared in *The National Review,* December 1, 1964, 1053–1055.

178. The conflict between religious and political conservatism is discussed in D. G. Hart, "Conservatism, the Protestant Right, and the Failure of Religious History," *Journal of the Historical Society,* 4:4 (2004), 447–493; and Andrew Sullivan, *The Conservative Soul: How We Lost It, How to Get It Back* (New York: HarperCollins, 2006).

179. Kirk, *The Conservative Mind*, 7.

180. The question of how conservative, and what kind of conservative, Ronald Reagan was has now become a contested issue of historical inquiry. Assessments from a variety of perspectives are contained in W. Elliot Brownlee and Hugh Davis Graham, eds., *The Reagan Presidency* (Lawrence: University Press of Kansas, 2003).

181. As President Reagan put it in concluding his 1989 Farewell Address from the Oval Office, "Younger parents aren't sure that an unambivalent appreciation of America is the right thing to teach modern children. And for those who create the popular culture, well-grounded patriotism is no longer the style. Our spirit is back, but we haven't reinstitutionalized it. . . . If we forget what we did, we won't know who we are. I'm warning of an eradication of the American memory that could result, ultimately, in an erosion of the American spirit. . . . And children, if your parents haven't been teaching you what it means to be an American, let 'em know and nail 'em on it. That would be a very American thing to do." I discuss the speech and Reagan's political ideas in "Ronald Reagan and the American Public Philosophy," in Brownlee and Graham, eds., *The Reagan Presidency*, 17–39.

182. Kevin Phillips, *American Theocracy: The Peril and Politics of Radical Religion, Oil, and Borrowed Money in the 21st Century* (New York: Viking, 2006), vi, xiii.

183. Fiorina, *Culture War?* 26, 55.

184. Wayne Baker, *America's Crisis of Values* (Princeton: Princeton University Press, 2003), 104. For a general discussion of the different value systems informing liberal and conservative political attitudes, see George Lakoff, *Moral Politics: How Liberals and Conservatives Think* (Chicago: University of Chicago Press, 2002).

185. John Evans, "Have Americans' Attitudes Become More Polarized?—An Update," *Social Science Quarterly*, 84 (2003), 71–90. On abortion, see Ted Mouw and Michael Soel, "Culture Wars and Opinion Polarizations," *American Journal of Sociology*, 106 (2001), 913–943.

186. Fiorina, *Culture Wars?* 83–87 and 118ff.

187. Ibid., 77.

188. These and other reality checks on exaggerated claims about the religious right's impact on election outcomes are contained in Greeley and Hout, *The Truth about Conservative Christians*, chap. 3, and

E. J. Dionne Jr., David Brady, and Pietro Nivola, eds., *Red and Blue Nation: Characteristics and Causes of America's Polarized Politics* (Washington: Brookings, 2007).

189. Ibid., 130–132; 179–181. This considers only whites since African-American citizens, regardless of religious attachments, continue to vote overwhelmingly Democratic.

190. Approximately a quarter of Americans are college graduates. This and related issues are discussed in James Q. Wilson, "How Divided Are We?" *Commentary*, February 2006, 15–22.

191. Sydney Ahlstrom, "Theology in America," in Smith and Jamison, *The Shaping of American Religion*, 317.

192. On those respective points, see Nancy Bermeo, *Ordinary People in Extraordinary Times: The Citizenry and the Breakdown of Democracy* (Princeton: Princeton University Press, 2003); Ernest Gellner, *Nations and Nationalism* (Ithaca: Cornell University Press, 1983); Benedict Anderson, *Imagined Communities* (London: Verso Editions and NLB, 1983).

193. Margaret Somerville, *The Ethical Canary: Science, Society, and the Human Spirit* (New York: Viking, 2000). Informative if rather breathless surveys are contained in Francis Fukuyama, *Our Posthuman Future: Consequences of the Biotechnology Revolution* (Gordonsville, Va.: Farrar, Straus and Giroux, 2002); Gregory Stock, *Redesigning Humans: Our Inevitable Genetic Future* (New York: Houghton Mifflin, 2002); and Joel Garreau, *Radical Evolution* (New York: Doubleday, 2005).

194. John H. Evans, *Playing God? Human Genetic Engineering and the Rationalization of Public Bioethical Debate* (Chicago: University of Chicago Press, 2002).

195. Debora L. Spar, *The Baby Business: How Money, Science, and Politics Drive the Commerce of Conception* (Cambridge, Mass.: Harvard Business School, 2005); Susannah Baruch, David Kaufman, and Kathy L. Hudson, *Genetic Testing of Embryos: Practices and Perspectives of U.S. IVF Clinics* (Washington, D.C.: Genetics and Public Policy Center, 2006), *www.dnapolicy.org* (accessed 10/5/06). Since the survey of 415 clinics produced only a 45 percent response rate (190 clinics), the figures cited for designer babies are probably underestimates.

196. Steve Bruce, *Politics and Religion* (Oxford: Polity Press, 2003).

197. For an insightful discussion of this argument, repeated before and af-

ter the 1960s in many quarters, see Bryan Wilson, *Religion in Secular Society: A Sociological Comment* (London: C. A. Watts, 1966).

198. See the comments of Nancy Rosenblum in Ceaser, *Nature and History*, 130–134.

199. In his first published work, Rawls used the Catholic Inquisition as an example of what, ten years later, he would call the failure to conduct public debate by means of public reason accessible to all. John Rawls, "Outline of a Decision Procedure for Ethics" (1951) and "Constitutional Liberty and the Concept of Justice" (1963), both in Rawls, *Collected Papers*, ed. Samuel Freeman (Cambridge, Mass.: Harvard University Press, 1999). On the legal orthodoxy, see Rawls's Harvard colleague Lawrence H. Tribe, "The Supreme Court 1972 Term," *Harvard Law Review*, 87 (1973). Barack Obama, "The Connection Between Faith and Politics," June 28, 2006. *Www.realclearpolitics.com* (accessed 7/7/06).

200. See Damon Linker, *The Theocons: Secular America under Siege* (New York: Doubleday, 2006); and Phillips, *American Theocracy*. Examples of the recent more hysterical fears can be found in Michelle Goldberg, *Kingdom Coming: The Rise of Christian Nationalism* (New York: W. W. Norton, 2006); Laurenn Sandler, *Righteous: Dispatches from the Evangelical Youth Movement* (New York: Viking, 2006); James Rudin, *The Baptizing of America: The Religious Right's Plans for the Rest of Us* (New York: Thunder's Mouth, 2006).

201. Many references to such derangement are in Thomas Frank's bestseller, *What's the Matter with Kansas? How Conservatives Won the Heart of America* (New York: Henry Holt, 2004). The irrationality of all traditional religions and the threat posed by moderates tolerating Bible-believing Christians is argued in Sam Harris, *The End of Faith: Religion, Terror, and the Future of Reason* (New York: W. W. Norton, 2004), with a reply to his Christian critics in *Letter to a Christian Nation* (New York: Knopf, 2007). The estimate of white voters' dislike of traditionalist Christians is in Bolce and De Maio, "Our Secularist Democratic Party," 13.

202. Fortunately, the "liberal" philosophical and legal orthodoxy on this subject is breaking down. See Christopher J. Eberle, *Religious Conviction in Liberal Politics* (Cambridge: Cambridge University Press, 2002), and the splendid collection of essays in the *Wake Forest Law Review*, 36:2 (2001).

203. Hugh Heclo, "Campaigning and Governing: A Conspectus," in Ornstein and Mann, *The Permanent Campaign*, 1–37; and "The Corruption of Democratic Leadership," in Robert Faulkner et al., eds., *American Democracy: The Great Dangers and What Can Be Done* (Ann Arbor: University of Michigan Press, 2007).

204. Michael McConnell quoted in Jean Bethke Elshtain, "A Response to Chief Justice McLachlin," in Douglas Farow, ed., *Recognizing Religion in a Secular Society* (Montreal: McGill Queen's University Press, 2004), 37.

205. Glenn Tinder, *The Political Meaning of Christianity* (Baton Rouge: Louisiana State University Press, 1989), 8. Thus relying heavily on biblical arguments, former President Jimmy Carter criticizes Christian fundamentalists, not least those leading the Southern Baptist Convention (from which he resigned in protest), for giving political encouragement to foreign policy unilateralism, neglect of human rights, economic inequality, and environmental degradation. Jimmy Carter, *Our Endangered Values: America's Moral Crisis* (New York: Simon and Schuster, 2005).

206. Unfortunately, every use of the term "fundamentalist" now sweeps up into one category all adherents to Christian, Jewish, and Muslim religions who adopt "a militant form of piety." Such militant piety among Christians would presumably include Martin Luther King Jr., John Paul II, Dietrich Bonhoeffer, Dorothy Day, and a host of other inspiring individuals. The option of subversion is more rightly called "post-fundamentalism," for it abandons the compassionate ethic of all world religions in favor of its own apocalyptic vision. Karen Armstrong, *The Battle for God* (New York: Random House, 2001).

207. On the recognition of this danger from two former leaders of the Moral Majority, see Cal Thomas and Ed Dobson, *Blinded by Might: Can the Religious Right Save America?* (Grand Rapids, Mich.: Zondervan, 1999). Along these same lines, Francis Schaeffer's son Franky, who produced his father's films, went on to renounce social activism, abandon Protestantism, and join the Eastern Orthodox Church. Since the mid-1990s, valuable examples of this worry from a more or less traditional Christian perspective are Michael S. Horton, *Beyond Culture Wars* (Chicago: Moody Press, 1994); James Montgomery Boice, *Two Cities, Two Loves: Christian Responsibility in a Crumbling Culture* (Downers Grove, Ill.: InterVarsity Press, 1996); and David Kuo, *Tempting Faith* (New York: Free Press, 2006).

208. John Persinos, "Has the Christian Right Taken Over the Republican Party?" *Campaigns and Elections,* September 1994, 21–24. *www. findarticles.com* (accessed 6/18/06).

209. Jeffrey Stout, *Democracy and Tradition* (Princeton: Princeton University Press, 2003).

210. William M. Shea, *The Lion and the Lamb: Evangelicals and Catholics in America* (Oxford: Oxford University Press, 2004), 283–294.

211. John Courtney Murray, *We Hold These Truths* (New York: Sheed and Ward, 1960), 10.

212. The signature work is Richard John Neuhaus, *The Naked Public Square: Religion and Democracy in America* (Grand Rapids, Mich.: Eerdmans, 1984). Neuhaus begins by observing, "Our quarrel with politicized fundamentalism is not that it has broken the rules of the game by 'going public' with Christian truth claims. Christian truth, if it is true, is public truth. It is accessible to pubic reason. . . . Our quarrel is primarily theological." He later raises the familiar democratic proceduralist objection: "The religious new right . . . *wants to enter the political arena making public claims on the basis of private truths. The integrity of politics itself requires that such a proposal be resisted. Public decisions must be made by arguments that are public in character. A public argument is transsubjective. It is not derived from sources of revelation or dispositions that are essentially private and arbitrary. . . . Fundamentalist morality, which is derived from beliefs that cannot be submitted to examination by public reason, is essentially a private morality. If enough people who share that morality are mobilized, it can score victories in the public arena. But every such victory is a setback in the search for a public ethic"* (19, 36–37; italics in the original).

213. See the symposium discussion on the twentieth anniversary of the publication of Richard John Neuhaus's *The Naked Public Square.* "The Naked Public Square Now," *First Things,* November 2004, 11–26. A more hopeful view of the potential role of natural law in contemporary America is carefully argued in Russell Hittinger, *The First Grace: Rediscovering the Natural Law in a Post-Christian World* (Wilmington, Del.: ISI Books, 2003).

214. Isserman and Kazin, *America Divided,* 241.

215. *First Things,* February 2004, 67.

216. Thomas B. Harbottle, ed., *Dictionary of Quotations (Classical)* (New York: Frederick Ungar, 1958), 308. For a more recent discus-

sion of this theme, see John Howard Yoder, *The Priestly Kingdom: Social Ethics as Gospel* (Notre Dame, Ind.: University of Notre Dame Press, 1984).

217. Trying to get an accurate reading of such points is obviously a murky business that should be approached carefully. The figures in the text are from George Barna, "Practical Outcomes Replace Biblical Principles as the Moral Standard," *Barna Research Online,* September 10, 2001, *www.barna.org* (accessed 6/8/04). The general thematics from Barna's opinion polling can be found in research report titles such as "Americans Are Most Likely to Base Truth on Feelings" (February 12, 2002); "Only Half of Protestant Pastors Have a Biblical Worldview" (January 12, 2004); "Most Americans Feel Accepted by God, But Lack a Biblical Worldview" (August 9, 2005); "The Concept of Holiness Baffles Most Americans" (February 20, 2006).

218. Alan Wolfe, *The Transformation of American Religion: How Americans Live Their Faith* (New York: Free Press, 2003).

219. George Barna and Mark Hatch, *Boiling Point* (Ventura, Calif.: Regal Books, 2001), 190–193; Luke Timothy Johnson, *The Creed: What Christians Believe and Why It Matters* (New York: Doubleday, 2003).

220. A hearty little tussle has developed in the social science literature in the attempt to pin down the extent of "over-reporting" in Americans' self-reported churchliness. Studies have shown a gap between opinion-poll-based and actual-count-based measures of attendance of over 80 percent. The over-reporting appears to be greatest among committed believers and active church members. See Andrew Walsh, "Church, Lies, and Polling Data," *Religion in the New,* 1:2 (1998), 1–8. A particularly careful case study of one well-established suburban evangelical church in the deep South showed a 59 percent rate of attendance over-reporting *by church members.* If one assumed that by "attending church" in the last week respondents meant attending the worship service, the over-reporting/lying rate was 83 percent. The rate of over-reporting for Sunday School attendance was 57 percent. Penny Long Marier and C. Kirk Hadaway, "Testing the Attendance Gap in a Conservative Church," *Sociology of Religion,* 60:2 (1999), 175–187.

221. Michael Horton quoted in a general review of the evidence: Ronald J. Sider, "The Scandal of the Evangelical Conscience," *Books and Culture,* January/February 2005, 8–9 and 39.

222. Donald Critchlow, *Intended Consequences: Birth Control, Abortion, and the Federal Government in Modern America* (New York: Oxford University Press, 1999), 132; Boice, *Two Cities, Two Loves*, 28.

223. Fiorina, *Culture Wars?* 81, 161–164.

224. Genetics and Public Policy Center, *Reproductive Genetic Testing: What America Thinks*, 2005. *www.dnapolicy.org* (accessed 9/22/06).

225. These and similar findings are in Christian Smith, *Christian America? What Evangelicals Really Want* (Berkeley: University of California Press, 2000), and Greeley and Hout, *The Truth about Conservative Christians*, 90.

226. In the 1970s, the government and various home-school groups estimated the home-school population to be between 10,000 and 20,000 students. The latest federal survey puts the number of students being home-schooled as of spring 2003 at approximately 1.1 million, or 2.2 percent of the student population in grades K–12. This represents a 10 percent annual growth rate, given the estimated 850,000 students (1.7 percent of the population) being home-schooled in the spring of 1999. In terms of the most important reason for home-schooling, 31 percent of the students had parents who cited concern about the environment of other schools (such as safety, drugs, or negative peer pressure), and 30 percent had parents who said the most important reason was to provide religious or moral instruction. Another 16 percent of students had parents who said dissatisfaction with the academic instruction available at other schools was their most important reason for home-schooling. National Center for Education Statistics, *Homeschooling in the United States: 2003, Statistical Analysis Report* (Washington, D.C.: NCES, February 2006).

227. See Colleen Carroll, *The New Faithful: Why Young Adults Are Embracing Christian Orthodoxy* (Chicago: Loyola Press, 2002); and Robert E. Webber, *The Younger Evangelicals: Facing the Challenges of the New World* (Grand Rapids, Mich.: Baker Book House, 2002). The substantial divide in religious outlooks of the coming generation can be gauged by comparing two recent books: Naomi Schaefer Riley, *God on the Quad: How Religious Colleges and the Missionary Generation are Changing America* (New York: St. Martin's, 2005); and Christian Smith, *Soul Searching: The Religious and Spiritual Lives of American Teenagers* (New York: Oxford University Press, 2005).

228. Stanley Hauerwas, *A Community of Character: Toward a Construc-*

tive Christian Social Ethic (Notre Dame: University of Notre Dame Press, 1986). A different separatist view emphasizes hierarchy of authority rather than democracy and human rights as a core Christian political teaching. Robert P. Kraynak, *Christian Faith and Modern Democracy* (Notre Dame: University of Notre Dame Press, 2001). On "chastened patriots," see Darrell Cole, *When God Says War Is Right: The Christian's Perspective on When and How to Fight* (Des Plaines, Ill.: WaterBrook Press, 2002). John Lukacs, *Confessions of an Original Sinner* (New York: Ticknor and Fields, 1990).

229. Jean Bethke Elshtain, *Democracy on Trial* (New York: Basic Books, 1995), xv.

230. R. R. Reno, *In the Ruins of the Church: Sustaining Faith in an Age of Diminished Christianity* (New York: Brazos, 2002). The Christian case for getting Christianity out of politics is forcefully presented in Darryl Hart, *A Secular Faith: Why Christianity Favors the Separation of Church and State* (Chicago: Ivan R. Dee, 2006).

231. Clifford Geertz, "A Life of Learning," The Charles Homer Haskins Lecture for 1999, Occasional Paper no. 45, American Council of Learned Societies. *www.acls.com* (accessed 7/7/06).

232. In May 2006 when 820 self-identified Christians were asked whether they thought of themselves first as American or as Christian, 42 percent said Christian first and 48 percent said American first (with 7 percent not responding). For those describing themselves as evangelicals, the proportion of "Christian first" rose to 62 percent. By contrast, 62 and 65 percent of Catholics and mainline Protestants respectively chose "American first." See "Christians First, Americans Second," Pew Research Center, *http:pewresearch.org/datatrends* (accessed 10/19/06).

2. DEMOCRACY AND CATHOLIC CHRISTIANITY IN AMERICA

1. See p. 79 of this volume.

2. My source for most data on religious affiliation is *www.adherents.com*.

3. See p. 27 of this volume.

4. My sources for this discussion of American Catholic history during the colonial and republican period include Jay P. Dolan, *In Search of An American Catholicism* (Oxford: Oxford University Press, 2002), chap. 1, 13–46; James T. Fisher, *Communion of Immigrants: A His-*

tory of Catholics in America (Oxford: Oxford University Press, 2002), chaps. 1 and 2, 1–42; Charles R. Morris, *American Catholic* (New York: Random House, 1997), chaps. 1 and 2, 3–53; and David J. O'Brien, *Public Catholicism* (Maryknoll, N.Y.: Orbis Books, 1996), chap. 2, 9–33.

5. Statistics on numbers of Catholics and percentage of the population that is Catholic, here and later, are from Roger Finke and Rodney Stark, *The Churching of America* (New Brunswick, N.J.: Rutgers University Press, 1992), primarily from chaps. 2 and 4.

6. This section relies on Dolan, *In Search,* chaps. 2 and 3, 47–126; Fisher, *Communion of Immigrants,* chaps. 3 and 4, 41–92; Morris, *American Catholic,* chaps. 3–6, 54–164; O'Brien, *Public Catholicism,* chap. 3, 34–61; and John T. McGreevy, *Catholicism and American Freedom: A History* (New York: W. W. Norton, 2003), Introduction through chap. 4, 7–126.

7. Morris, *American Catholic,* 40–47.

8. Richard McBrien, in his comprehensive survey *Catholicism* (San Francisco: HarperSanFrancisco, 1994), describing the nineteenth-century reaction to the Enlightenment, says: "A rigid traditionalism developed in France (going by the names of Integralism and Fideism), distrustful of all rational reflection in theology and excessively dependent on Papal direction (*Ultramontanism,* literally those who look 'beyond the mountains,' the Alps, to Rome)" (p. 644).

9. This discussion relies to some extent on the sources cited in note 4, but mainly relies on and quotes from a masterful study by John Noonan, *A Church That Can and Cannot Change* (Notre Dame: University of Notre Dame Press, 2005), primarily chaps. 21, 22, and 23, 145–158. The encyclical quoted by Noonan is Leo XII, *Mirari Vos.* (Papal encyclicals take their names from their first few words in the Latin original. The meaning here is "You wonder.")

10. Noonan, *Church That Can and Cannot Change,* 149.

11. Morris, *American Catholic,* 54–60.

12. Leo XIII, *Longinqua,* Encyclical on Catholicism in the United States, 1895, paragraphs 1 (on esteem and love) and 6. Available on the Vatican website: *www.vatican.va/holy_father/leo_xiii/encyclicals/documents/hf_l-xiii_enc_06011895_longinqua_en.html.*

13. Pope Leo XIII, *Immortale Dei,* Encyclical on the Christian Constitution of States, 1885, paragraphs 23 and 24, available on the Vatican

website: *www.vatican.va/holy_father/leo_xiii/encyclicals/documents/
hf_l-xiii_enc_01111885_immortale-dei_en.html.*

14. Leo XIII, *Immortale Dei,* paragraph 6.

15. Vatican Council II, Declaration on Religious Liberty (*Dignitatis Humanae*), 1965, paragraph 2. My source for all Vatican Council II documents is Austin Flannery, O.P., ed., *Vatican Council II: The Basic Sixteen Documents* (Northport, N.Y.: Costello, 1996).

16. Vatican Council II, Declaration on Religious Liberty, paragraph 1.

17. This history is thoroughly documented in Noonan, *Church That Can and Cannot Change.*

18. Murray quoted by Xavier Rynne, *Vatican Council II* (Maryknoll, N.Y.: Orbis Books, 1968 and 1996), 460. Xavier Rynne is the pseudonym for the Redemptorist priest Francis X. Murphy, who was present at the Council as an expert adviser and wrote a series of articles for the *New Yorker,* later published as a book, describing in great detail the workings and debates of the Council.

19. Vatican Council II, Pastoral Constitution on the Church in the Modern World (*Gaudium et Spes*), 1965, paragraph 27.

20. Noonan, *Church That Can and Cannot Change,* chaps. 24–27, 161–190.

21. Ibid., 215.

22. A description of the arguments about religious freedom at the Council can be found in Rynne, *Vatican Council II,* 298–303 and 454–456.

23. Joseph Ratzinger, now Pope Benedict XVI, and Marcello Pera, *Without Roots: The West, Relativism, Christianity, Islam* (New York: Basic Books, 2006), 112–113.

24. This discussion relies on Andrew Greeley, *The Catholic Revolution* (Berkeley: University of California Press, 2004). Excellent analyses of the current state of Catholicism in America are provided in Peter Steinfels, *A People Adrift* (New York: Simon and Schuster, 2005), and David Gibson, *The Coming Catholic Church* (San Francisco: HarperSanFrancisco, 2003).

25. Greeley, *Catholic Revolution,* 34–40.

26. Ibid., 41–60.

27. John C. Green, Corwin E. Smith, James L. Guth, and Lyman A. Kellstedt, "The American Religious Landscape and the 2004 Presidential Vote: Increased Polarization," report to the Pew Forum on

Religion and Public Life, 2005, *http://pewforum.org/publications/ surveys/postelection.pdf.*

28. Ibid.

29. Pope Benedict XVI, *Deus Caritas Est* (God is Love), 2005, available through the Vatican website: *www.vatican.va/holy_father/benedict_ xvi/encyclicals/documents/hf_ben-xvi_enc_20051225_deus-caritas- est_en.html.*

30. The most recent exposition of Benedict's thinking on these issues is Joseph Cardinal Ratzinger, *Truth and Tolerance: Christian Belief and World Religions* (San Francisco: Ignatius Press, 2004).

31. Pope Benedict XVI, *Without Roots.*

32. Pope Benedict XVI, *Deus Caritas Est,* paragraph 28.

33. Congregation for the Doctrine of the Faith, "Doctrinal Note on Some Questions regarding the Participation of Catholics in Political Life," 2002, *www.vatican.va/roman_curia/congregations/cfaith/doc- uments/rc_con_cfaith_doc_20021124_politica_en.html.*

3. Pluralism Is Hard Work

1. Richard Hofstadter, *The Progressive Historians* (New York: Knopf, 1968), 463. For an insightful discussion of his arguments, see David S. Brown, *Richard Hofstadter: An Intellectual Biography* (Chicago: University of Chicago Press, 2006), 188–206.

2. William McLoughlin, *Revivals, Awakenings, and Reform* (Chicago: University of Chicago Press, 1980); Nathan O. Hatch, *The Democra- tization of American Christianity* (New Haven: Yale University Press, 1989); Mark Noll, *America's God: From Jonathan Edwards to Abra- ham Lincoln* (New York: Oxford University Press, 2002); Richard Wightman Fox, *Jesus in America* (New York: HarperSanFrancisco, 2004); D. G. Hart, *The Lost Soul of American Protestantism* (Lanham, Md.: Rowman and Littlefield, 2002).

3. Alan Wolfe, "Religious Diversity: The American Experiment That Works," in *Americanism: New Perspectives on the History of an Ideal,* ed. Michael Kazin and Joseph A. McCartin (Chapel Hill: Uni- versity of North Carolina Press, 2006), 159–160.

4. On the utilitarianism of American religion, see Hart, *Lost Soul.*

5. Quoted in Gary Gerstle, *American Crucible: Race and Nation in the Twentieth Century* (Princeton: Princeton University Press, 2001), 53.

6. Jon Butler, *Awash in a Sea of Faith: Christianizing the American People* (Cambridge, Mass.: Harvard University Press, 1990), 197–199.

7. Benjamin Justice, *The War That Wasn't: Religious Conflict and Compromise in the Common Schools of New York State, 1865–1900* (Albany: State University of New York Press, 2005).

8. John T. McGreevy, *Catholicism and American Freedom: A History* (New York: W. W. Norton, 2003), 123.

9. Leonard J. Moore, "Historical Interpretations of the 1920s Klan: The Traditional View and the Populist Revision," in *The Invisible Empire in the West: Toward a New Historical Appraisal of the Ku Klux Klan of the 1920s*, ed. Shawn Lay (Urbana: University of Illinois Press, 1991), 17–38; Michael Kazin, *A Godly Hero: The Life of William Jennings Bryan* (New York: Knopf, 2006), 166–167; *Letters of Eugene V. Debs*, Vol. 1, 1874–1912, ed. J. Robert Constantine (Urbana: University of Illinois Press, 1990), 560.

10. Many Catholic intellectuals were not happy with JFK's position but held their tongues. See McGreevy, *Catholicism and American Freedom*, 213–214. On anti-Catholicism in the mid-century, see ibid., 166–188.

11. See David Hollinger, *Science, Jews, and Secular Culture: Studies in Mid-Twentieth-Century American Intellectual History* (Princeton: Princeton University Press, 1996), and Diana Selig, "Cultural Gifts: American Liberals, Childhood, and the Origins of Multiculturalism, 1924–1945," Ph.D. diss., University of California, Berkeley, 2001.

12. Contrary to conventional wisdom, Eisenhower was a deeply pious man who considered becoming a minister and told a friend, during the 1952 campaign, "The farther I proceed in political life, the more I believe that I should have striven to be worthy of the pulpit as an avenue of public service instead of the political podium." No president since Wilson shared that sentiment, and Ike's much-derided statement may have helped stir the revival of political religiosity that would become commonplace by the 1970s. See Ira Chernus, "Faith and Fear in the Fifties," *www.spot.colorado.edu*.

13. Coffin, undated quote, cited by Edith Guffey, "Celebrate Micah's Call," Address to New England Women's Gathering of the UCC, March 22, 2006, at *www.news.ucc.org*. Also see Warren Goldstein, *William Sloane Coffin, Jr.: A Holy Impatience* (New Haven: Yale University Press, 2004).

14. Michael Lacey and William M. Shea, "Catholics and the Liberal Tradition: Still Compatible," *Commonweal*, October 11, 2003.

15. Quoted in Garry Wills, "Did Tocqueville 'Get' America?" *New York Review of Books*, April 29, 2004. In much of this piece, Wills, in his debunking zeal, misses the brilliance of *Democracy in America*. But that is not the case with the subject of race.

16. Gustave de Beaumont, *Marie, or Slavery in the United States*, trans. Barbara Chapman (Stanford: Stanford University Press, 1958), 5, 33–34.

17. Albert J. Raboteau, *A Fire in the Bones: Reflections on African-American Religious History* (Boston: Beacon Press, 1995), 63. Some American Indians voiced an analogous critique. In 1916, the Santee missionary Charles Eastman wrote about an elderly Indian on the Great Plains who, after attending Bible study for a week, declared, "I have come to the conclusion that this Jesus was an Indian. He was opposed to material acquirement and to great possessions. He was inclined to peace. He was as unpractical as any Indian and set no price upon his labor of love. These are not the principles upon which the white man has founded his civilization. It is strange that he could not rise to these simple principles which were commonly observed among our people." Quoted in *Talking Back to Civilization: Indian Voices from the Progressive Era*, ed. Frederick E. Hoxie (Boston: Bedford/St. Martins, 2001), 76–77.

18. Jim Wallis, *God's Politics: Why the Right Gets It Wrong and the Left Doesn't Get It* (San Francisco: HarperSanFrancisco, 2005), 155–157.

19. Wade Clark Roof, *A Generation of Seekers: The Spiritual Journeys of the Baby Boom Generation* (San Francisco: HarperSanFrancisco, 1993).

20. Peter Steinfels, "Hard and Soft Secularism," *Religion in the News*, 8 (Winter 2006), Supplement, 6, 11–12. For a counter-argument that mirrors Heclo's, see James Q. Wilson, "How Divided Are We?" *Commentary*, February 2006, 15–21.

21. F. Scott Fitzgerald, *The Crack-Up, with other uncollected pieces, note-books and unpublished letters* (New York: New Directions, 1945).

4. Whose Christianity? Whose Democracy?

1. R. Stephen Warner, "The Place of the Contemporary American Religious Congregation," in James P. Wind and James W. Lewis, eds.,

American Congregations, vol. 2, *New Perspectives in the Study of Congregations* (Chicago: University of Chicago Press, 1994).

2. Anatol Lieven, *America Right or Wrong: An Anatomy of American Nationalism* (New York: Oxford University Press, 2004).

3. For more on this debate see James Davison Hunter and Alan Wolfe, *Is There A Culture War? A Dialogue on Values and American Public Life* (Washington, D.C.: Brookings Institution Press, 2007).

4. For more on this point, see Melinda Bollar Wagner, "Generic Conservative Christianity: The Demise of Denominationalism in Christian Schools," *Journal for the Scientific Study of Religion,* 36 (1997), 13–24.

5. Daniel Walker Howe, *The Political Culture of the American Whigs* (Chicago: University of Chicago Press, 1979), 150.

6. Peter Dobkin Hall, "The Rise of the Civic Engagement Tradition," in Mary Jo Bane, Brent Coffin, and Richard Higgins, eds., *Taking Faith Seriously* (Cambridge, Mass.: Harvard University Press, 2005), 57.

7. Nathan Hatch, *The Democratization of American Christianity* (New Haven: Yale University Press, 1989).

8. R. Stephen Warner, *New Wines in Old Wineskins: Evangelicals and Liberals in a Small-Town Church* (Berkeley: University of California Press, 1988).

9. Bernard Henri Lévy, *American Vertigo: Traveling America in the Footsteps of Tocqueville* (New York: Random House, 2006).

10. Alan Wolfe, *The Transformation of American Religion: How We Actually Live Our Faith* (New York: Free Press, 2003).

11. Vincent Crapanzano, *Serving the Word: Literalism in America from the Pulpit to the Bench* (New York: New Press, 2000), 394–395.

12. Stephen Macedo, "Liberal Civic Education and Religious Fundamentalism: The Case of God v. John Rawls?" *Ethics,* 105 (April 1995), 478.

13. Stanley Hauerwas and William Willimon, *Resident Aliens: A Provocative Christian Assessment of Culture and Ministry for People Who Know That Something Is Wrong* (Nashville: Abingdon Press, 1989).

14. Wagner, "Generic Conservative Christianity."

15. See, for example, *First Things* editors, "Introduction," *First Things,* 67 (November 1996), 21–24.

16. Donald E. Miller, *Reinventing American Protestantism: Christianity in the New Millennium* (Berkeley: University of California Press, 1997).

17. See, for example, Grant Wacker, *Heaven Below: Early Pentecostals and American Culture* (Cambridge, Mass.: Harvard University Press, 2001), 28.

18. Rodney Stark, *The Victory of Reason: How Christianity Led to Freedom, Capitalism, and Western Success* (New York: Random House, 2005).

5. RECONSIDERING CHRISTIANITY AND AMERICAN DEMOCRACY

1. Kevin Phillips, *American Theocracy* (New York: Viking, 2006).

2. Jaroslav Pelikan, *The Christian Tradition: A History of the Development of Doctrine* (Chicago: University of Chicago Press, 1984).

3. G. K. Chesterton, *St. Thomas Aquinas: "The Dumb Ox"* (New York: Sheed and Ward, 1954), 13.

4. Jaroslav Pelikan, *Credo: Historical and Theological Guide to Creeds and Confessions of Faith in the Christian Tradition* (New Haven: Yale University Press, 2003), 7 and 377–378.

5. See, for example, C. S. Lewis, *Mere Christianity* (New York: HarperCollins, 2001); N. T. Wright, *Simply Christian: Why Christianity Makes Sense* (San Francisco: HarperSanFrancisco, 2006); Joseph Ratzinger (Pope Benedict XVI), *Introduction to Christianity* (Fort Collins, Colo.: Ignatius Press, 2004).

6. Robert A. Dahl, *On Democracy* (New Haven: Yale University Press, 1998), 93–94, 103–106.

7. Thomas T. McAvoy, "The Formation of the Catholic Minority in the United States 1820–1860," *Review of Politics*, 10:1 (1948), 15. The Catholic population estimate is from Sister M. Augustina Ray's *American Opinion of Roman Catholicism in the Eighteenth Century* (New York, Columbia University Press, 1936), which describes the general decline in political opposition to Catholicism in the Revolutionary era.

8. Michael Lacey, personal communication, February 10, 2006. I am deeply grateful to Mike for these and his many other insightful comments on the draft text of my lecture.

9. As the Pope put it, "If there is no ultimate truth to guide and direct political activity, then ideas and convictions can easily be manipulated for reasons of power . . . A democracy without values easily turns into open or thinly-disguised totalitarianism." John

Paul II, *Centesimus Annus,* 46, quoted in George Weigel, "Catholicism and Democracy in the Age of John Paul II," *Logos,* 4:3 (2001), 48.

10. Congregation for the Doctrine of the Faith, "Doctrinal Note on Some Questions Regarding the Participation of Catholics in Political Life," November 24, 2002. *www.vatican.va/roman* (accessed 5/10/06).

11. U.S. Conference of Catholic Bishops, "Faithful Citizenship: A Catholic Call to Political Responsibility," Washington, 2003. *www.nccbuscc.org* (accessed 5/11/06).

12. H. Richard Niebuhr, *The Social Sources of Denominationalism* (New York: Henry Holt, 1929).

13. Recent evidence on this subject is in Andrew Greeley and Michael Hout, *The Truth about Conservative Christians: What They Think and What They Believe* (Chicago: University of Chicago Press, 2006), 43–44.

14. Ibid., 66. For an account of Republican skill on this score, see Thomas B. Edsall, *Building Red America: The New Conservative Coalition and the Drive for Permanent Power* (New York: Basic Books, 2006).

15. Rudolf Otto, *The Idea of the Holy* (New York: Oxford University Press, 1958), first published 1923; Stephen G. Post, *Human Nature and the Freedom of Public Religious Expression* (Notre Dame, Ind.: University of Notre Dame Press, 2003).

16. Karl Lowith, *Meaning in History: The Theological Implications of the Philosophy of History* (Chicago: University of Chicago Press, 1949), 112; Reinhold Niebuhr, *The Nature and Destiny of Man: A Christian Interpretation,* vol. 2 (New York: Charles Scribner's Sons, 1943), 87.

17. Arguments generally favorable to this future possibility are in Mark A. Noll and Carolyn Nystrom, *Is The Reformation Over? An Evangelical Assessment of Contemporary Roman Catholicism* (Grand Rapids, Mich.: Baker Academic, 2005). Pointing in the opposite direction is evidence of lingering anti-Catholicism among white conservative Protestants and an enduring difference between the individualistic versus communitarian ways in which conservative Protestants and conservative Catholics see the world respectively. See Greeley and Hout, *The Truth about Conservative Christians,* 175–177; and Damon Linker, *The Theocons: Secular America under Siege* (New York: Doubleday, 2006).

18. Wilfred M. McClay, "Pilgrims Giving Thanks," *Touchstone*, November 2005, 4.

19. Roy Hattersley, "Faith Does Breed Charity," *The Guardian*, September 12, 2005, 8. Taking a larger view, the philosopher and self-described "methodological atheist" Jürgen Habermas argues that Christianity must remain a fundamental source of nourishment for any European civilization of liberty, human rights, and democracy. See Jürgen Habermas, *Time of Transitions* (Oxford: Blackwell, 2006).

20. John Witte, Jr., and Frank Alexander, eds., *The Teachings of Modern Christianity on Law, Politics, and Human Dignity* (New York: Columbia University Press, 2006). On a popular level, there is a growing chorus of voices calling for a Christian civic engagement from the liberal side of the political spectrum. See Peter Laarman, ed., *Getting on Message: Challenging the Christian Right from the Heart of the Gospel* (Boston: Beacon Press, 2006); Jim Wallis, *God's Politics: Why the Right Gets It Wrong and the Left Doesn't Get It* (New York: HarperCollins, 2005); Jimmy Carter, *Our Endangered Values: America's Moral Crisis* (New York: Simon and Schuster, 2005); Randall Balmer, *Thy Kingdom Come: How the Religious Right Distorts the Faith and Threatens America* (New York: Basic Books, 2006); Michael Lerner, *The Left Hand of God: Taking Back Our Country from the Religious Right* (San Francisco: HarperSanFrancisco, 2006); Bob Edgar, *Middle Church: Reclaiming the Moral Values of the Faithful Majority from the Religious Right* (New York: Simon and Schuster, 2006); Obery M. Hendricks, Jr., *The Politics of Jesus: Rediscovering the True Revolutionary Nature of the Teachings of Jesus and How They Have Been Corrupted* (New York: Doubleday, 2006); and Brian D. McLaren, *The Secret Message of Jesus: Uncovering the Truth That Could Change Everything* (Nashville: W Publishing Group, 2006).

21. Pierre Manent, "Christianity and Democracy: Some Remarks on the Political History of Religion, or, on the Religious History of Modern Politics," in his *Modern Liberty and Its Discontents* (Oxford: Rowman and Littlefield, 1998), 97–115.

22. Glenn Tinder, *The Political Meaning of Christianity* (Baton Rouge: Louisiana State University Press, 1989), 8. Tinder's theme is carried forward in David Dark, *The Gospel According to America: A Meditation on a God-blessed, Christ-haunted Idea* (Louisville, Kentucky:

Westminster John Knox Press, 2005), and in a more secular vein by the PBS journalist Ray Suarez's *The Holy Vote: The Politics of Faith in America* (New York: Rayo/Harper Collins, 2006). For a more personal appeal to Christians in the current regime of deliberately managed divisiveness, see Senator John Danforth, *Faith and Politics: How the Moral Values Debate Divides America and How to Move Forward Together* (New York: Viking, 2006).

ACKNOWLEDGMENTS

I am immensely grateful to Theda Skocpol and Harvard's Center for American Political Studies for giving me the opportunity to present this Tocqueville Lecture and to respond to its thoughtful critics. The result, for better or worse, is something that I probably never would have written otherwise. I also naturally applaud any publication project that allows me the last word by way of rejoinder. Of course, given the length of what is trying to pass itself off as a "lecture," others may just as naturally feel that I have already been allowed far too many words. The three distinguished commentators had originally signed on to respond to a lecture of 12,000 to 15,000 words, but they ended up, without a grumble, being subjected to something well over twice that size. They are indeed noble souls.

While the oral lecture was presented only in outline form at Harvard in March 2006, the full text was made available to the commentators prior to the lecture. The text of the lecture published here has since been elaborated in places and edited for purposes of clarity and accuracy. However, no points of substance have been altered in order to anticipate the three respondents' subsequent comments—a heroic abstention given one's authorial yearning for omniscience. Once engaged in writing my rejoinder, it became clear to me just how indebted I am to Professors Bane, Kazin, and Wolfe for helping me think about this subject. The same debt is due to my friend Mike Lacey and an outside reader for Harvard University Press. Their gracious comments on the entire manuscript saved me from at least some of the worst consequences of my own ignorance. Likewise, the Press's splendid editor, Mary Ellen Geer, helped me appear to be a much more polished writer than I really am. Still farther behind the scenes, deserving but not seeking the honor that should fall to public-spirited people, there are Terry and Betsy Considine. Their support made this book possible.

Finally, I wish to thank my wife, Beverley, for putting up with me during the many times of frustration and ill-temper as I worked on this project. I am sure it seemed like I should be the last person to be writing about Christianity, which is probably true.

Hugh Heclo
White Post, Virginia
October 2006

ABOUT THE AUTHORS

MARY JO BANE is Thornton Bradshaw Professor of Public Policy and Management, Academic Dean, and Chair of the Management and Leadership area at Harvard University's Kennedy School of Government. From 1993 to 1996 she was Assistant Secretary for Children and Families at the U.S. Department of Health and Human Services. From 1992 to 1993 she was Commissioner of the New York State Department of Social Services, where she had previously served as Executive Deputy Commissioner from 1984 to 1986. From 1987 to 1992, at the Kennedy School, she was Malcolm Wiener Professor of Social Policy and Director of the Malcolm Wiener Center for Social Policy. She is the author of a number of books and articles on poverty, welfare, families, and the role of churches in civic life, and the coeditor, most recently, of *Taking Faith Seriously.* She is currently doing research on poverty in the United States and internationally.

HUGH HECLO is Robinson Professor of Public Affairs at George Mason University, a former Professor of Government at Harvard University, and prior to that a Senior Fellow at the Brookings Institution in Washington. Most recently he has been contributing coeditor with Wilfred McClay of *Religion Returns to the Public Square.* He currently serves on the 12-member Scholars' Council advising the Librarian of Congress, and in 2002 was honored by the American Political Science Association with the John Gaus

Award for lifetime achievement in the fields of political science and public administration. For the past twenty-five years, he, his wife, and daughter have operated a Christmas tree farm in the northern Shenandoah Valley.

MICHAEL KAZIN is Professor of History at Georgetown University. He is the author of *Barons of Labor: The San Francisco Building Trades and Union Power in the Progressive Era; The Populist Persuasion: An American History;* and *A Godly Hero: The Life of William Jennings Bryan.* He is also the coauthor, with Maurice Isserman, of *America Divided: The Civil War of the 1960s;* the coeditor, with Joseph A. McCartin, of *Americanism: New Perspectives on the History of an Ideal;* and editor-in-chief of the forthcoming Princeton Encyclopedia of American Political History.

ALAN WOLFE is Professor of Political Science and Director of the Boisi Center for Religion and American Public Life at Boston College. His most recent books include *Does American Democracy Still Work?; Return to Greatness: How America Lost Its Sense of Purpose and What It Needs to Do to Recover It; The Transformation of American Religion: How We Actually Live Our Faith;* and *An Intellectual in Public.* Wolfe currently chairs a task force of the American Political Science Association on "Religion and Democracy in the United States." He serves on the advisory boards of Humanity in Action and the Future of American Democracy Foundation, and on the president's advisory board of the Massachusetts Foundation for the Humanities. In the fall of 2004, Professor Wolfe was the George H. W. Bush Fellow at the American Academy in Berlin.

INDEX

Abolition movement, 19, 74, 76, 131, 173, 194

Abortion, 137, 178, 238; Catholic opposition to, 112, 164, 166, 226; and Democratic Party, 115, 163; public debate on, 120, 124, 127, 140

Ahlstrom, Sydney, 61, 63, 102, 123, 214, 216

Alcuin, 137

American Revolution, 10, 30, 114; Christian context of, 31, 42, 69, 77; Catholics and, 149, 173

Amillennialism, 45

Anti-Catholicism, 4, 215, 131, 281n17; and John F. Kennedy's presidential candidacy, 110, 176, 264n164; in the nineteenth century, 152, 173, 175, 191, 224; in the 1920s, 174–175

Anti-communism, 97, 106, 109, 111, 117, 118

Anti-Saloon League, 174

Apostles' Council, Jerusalem, 22

Aristocracy, 10, 48, 53, 234, 244n9

Augustine, 45, 56, 78, 131, 201

Awakenings: Second, 19, 40–41, 114, 171, 183; First Great, 40, 42, 68–69; and civil rights movement, 97–98, 132; Sixties as a secular, 99–101, 182, 214,

230; contemporary evangelical, 204. *See also* Revivalism

Baby Boomers, 81, 96

Backus, Isaac, 26

Bane, Mary Jo, 147–166, 190, 215, 221, 222–227

Baptists, 24, 188, 228, 229

Baxter, Richard, 240

Beaumont, Gustave de, 180–181

Beecher, Henry Ward, 38, 175

Beecher, Lyman, 58, 175, 193, 194

Benedict XVI (Pope), 160, 164–165, 224–226

Benevolent societies, 19, 70–74, 131, 194, 237–238

Birth control, 74, 112, 140, 160, 224

Black churches, 74, 97, 121, 181

Black power movement, 98, 182

Boaz, Franz, 177

Boice, James Montgomery, 139–140

Boorstin, Daniel, 169

Boykin, William, 182

Bryan, William Jennings, 84, 175, 176

Buckley, William F., Jr., 111, 116

Bush, George, 117

Bush, George W., 42, 43, 162, 163, 196, 201, 251n58

Bush, Laura, 196

289